Lecture Notes in Computer Science 9661

Commenced Publication in 1973
Founding and Former Series Editors:
Gerhard Goos, Juris Hartmanis, and Jan van Leeuwen

More information about this series at http://www.springer.com/series/7409

Jeffrey Parsons · Tuure Tuunanen
John Venable · Brian Donnellan
Markus Helfert · Jim Kenneally (Eds.)

Tackling Society's Grand Challenges with Design Science

11th International Conference, DESRIST 2016
St. John's, NL, Canada, May 23–25, 2016
Proceedings

 Springer

Editors
Jeffrey Parsons
Memorial University of Newfoundland
St. John's
Canada

Tuure Tuunanen
University of Jyväskylöä
Jyväskylä yliopisto
Finland

John Venable
Curtain University
Bentley
Australia

Brian Donnellan
Innovation Value Institute
Maynooth University
Maynooth, Co., Kildare
Ireland

Markus Helfert
School of Computing
Dublin City University
Dublin 9
Ireland

Jim Kenneally
Intel Labs Europe
Leixlip
Ireland

ISSN 0302-9743   ISSN 1611-3349   (electronic)
Lecture Notes in Computer Science
ISBN 978-3-319-39293-6   ISBN 978-3-319-39294-3   (eBook)
DOI 10.1007/978-3-319-39294-3

Library of Congress Control Number: 2016939374

LNCS Sublibrary: SL3 – Information Systems and Applications, incl. Internet/Web, and HCI

Printed on acid-free paper

This Springer imprint is published by Springer Nature
The registered company is Springer International Publishing AG Switzerland

Preface

This volume contains selected research papers and descriptions of prototypes and products presented at DESRIST 2016 - the 11th International Conference on Design Science Research in Information Systems and Technology held from May 23–25, 2016, in St. John's, Newfoundland, Canada.

The DESRIST conference continued the tradition of advancing and broadening design research within the information systems discipline. DESRIST brings together researchers and practitioners engaged in all aspects of design science research, with a special emphasis on nurturing the symbiotic relationship between design science researchers and practitioners. As in previous years, scholars and design practitioners from various areas, such as information systems, computer science, industrial design, design thinking, innovation management, service science, and software engineering, came together to discuss and solve design problems through the innovative use of information technology and applications. The outputs of DESRIST, new and innovative constructs, models, methods, processes, and systems provide the basis for novel solutions to design problems in many fields. The conference further built on the foundation of ten prior highly successful international conferences held in Claremont, Pasadena, Atlanta, Philadelphia, St. Gallen, Milwaukee, Las Vegas, Helsinki, Miami, and Dublin.

The title of this volume is "Tackling Society's Grand Challenges with Design Science." Information systems continue to play increasingly important roles in our lives, in areas as diverse as social media, health care, and embedded technology. At the same time, society faces growing challenges, including demands on health-care systems, climate change, and security. Consequently, there is a need to address these topics in design research. The agenda of DESRIST 2016 reflected this approach. By accommodating a range of diverse design perspectives, the intent of the conference was to stimulate discussion and enable cross-discipline collaboration.

Overall we received 62 submissions (31 research manuscripts, 10 prototypes and products and 21 research-in-progress and poster papers) for review. Each research paper was reviewed by a minimum of two referees. For these proceedings, 11 full papers and two short papers were accepted, together with nine short papers describing prototypes and products. The accepted papers were distributed between ranges of diverse design perspectives. As in previous years, a substantial number of papers discussed methodological aspects of design science and described the application of design science research to real-world design problems.

We would like to thank the authors who submitted their papers to DESRIST 2016, and we trust that the readers will find them as interesting and informative as we did. We would like to thank the members of the Program Committee, as well as the additional reviewers who took the time to provide detailed and constructive reviews for the authors. We appreciate the efforts of the other members of the Organizing Committee, as well as the volunteers whose dedication and effort helped bring about another successful conference. We would like to take this opportunity to thank Professors Alan Hevner and Samir Chatterjee for their encouragement and guidance, and Dr. Rob Gleasure, proceedings chair, without whom this volume would not have been possible. Furthermore, we thank the sponsoring organizations, in particular, Maynooth University, University of Jyväskylä, Claremont Graduate University, and Memorial University of Newfoundland, for their financial support.

We believe the papers in these proceedings provide several interesting and valuable insights into the theory and practice of design science, and they open up new and exciting possibilities for research in the discipline.

May 2016

Jeffrey Parsons
Tuure Tuunanen
John Venable
Markus Helfert
Brian Donnellan
Jim Kenneally

Organization

General Chairs

Markus Helfert
Brian Donnellan
Jim Kenneally

Program Chairs

Jeffrey Parsons
Tuure Tuunanen
John Venable

Products and Prototypes Chair

Paul Ralph

Proceedings Chair

Rob Gleasure

Panel Chairs

Monica Chiarini Tremblay
Carson Woo

Doctoral Consortium Chairs

Joerg Evermann
Matti Rossi

Website and Review System Coordinator

Roman Lukyanenko

Program Committee

Tero Päivärinta   Luleå University of Technology, Sweden
Helmut Krcmar   Technische Universität München, Germany
Frederik Ahlemann   University of Duisburg-Essen, Germany

Brian Donnellan	Maynooth University, Ireland
Stephan Aier	University of St. Gallen, Switzerland
Balaji Padmanabhan	University of South Florida, USA
Hemant Jain	University of Wisconsin-Milwaukee, USA
Anindya Datta	National University of Singapore

Additional Reviewers

Jannis Beese	David Hoffmann	Josef-Michael Schwaiger
Michael Blaschke	Xingzhi Jia	Michael Walch
Dominik Bork	Markus Lang	Seokjun Youn
Kevin Clees	Rakesh Mallipeddi	
Yating Feng	Prabu Ramachandran	

Contents

Short Papers

Prototypes

Full Papers

Design of an Awareness Smartphone Platform Based on Direct and Indirect Persuasion for Energy Conservation

Olayan Alharbi[✉] and Samir Chatterjee

Innovation Design and Empowerment Applications Lab (IDEA),
Center for Information Systems and Technology,
Claremont Graduate University, 130 E. 9th Street, Claremont, CA 91711, USA
{Olayan.alharbi,samir.chatterjee}@cgu.edu

Abstract. Direct and indirect persuasions are well known routes for delivering persuasive messages. However, designing and building IS&T artifacts that deliver a persuasion message indirectly is not explored enough yet. This DSR study reports the design, building and evaluation of an indirect persuasion technology. We focus on energy conservation application. Four principles of direct and indirect persuasive design are presented. In addition, these principles are utilized to design and build two different IS&T artifacts: an e-fotonovela application as an indirect persuasion route and the text messaging system as a direct persuasion route. A field study was conducted to evaluate each route. The immediate route effectiveness was measured by a post-survey. Furthermore, results from a longitudinal survey (after one year) showed that indirect persuasion is better remembered than the direct persuasion. This is a significant finding with important implications.

Keywords: Design science · Energy informatics · Persuasion technology · Direct persuasion · Indirect persuasion

1 Introduction

Individuals in the U.S. use energy six times more than the average of the world according to per capita consumption [1]. U.S. households closely follow second to Norway in generating the highest average electricity consumption among the OECD countries (Industrial countries) [2]. Excessive electricity consumption presents numerous financial and environmental threats. These threats impact most wildlife and environments by creating high negative risks for the earth's ecosystem [1, 3, 4]. These threats encourage scientists from different disciplines to explore areas of research to reduce electricity waste. With the focus on reducing energy consumption, two solutions are commonly presented: promoting energy-efficiency and change energy conservation behaviors [3]. Most of these studies are experimental studies for designing, building, and evaluating persuasion intervention that promote pro-environmental behavior [3]. These interventions include eco-feedback [5, 6], setting goals [7], peer comparisons [8], and other interventions that aim to educate and motivate users to be more efficient and conservative in using energy. These energy reduction studies share a common desired

© Springer International Publishing Switzerland 2016
J. Parsons et al. (Eds.): DESRIST 2016, LNCS 9661, pp. 3–18, 2016.
DOI: 10.1007/978-3-319-39294-3_1

behavior, a pro-environmental behavior. Most ICT systems that are designed to change user behavior provide users with a tool (e.g. setting goals) to reach the desired behavior [3]. These systems are considered persuasive technology [9].

In general, persuasion includes two strategies to deliver a persuasive intervention: direct and indirect persuasion [10]. Direct persuasion occurs when a persuader directly sends advocated information to persuadees. Aleahmad et al. [11] defines direct persuasion as persuasion that has clear and apparent intentions. Direct persuasion uses clear persuasion argument [12]. Comparatively, indirect persuasion (self-persuasion) is based on self-generated information that persuadees use and form opinions based on their interpretation of the messages. Indirect persuasion allows persuadees to observe positive impacts of targeted behavior/attitude and/or negative impacts of risky behaviors.

IST designers apply both persuasion strategies to deliver their message. However, Torning and Oinas-Kukkonen [13] state that a majority of studies do not reveal details of persuasion routes. Studies typically illustrate the process of designing persuasive tools, but there are limited studies on direct and indirect routes.

Although, distinct differentiations lie between direct and indirect persuasion, the field lacks studies that provide extensive illustrations about persuasion message routes. The lack of details surrounding persuasion messages provide minimal help to readers in correctly identifying messages routes [13]. However, there are studies regarding customizing and personalizing persuasion messages but not enough information about designing an indirect persuasion or comparing the impacts of direct and indirect persuasion.

This paper specifically focuses on utilizing Design Science Research (DSR) method to address how to design, build, and evaluate direct and indirect persuasive interventions? In addition, it presents results from a longitudinal survey. A post-survey (immediate following the intervention) and a follow-up survey (1-year later) were administered. A report of immediate survey results was presented [14]. This study measures long-term effectiveness and includes design and evaluation process of indirect persuasion routes. Moreover, it measures the lasting impact of routes (direct and indirect) through implementing an awareness intervention. e-fotonovela (comic book style storytelling) is used as an indirect intervention to demonstrate the targeted behavior and its positive consequences and SMS messages is used as a direct persuasion route. The content of e-fotonovela solely demonstrates how people are using conservative tips to reduce their electricity consumption and presenting benefits of their conservative behavior. Implementing both routes simultaneously aids in the comparison of each routes' immediate and long-term effectiveness.

The rest of the paper is structured as follows: Sect. 2 provides background information on energy informatics and persuasion. Then, the research method and the kernel theoretical model is presented. Section 3.1 includes the design and building phase for direct and indirect persuasion. Section 3.3 discusses the study evaluation phase that consists of evaluation process and results decisions. The final section concludes the paper and presents study limitations and potential for future studies.

2 Background

Most energy efficiency and energy curtailment studies are interdisciplinary studies. They include different disciplines such as energy informatics and psychology [3]. Our study falls into an energy informatics research that utilizes persuasive interventions and a pro-environmental model to reduce household electricity waste. It focused on two different persuasion routes: direct and indirect persuasion.

2.1 Energy Informatics

Energy informatics is an interdisciplinary field that includes mainly energy and IS&T studies. According to Watson and Boudreau [15], energy informatics is "analyzing, designing and implementing systems to increase the efficiency of energy demand and supply systems." Energy informatics targets to achieve the following equation:

$$Energy + information < energy$$

As aforementioned, global warming is a serious issue. A sustainable society needs to reduce energy consumption. Energy informatics seeks saving energy in two different levels: distribution and consumption. Energy waste during delivery process are bigger than waste at consumption level. Watson divides the role of IS&T in the supplier side into areas managing and administrating energy flow network and sensors network for the energy distribution [15]. Smart meter solutions for tracking consumption are examples of how energy informatics is utilized in the energy sector.

On the other hand, Information Systems plays a major role in reducing energy waste. IS&T helps in changing social norms to promote energy efficiency [15]. Moreover, energy-efficient products are enhanced by IS&T solutions. Smart Thermostat and smart lighting systems are examples of how IS&T are able to provide energy-efficient products with relative information to maximize these product efficiency. Energy efficiency is reducing energy consumption without changing energy consumption. Goebel et al. [16] explicitly emphasized the need to include end users consumption behavior as one of energy informatics research goals to avoid rebound effect issues. Rebound effect occurs when people use energy efficient-products with an excessive consumption. This behavior can minimize benefits of energy efficient-products because excessive consumption behavior. To that end, IS&T is producing promising solutions to increase energy curtailment and decrease energy waste by targeting consumer behavior [3].

Finally, new energy informatics research is reducing energy waste by changing consumers behavior. Promising results have been reported [3, 17]. Studies show up to 40 % electricity saving in offices and 21 % in the residential level [3, 18]. IS&T have utilized different strategy to change people's behavior such as providing real time feedback, comparison (social support), setting goals and reminders (tool systems).

Based on Goebel's scope of energy informatics research [16] (see Fig. 1), our research provides households with an instructional intervention to raise their awareness about electricity consumption. This paper's main focus is to contrast two different designs having two different persuasion routes: direct and indirect persuasion.

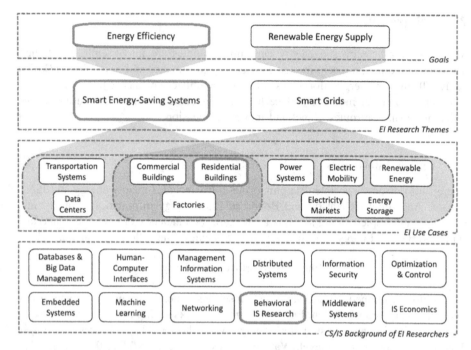

Fig. 1. Scope of energy informatics. Green cell is the scope of this study. (Source [16]) (Color figure online)

2.2 Persuasion

Our daily conversation with our managers, professors, friends, and pets can be considered as persuasive conversations. Persuasion occurs whenever speakers have the intention to persuade the receivers about certain issues. Historically, humans have been using rhetoric as a mean for persuasion. Kennedy [19], explores Aristotle, Cicero and Plato's works about rhetoric and persuasion that was accomplished during the period of 400 B.C. Persuasion is considered as one of the most common sciences that has been studied in social psychology [20]. Simons [21] define persuasion as "human communication designed to influence the autonomous judgments and actions of others."

In general, there are two routes used to persuade people: direct and indirect persuasion routes. These routes differ in the way arguments are presented. Direct persuasion occurs when the persuader sends persuasion information to the persuadees directly. Aleahmad et al. [11] defines direct persuasion as persuasion that has clear and apparent intentions. Direct persuasion uses a clear persuasion argument [12]. The desired behavior/attitude is presented directly. The persuasion process components (persuader, persuadee, and message) are clear. Direct persuasion has a direct route to the persuadees. However, direct persuasion does not produce a direct experience. Persuasive messages have required information to persuade persuadees clearly. Thus, direct persuasion does not allow persuadees to make self-persuasion process. Persuasion information are explicitly mentioned in the message. They are not conclude by the persuadees. Most of the advertisements use direct persuasion by listing the positive consequences of buying their products. Aronson [22] reveals that direct persuasion is helpful if the message seeks an immediate action rather than a long-lasting change.

Indirect persuasion is based on self-generated information where persuadees build their opinions based on their own explanations of a persuasion message. Indirect persuasion strategy allows persuadees to observe positives impacts of targeted behavior/attitude and negative impacts of current behavior. Aronson [22] states that the power of indirect persuasion is a result of allowing persuadees to produce their motivations for change based on their understanding of the message. As a result, indirect persuasion helps people adopt change as if they are persuaders of themselves. Indirect persuasion studies reveal that people adopt persuasion message, as it is their own message [22]. Hence, a targeted behavior/attitude does not fade after a persuasion intervention ends. However, [23] impacts of persuasion vary based on how people evaluate and receive persuasion message. Direct persuasion works better with individuals who receive the persuasion message with complete attention and evaluate its content carefully. Indirect persuasion is more successful with people who are less thoughtful and superficial evaluation for the content.

Persuasive Technology

In the past, persuasion has been done mostly by humans. Recently, scientists (e.g. [9, 12, 24]) have utilized technology to persuade people. Technology has several advantage over humans such reachability, scalability, and customization features.

Persuasive technology studies present different design techniques (e.g. such as tailoring, suggestions, and self-monitoring) to change behavior [13]. Persuasive technology solutions present persuasion message in different media formats (web application, mobile application) using various strategies (awareness, motivation, social support, and social comparison). Baby Think It Over is a persuasive simulator that provides real infant care experience. It was successful in demonstrating parents' responsibilities to teenagers to decrease teen pregnancy [25]. It was built to raise awareness in teenager about the consequence of unplanned pregnancy.

Even utilizing technology, persuadees' receive persuasion interventions through one of two routes: directly and indirectly. Both persuasion routes have been implemented in previous studies examining persuasive technology (e.g. [26, 27]). However, most of existing studies mainly focus on measuring the effectiveness of persuasion techniques (experimental studies) [13]. According to a review by Torning and Oinas-Kukkonen [13], all PT studies do not present how persuasion routes are designed. Few of them have enough detail about persuasion messages that may help readers to figure out which persuasion route has been utilized. Thus, there is little general information regarding persuasion routes and it scarcity for studies addressing how to design indirect persuasive technology?

2.3 Geller Behavioral Change Model

Changing behavior is the target of this work. Direct and indirect persuasion are routes to deliver persuasion interventions. Several well-known theoretical models have been developed to change behavior (e.g. [10]). There are models that are built for changing general attitude or/and behavior. However, Geller has developed a model that specifically focuses on encouraging a pro-environmental behavior [28]. In this study we adopt Geller's behavioral model. The model presents four stages for people who excessively consume energy (unconscious incompetence, conscious incompetence, conscious competence, and unconscious competence). Hence, there are three interventions that can help people attain conservative behavior. These interventions are instructional, motivational, and supportive. Instructional interventions help people in conscious incompetence stage. Instructional interventions raise people's awareness about their risky habits. Motivational interventions encourages people to apply what they learn from instructional intervention. Supportive intervention helps people to maintain and remain engaged.

Many people are in the "unconscious incompetence" stage where they are not aware of the risks of their habits. They usually perform subconsciously without thinking about their bad habits. With instructional intervention, people become aware of the risks of their habit, and they understand the desired behavior. People with risky habits need to have instructions about the problem and about the available solutions. Awareness programs are required to help people understand the desired behavior and ways to perform it. This study explores two persuasion routes for designing an instructional intervention.

3   Research Method

DSR is an iterative research approach to design, develop and evaluate ICT artifacts. DSR has three phases: design, build, and evaluate artifacts [29]. DSR has two iterative cycles: rigor cycle and relevance cycle. Rigor cycle helps in accessing existing knowledge and relevance cycle ensures the problem has societal relevance.

3.1   Design Principles for Direct and Indirect Persuasion

There are several design principles that differ based on persuasion routes [10, 22, 23] (see Table 1).

> **DP1:** Persuasion argument: Persuasion messages carry an argument to convince persuadees. A persuasion argument can be a clear solid argument or peripheral cues arguments [10]. Indirect persuasion requires peripheral cues arguments [12]. According to [10], an indirect persuasion message may include several arguments rather than one logical argument. Additionally, credibility and attractiveness of persuaders may be more convincing to people.
>
> **DP2:** Consequences: The positive consequences or benefits of the targeted actions can be explicit (direct) or implicit (indirect) for persuadees to interpret. Although, most commercial advertisements develop a direct persuasion, some utilize metaphors and photos to develop indirect persuasion. Metaphors and photos implicitly shows benefits of purchasing the advertised products [30].

DP3: Required actions: Designers can explicitly or implicitly ask persuadees to do certain actions. For instance, [27] utilized text messaging systems to encourage oral patients to brush their teeth twice a day. In indirect persuasion scenario, Aronson [22] states that messages may not explicitly require persuadees to apply certain actions or advices.

DP4: Persuasion intent: This design principle cares about persuadees' opinion after accepting the persuasion message. Do they believe that they made their own decision or that someone mediated their decision? The answer for this question has a significant impact on creating a habit rather than temporary actions [22]. Indirect persuasion helps self-persuasion [22].

Table 1. Direct and indirect persuasion design principles

Persuasion elements		Persuasion design principles	
		Direct persuasion	Indirect persuasion
DP1:	Persuasion argument	Central argument	Peripheral (Cues) argument
DP2:	Consequences	Explicit	Implicit
DP3:	Required actions	Explicit	Implicit
DP4:	Persuasion intent	Mediated persuasion	Self-persuasion

3.2 Design and Build Phase

To test our idea, we built a mobile persuasion platform. It includes two main applications: a smartphone (e-fotonovela) for the indirect persuasion route and a text messaging system for the direct persuasion route.

Indirect Persuasion Design and Build Phase

A fotonovela is a comic style storytelling book. It is usually developed by having two or more actors that are involving in a discussion or a story. It has been used in health care studies to demonstrate a desired behavior [31–33]. It is suitable for developing indirect persuasion for three reasons: First, the fotonovela content is controlled by its writers. Thus, the content can be developed to meet indirect persuasion message principles **(DP1)**. The fotonovela story or argument can be developed to include multiple peripheral cues (e.g. expert opinions, attractive actors) rather than one solid logical argument. The fotonovela persuasion argument can indirectly refer to required actions and positive consequences for the targeted behavior **(DP2)** and **(DP3)**.

Second, a fotonovela as a template for persuasion message allows us to demonstrate the targeted behavior without targeting the fotonovela readers. Thus, fotonovela can indirectly and subtly persuade its readers without targeting them. Third, considering these reasons and the fact that comic books are known as a source of pleasure, fotonovela may help readers develop their own persuasion decision. In addition, the fotonovela content allows readers to make their choices regarding required actions toward the targeted behavior. Thus, fotonovela as an indirect persuasion route helps readers develop persuasion process for themselves **(DP4)**.

Fig. 2. A pre-survey to determine main concern

Thus, significant elements of a fotonovela are content and actors. Below, an explanation for utilizing the fotonovela content and actors to implement indirect persuasion. As mentioned above, the content has to have peripheral cues. In addition, the required actions and positive consequence should be mentioned implicitly.

Customized e-fotonovela
A smartphone application was developed to view the e-fotonovela. It was built for the Android operating system. Customization is a vital factor in increasing persuasion process success rate [12, 27]. In addition, cost and environmental concerns are the most common motivators for households to decrease energy consumption. Therefore, two versions of the e-fotonovela were developed (cost and environmental concern). The smartphone application has a novel feature that determines users main concern and then provides them with the suitable version (cost or environmental). After downloading the smartphone application, users complete a very short pre-survey (Fig. 2). Based on the response to the pre-survey, the customized version of the fotonovela is loaded into the application (Figs. 3 and 4).

The e-fotonovela as a Design Technique for Indirect Persuasion
Both fotonovela versions (cost and environmental) have the same amount of scenes (25 scenes for each, total 50). The scenario of both versions is similar including three actors (two workmates: Peter and Michael and Peter's wife Sarah). The e-fotonovela persuasion arguments occur in two locations (work and at Sarah and Peter's house). The e-fotonovela starts by a discussion between the two workmates (Peter and Michael). During their conversation, Peter expressed his family's concern about negative impacts of excessive electricity consumption. Then, Michael joins the conversation by telling how he has been able to reduce electricity consumption. He explains several attainable tips to reduce electricity waste. In addition, they discuss several barriers towards electricity conservation such as level of comfortable, laziness, and forgetfulness. Then, the e-fotonovela moves to the other location (Peter's house). At Peter's home, he starts

Fig. 3. The e-fotonovela version of cost concern

Fig. 4. The e-fotonovela version of environmental concern

a conversation with his wife about Michael's success story in reducing electricity waste. Sarah joins the conservation by defending their consumption and explaining how little waste they produce. However, in the end, she is persuaded about their high amount of waste and how it is possible to limit it. In the closing scene, Peter tells his wife how to enroll in a text messaging system (Fig. 5). The text message system is the second application that was built following a direct persuasion design principle.

Fig. 5. Closing scene: an invitation for the texting message program

The e-fotonovela scenario follows recommended indirect persuasion principles by designing and building the following techniques. **(DP1)** fotonovela was not built based on one solid conversation. It includes several arguments. All of them lead to the targeted behavior (electricity conversation). In addition, Michael's role is a source of credibility. His success story presents his expertise in reducing electricity consumption. According [10, 12], source of credibility is a technique to persuade people indirectly.

Although, the content includes facts, tips to save electricity, and positive consequences (cost reduction or pro-environmental behavior), these tips **(DP3)** and positive consequences **(DP2)** are not the main focus of the fotonovela. It is linked to Michael success story. The required actions to reach the targeted behavior and its positive consequences are implicitly mentioned in the e-fotonovela.

The story in the fotonovela is customized based on the reader's main concern for reducing electricity consumption (cost or environment). However, all the persuasion conversations (reasons, barriers, tips, consequences) are not guaranteed to be applicable for readers. For instance, Sarah talked about how often she leaves Cable TV on stand-by mode. Readers may or may not have a Cable TV. Thus, this persuasion process allows readers to have their own persuasive conversation. Readers are aware that they are not part of the fotonovela. The fotonovela raises their awareness about excessive electricity consumption and helps them consider their own consumption **(DP4)**.

However, **DP4** relies on readers' perception regarding persuasion source and are they targeted or not. Based on our review for existing scientific knowledge regarding indirect persuasion (e.g. [10, 12, 22]), the fotonovela content is crafted carefully to avoid possibility of positioning readers as persuadees.

Direct Persuasion Design and Build Phase

Based on the above design principles, direct persuasion relies on a direct message that includes logical arguments with explicit required actions and positive consequences for the targeted behavior. A messaging system was adopted to be the direct persuasion artifact: BulkSMS. The messaging system has relevant tips and suggestions for the cost or environmental group and has the ability to send and receive messages automatically.

As mentioned, last scene of the e-fotonovela has a subscription invitation for a daily awareness messages program (Fig. 5). If a user accepts the invitation, his/her contact information and best time to receive messages, and main concern are collected. Then, the messages system is programed to send two messages daily with an exception of the first and last day of the experiment. The daily messages are: an awareness and a follow up message (Fig. 6).

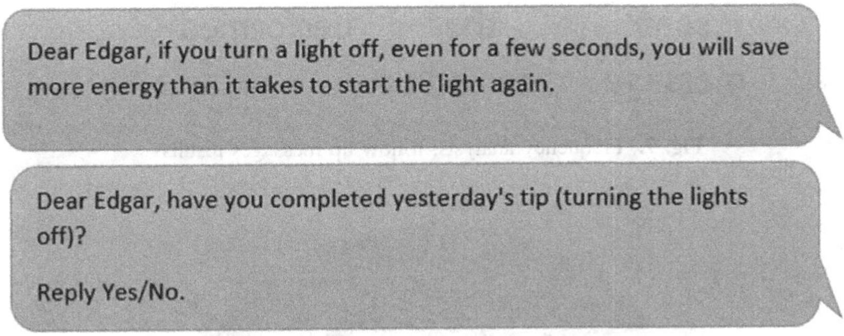

Dear Edgar, if you turn a light off, even for a few seconds, you will save more energy than it takes to start the light again.

Dear Edgar, have you completed yesterday's tip (turning the lights off)?

Reply Yes/No.

Fig. 6. Examples of an awareness and follow-up text message

A Text Messaging System as a Design Technique for Direct Persuasion

A text message is a personal communication tool. Subscribers know that they subscribed to an awareness program to change their electricity consumption behavior. The awareness messages address the subscriber by first name. The message explicitly asks persuadees (subscribers) to conduct a specific saving tip (**DP2**). In addition, it motivates persuadees by specifying the positive consequences for each saving tips (**DP3**). Each message is a logic argument that directly explains how to save electricity and the benefits of the electricity conservation behavior (**DP1**). A follow up message is sent one day later after each awareness message. It directly asks subscribers if they did the required actions (**DP4**) (Fig. 6).

3.3 Evaluation and Results

The effectiveness and usability for the solution as a persuasive technology were reported in a previous paper [14] (see Figs. 7 and 8). This paper provides results and findings for direct and indirect persuasive technology. Specifically, the evaluation phase measures the immediate and long-term effectiveness of each persuasion route (longitudinal survey). A field study was conducted with actual households. 50 households were recruited.

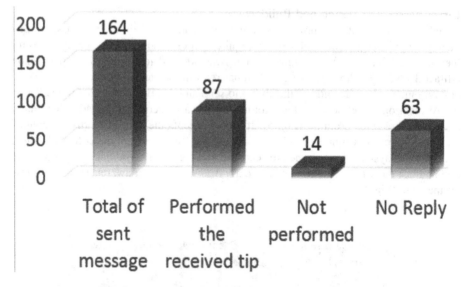

Fig. 7. Frequency analysis: follow up messages results

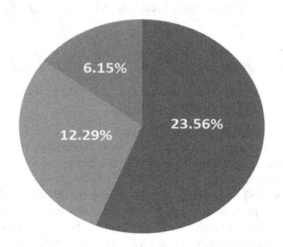

Fig. 8. Participant reports of electricity reduction rate

A member from each household downloaded the e-fotonovela application. However, only 46 users completed the pre-survey. Thus, data from 4 households was not used.

As explained above, the last scene of the e-fotonovela is an invitation for the texting message awareness program. The e-fotonovela (indirect route) was successful in persuading 38 out of 46 householders to accept the invitation and subscribe in the text messaging awareness program. The texting messages awareness program (direct route) was run for five days. Each household receives 8 messages including a daily awareness message and a daily follow up messages. On the last day, they were asked to answer an exit survey (Post-survey).

The post-survey evaluates the solution effectiveness and persuasion routes. However, there are questions that focus on each persuasion routes. 84 % found the e-fotonovela to be a persuader for electricity conservation behavior. Similarly, 85 % of participants believe that the text messages remind them to take actions. These results are consistent with Aronson's study [22] that shows how indirect persuasion has better results in changing behavior where direct persuasion is helpful in encouraging people to take action.

Based on **DP2**, the e-fotonovela indirectly includes advices and tips for reducing electricity waste. 86 % of participants were able to observe these indirect conservation tips. (**DP3**) Customized positive consequences (reducing cost or reducing the rate of CO_2 emission) are implicitly included in the e-fotonovela. 29 people found that fotonovela content matched their main concern.

Finally, after a year, a longitudinal follow up survey was sent out to 38 households who had completed post-survey. Only 18 completed responses were received. 80 % responses confirmed that they remember the e-fotonovela and its saving tips. Each of the interventions (the fotonovela and text messages) includes four saving tips. Two of them are common in both interventions. In total, each participant read six saving tips. Half of the longitudinal follow up survey responses (9 out of 18) revealed that they often perform the saving tips that presented on both interventions.

When asked which of the two (e-fotonovela and text message) do they remember, most respondents remember the e-fotonovela. With respect to saving tips, the results are shown in Table 2. The most performed saving tip is turning light off. Turning light off was mentioned in a text message. There are two reasons that may explain the difference. Turning lights off is one of common saving tips. It is also easy to perform in a regular basis. In addition, the fotonovela visualizes the saving tips. Participants may remember the experience of exploring the e-fotonovela but they don't remember each saving tip where it was exactly mentioned.

Table 2. Frequency table for saving tips performance after a year (the longitudinal follow up survey)

Saving tip	Delivered by	Performed by
Turn off appliances on standby mode	Both direct and indirect persuasion	8
Unplugging unnecessary plugged cables	Both direct and indirect persuasion	6
Programming the air-conditioning thermostat	Indirect persuasion (e-fotonovela)	6
Lowering your water heater thermostat to 120 degrees	Indirect persuasion (e-fotonovela)	1
Using cold water when washing clothes	Direct persuasion (text message)	3
Turning lights off	Direct persuasion (text message)	12
None of them	NA	4

4 Conclusion and Future Work

Although, there are several studies that intervene to raise household awareness about electricity waste, there is a shortage of knowledge about persuasion routes for those interventions. Direct and indirect persuasion are well known routes for delivering persuasive messages. The differences between each route and how people process them have been a discussion topic for long time [10, 22, 30]. However, knowledge about designing, building, and evaluating direct and indirect persuasive technology is lacking. This paper follows DSR guidelines to design direct and indirect persuasion routes. In addition, it evaluates immediate and long-term effectiveness for each route. Four design principles are presented to aid in design of direct and indirect persuasion technology.

The e-fotonovela application served as an indirect persuasion route and the text messaging system as a direct persuasion route. Together they form an awareness system. These applications share the same goal: raising household awareness regarding electricity conservation behavior. The e-fotonovela implemented the design principles by demonstrating the targeted behavior (required actions and positive consequences).

Direct persuasion has been delivered through a text messaging awareness program. In contrast to the e-fotonovela, the text messages provide households with explicit persuasion messages. Finally, implementing both strategies (direct and indirect route) aids in comparing these routes and their design principles. In addition, it allows to measure the effectiveness for each on delivering same intervention (an awareness intervention).

The four design principles are drawn from previous psychological and persuasive technology studies. They can be considered as a level-1 contribution to design theory as stated in Gregor and Hevner [34].

References

1. U.S. Energy Information Administration (EIA) (2006). http://www.eia.gov/totalenergy/data/annual/archive/
2. OECD.org: Electricity Information 2015. Organisation for Economic Co-operation and Development, Paris (2015)
3. Abrahamse, W., Steg, L., Vlek, C., Rothengatter, T.: A review of intervention studies aimed at household energy conservation. J. Environ. Psychol. **25**, 273–291 (2005)
4. Fernandez, R., Watterson, J.: End-user GHG emissions from energy. Reallocation of Emissions from Energy Industries to End Users 2005–2009 (2011)
5. Froehlich, J., Findlater, L., Landay, J.: The design of eco-feedback technology. In: Proceedings of SIGCHI Conference on Human Factors in Computing Systems, pp. 1999–2008. ACM (2010)
6. Alahmad, M.A., Wheeler, P.G., Schwer, A., Eiden, J., Brumbaugh, A.: A comparative study of three feedback devices for residential real-time energy monitoring. IEEE Trans. Ind. Electron. **59**, 2002–2013 (2012)
7. Shiraishi, M., Washio, Y., Takayama, C., Lehdonvirta, V., Kimura, H., Nakajima, T.: Using individual, social and economic persuasion techniques to reduce CO2 emissions in a family setting. In: Proceedings of 4th International Conference on Persuasive Technology, pp. 13:1–13:8. ACM, New York, NY, USA (2009)

8. Foster, D., Blythe, M., Cairns, P., Lawson, S.: Competitive carbon counting: can social networking sites make saving energy more enjoyable? In: CHI 2010 Extended Abstracts on Human Factors in Computing Systems, pp. 4039–4044. ACM (2010)

9. Fogg, B.J.: Persuasive technology: using computers to change what we think and do. Ubiquity 2002 (2002)

10. Petty, R.E., Cacioppo, J.T.: The Elaboration Likelihood Model of Persuasion. Springer, Heidelberg (1986)

11. Aleahmad, T., Balakrishnan, A.D., Wong, J., Fussell, S.R., Kiesler, S.: Fishing for sustainability: the effects of indirect and direct persuasion. In: CHI 2008 Extended Abstracts on Human Factors in Computing Systems, pp. 3021–3026. ACM (2008)

12. Oinas-Kukkonen, H., Harjumaa, M.: Persuasive systems design: key issues, process model, and system features. Commun. Assoc. Inf. Syst. **24**, 28 (2009)

13. Torning, K., Oinas-Kukkonen, H.: Persuasive system design: state of the art and future directions. In: Proceedings of 4th International Conference on Persuasive Technology, p. 30. ACM (2009)

14. Alharbi, O., Chatterjee, S.: BrightDark: a smartphone app utilizing e-fotonovela and text messages to increase energy conservation awareness. In: MacTavish, T., Basapur, S. (eds.) PERSUASIVE 2015. LNCS, vol. 9072, pp. 95–106. Springer, Heidelberg (2015)

15. Watson, R., Boudreau, M.-C.: Energy Informatics. Green ePress, Athens (2011)

16. Goebel, C., Jacobsen, H.-A., Del Razo, V., Doblander, M.F.C., Rivera, D.-I.J., Ilg, D.-I.W. J., Flath, C., Schmeck, H., Weinhardt, C., Pathmaperuma, D.-I.D., et al.: Energy Informatics. Bus. Inf. Syst. Eng. **6**, 25–31 (2014)

17. Steg, L., Gardner, G.T., Stern, P.C.: Environmental problems and human behavior, 2nd edn. Pearson Custom Publishing, Boston (2005). ISBN 0-536-68633-5, $57.33, 2002 (371 pp.). Nickerson, R.S.: Psychology and Environmental Change. Lawrence Erlbaum Associates, Mahwah, ISBN 0-8058-4096-6, $89.95(cloth), $37.50(paper), 2003 (318 pp.). J. Environ. Psychol. **25**, 120–123

18. PIER: Office Plug Loads: Energy Use and Opportunities. Public Interest Energy Research (2012)

19. Kennedy, G.A.: The Art of persuasion in Greece. Princeton University Press, Princeton (1963)

20. Roloff, M.E., Miller, G.R.: Persuasion: New Directions in Theory and Research. Sage, Beverly Hills (1980)

21. Simons, H.W.: Requirements, problems, and strategies: a theory of persuasion for social movements. Q. J. Speech **56**, 1–11 (1970)

22. Aronson, E.: The power of self-persuasion. Am. Psychol. **54**, 875 (1999)

23. Oinas-Kukkonen, H., Harjumaa, M.: Towards deeper understanding of persuasion in software and information systems. In: 2008 First International Conference on Advances in Computer-Human Interaction, pp. 200–205. IEEE (2008)

24. Chatterjee, S., Byun, J., Pottathil, A., Moore, M.N., Dutta, K., Xie, H.Q.: Persuasive sensing: a novel in-home monitoring technology to assist elderly adult diabetic patients. In: Bang, M., Ragnemalm, E.L. (eds.) PERSUASIVE 2012. LNCS, vol. 7284, pp. 31–42. Springer, Heidelberg (2012)

25. Somers, C.L., Fahlman, M.M.: Effectiveness of the "Baby Think It Over" teen pregnancy prevention program. J. Sch. Health **71**, 188 (2001)

26. Miranda, B., Jere, C., Alharbi, O., Lakshmi, S., Khouja, Y., Chatterjee, S.: Examining the efficacy of a persuasive technology package in reducing texting and driving behavior. In: Berkovsky, S., Freyne, J. (eds.) PERSUASIVE 2013. LNCS, vol. 7822, pp. 137–148. Springer, Heidelberg (2013)

27. Ojo, A., Chatterjee, S., Neighbors, H.W., Piatt, G., Moulik, S., Neighbors, B.D., Abelson, J., Krenz, C., Jones, D., et al.: OH-BUDDY: mobile phone texting based intervention for diabetes and oral health management. In: 2015 48th Hawaii International Conference on System Sciences (HICSS), pp. 803–813. IEEE (2015)
28. Geller, E.S.: The challenge of increasing proenvironment behavior. In: Handbook Environment Psychology, pp. 525–540 (2002)
29. Hevner, A., Chatterjee, S.: Design Science Research in Information Systems, pp. 23–31. Springer, Boston (2010)
30. McQuarrie, E.F., Phillips, B.J.: Indirect persuasion in advertising: how consumers process metaphors presented in pictures and words. J. Advert. **34**, 7–20 (2005)
31. Hernandez, M.Y., Organista, K.C.: Entertainment–education? A fotonovela? A new strategy to improve depression literacy and help-seeking behaviors in at-risk immigrant Latinas. Am. J. Community Psychol. **52**, 224–235 (2013)
32. Unger, J.B., Molina, G.B., Baron, M.: Evaluation of sweet temptations, a fotonovela for diabetes education. Hisp. Health Care Int. **7**, 145–152 (2009)
33. Valle, R., Yamada, A.-M., Matiella, A.C.: Fotonovelas: a health literacy tool for educating Latino older adults about dementia. Clin. Gerontol. **30**, 71–88 (2006)
34. Gregor, S., Hevner, A.R.: Positioning and presenting design science research for maximum impact. MIS Q. **37**, 337–356 (2013)

PADRE: A Method for Participatory Action Design Research

Amir Haj-Bolouri[1(✉)], Lennarth Bernhardsson[1], and Matti Rossi[2]

[1] Department of Informatics, University West, Trollhattan, Sweden
{amir.haj-bolouri,lennarth.bernhardsson}@hv.se
[2] Information Systems, Aalto University, Espoo, Finland
matti.rossi@aalto.fi

Abstract. Action Design Research (ADR) is a Design Research (DR) method that enriches the Design Science Research (DSR) paradigm, by providing stages and principles for designing artifacts and allowing for their emergence in an organizational context. The method has been used and elaborated by scholars, extending the mode of the method and its stages, incorporating and adopting knowledge from related approaches such as Participatory Action Research (PAR) and Participatory Design (PD). In this paper, we have adopted principles and philosophy from PAR and PD to extend and elaborate the ADR method, by providing a front-end of Action Research (AR) that emphasizes learning through incremental iteration. We will introduce our elaborated method as Participatory Action Design Research (PADRE) and demonstrate how we have used it in our own research. We argue that the ADR method can benefit from incorporating learning within and across each and every stage iteratively. We also argue that learning can be used as a learning nexus, which informs and gets accumulated for formalization of learning that can be re-used within different cycles of ADR. Hence, we introduce PADRE and provide a model that consists of a set of key-components, which extends and elaborates the ADR method.

Keywords: Action design research · Participatory action design research · Design science research

1 Introduction

Since Hevner et al's [1] seminal paper in MISQ, the Design Science Research (DSR) paradigm has flourished and the volume of DSR publications has increased dramatically [2]. As a research approach, DSR provides and enables researchers to develop a body of knowledge based on technology invention [3], which practitioners (e.g. system designers) can use as technology application (e.g. systems design) [4]. In terms of generating scientific knowledge, DSR generates abstract and practical knowledge, where the first-mentioned deals with development of design principles and design theories [5–7], and the latter emphasizes ways of building and of evaluating IT-artifacts to address a general class of problems [8, 9].

As a further development to the DSR paradigm, Sein et al. [10] introduced the Action Design Research (ADR) method. The ADR-method is a design-research

© Springer International Publishing Switzerland 2016
J. Parsons et al. (Eds.): DESRIST 2016, LNCS 9661, pp. 19–36, 2016.
DOI: 10.1007/978-3-319-39294-3_2

method for generating prescriptive design knowledge through building and evaluating ensemble IT artifacts in an organizational setting [10]. More specifically, the ADR-method emphasizes two major challenges: **(1)** addressing a problem situation encountered in a certain organizational setting by intervening and evaluating; **(2)** constructing and evaluating an IT-artifact, which addresses the class of problems typified by an encountered situation. Sein et al [10, p. 4] state that: "*A new research method is needed to conduct Design Research that recognizes that the artifact emerges from interaction with the organizational context even when its initial design is guided by the researchers' intent. We propose ADR as such a method*". In other words, Sein et al [10] propose that new information systems are or should not be designed and developed in isolation from the organizational environment(s) that they would be used in. Instead, they propose that there should be a tight relation between the research activities of building, intervention, and evaluation (BIE) in a cycle, together with extensive participation by key stakeholders such as researchers, practitioners and end-users. Hence, they provide a research model emphasizing four different stages incorporated with guiding principles (shown in Fig. 1).

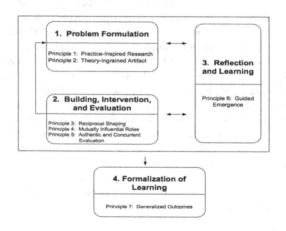

Fig. 1. ADR method: stages and principles [1]

In the course of our own research [11], we conducted research activities adopting the stages and principles of the ADR method (shown in Fig. 1). Thus, an intervention project was initiated in 2013 and ended in 2015, emphasizing building, intervening and evaluating an IT-artifact for conducting and distributing civic orientation through E-Learning [12–14]. The intervention project was conducted at a municipality in Sweden in close cooperation with stakeholders (e.g. practitioners, end-users) involved in the project, both on a conceptual and practical level, designing and evaluating the IT-artifact [13].

After conducting our first ADR-cycle, we discovered that we had applied the ADR method, incorporating activities for reflection and learning from the beginning to the end. Doing so, we had established a reciprocal space for interaction with the stakeholders. Such reciprocal space involved stakeholders from day one through participatory workshops, design workshops, and collaborative activities emphasizing early learning outcomes. We also realized that we had applied ADR to a complex, "wicked" problem, where no explicit artifact existed to address the problem of replicating the distribution of civic orientation through E-Learning. Thus, we were forced to re-examine how the ADR method provides necessary means for encapsulating and distributing early learning outcomes, which can incrementally and iteratively be formalized and used to resolve emerging challenges throughout the process of one to many ADR-cycles.

1.1 Problem

After our first conducted ADR-cycle, we studied further how the ADR method emphasizes reflection and learning in terms of guided emergence, where researchers "*move conceptually from building a solution for a particular instance, to actually applying that learning to a broader class of problems*" [1, p. 8]. This guidance is incorporated throughout the third stage of ADR, where reflection and learning is regarded as a separate stage. However, our learning outcomes from the first ADR cycle provided us insights for how to conduct the second cycle by deliberately establishing an early space for reciprocal reflection and learning with the stakeholders. Hence, we implemented our idea throughout the second cycle, and formulated the following research question for this paper:

- **RQ:** *How can the ADR method be elaborated to incorporate reflection and learning through early-embedded cycles of iteration, providing actively involved stakeholders and researchers an early reciprocal space for reflection, learning and action iteratively?*

1.2 Purpose

Based on the research question and our own experiences adopting the ADR-method, we started reading literature about how participatory research approaches, such as Participatory Action Research (PAR) and Participatory Design (PD), advocate solving problems and encapsulating learning outcomes during early stages of research activities [15–17]. We also identified how other scholars have approached extending the ADR method into flexible modes of elaboration [18], imposing participatory action research as a complementary for ADR [19]. Hence, the purpose of this paper is to present our findings as an elaborated version of the ADR method, and to advocate how early reflection and learning can be integrated into each and every stage of the ADR-model.

We emphasize the need for: (**1**) a participatory approach with researchers and practitioners co-creating knowledge at each step in the ADR-cycle; (**2**) a need for a learning activity at each stage in the ADR-cycle that informs participants in that stage and informs the planning for the next stage in the ADR-cycle. We believe that two points are crucial for our elaboration, which we will present as PADRE (a method for Participatory Action Design Research). But before doing so, we will present related research emphasizing Mullarkey and Henver's [18] and Bilandzic and Venable's [19] contributions. We stress that their contributions are important elaborations of the ADR method in general, and serve as source of inspiration for this paper in particular. Thus, the rest of this paper is structured as following: (1) we present related research; (2) we introduce PADRE; (3) we frame PADRE by describing how we have applied it in our own research; (4) we will discuss PADRE through an concluding discussion about PADRE's significance for practice and research.

2 Related Research

ADR as a method has been used to build and intervene ensemble artifacts within a wide range of application areas stretching from museums [20], to service development [21], to end-user development [22, 23] and other interconnected areas, which justifies ADR in practice and theory [24, 25]. But more relevantly, scholars have also suggested extending the ADR method through various forms of elaboration [18, 19]. However, we have through literature reading identified two works that we address as highly relevant for this paper. Hence, we will in the upcoming sub-sections present and discuss these two relevant works. Our choice with choosing and presenting the following two works is based upon their conceptual relevance to our own conducted research, and their significance in terms of inspiration, rigor and research within the frame of DSR in general, and ADR in particular.

2.1 Developing Action Design Research Further

Recently, Mullarkey and Hevner [18] presented an extended model of the ADR method, by expanding the method with two up-front activities and multiple entry points for entering the ADR method. They argue that: "*ADR tends to suggest a single design science research entry point focused on an existing information system using an action research cycle from problem formulation to build, intervention and evaluation*" [18, p. 133]. They proposed an extension to the original ADR model by introducing a problem diagnosing and concept design stage, together with the possibility of multiple DSR entry points shown in Fig. 2.

Figure 2 depicts for an ADR-process that provides multiple entry points for researchers to flexibly facilitate their research contributions, often required to obtain publication in top tier journals. Mullarkey and Hevner's [18] model incorporates the DSR model presented by Peffers et al [26] and elaborates the ADR method to be effective at the earliest possible entry point in Peffers et al's [26] model. The model also suggest that the activities of intervention, evaluation and reflection on learning cycles, can exist across stages as well as at each stage in the artifact development. The triangles in the model indicate a modification of Sein et al's [10] original BIE-triangles, offering to describe the activity at each stage of the fully elaborated ADR together with each entry point. However, Mullarkey and Hevner's [18] model puts less focus on *how* to actually involve stakeholders and engage them early on throughout an ADR cycle. The model does not explicitly emphasize any methodological constraints in terms of

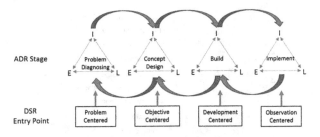

Fig. 2. ADR continuum with stages and entry points [18]

incorporating other relevant research approaches (e.g. PAR) as an extended component for the ADR method. However, the model is an excellent contribution in terms of facilitating flexible entry points for conducting ADR at various levels of engagement (e.g. objective centred, development centred). But the model could benefit from incorporating guidelines and principles on *how* to actually establish embedded cycles of iteration throughout the process of intervention, evaluation and reflection on learning. We will elaborate further on such notion through the idea of PADRE. But before doing so, we will in the next section present the relevant works of Bilandzic and Venable [19].

2.2 Towards Participatory Action Design Research for Urban Informatics

Bilandzic and Venable [19] propose a new research method for studies in the urban informatics domain. They introduce their research method as PADR (Participatory Action Design Research) for urban informatics. Their research method supports urban informatics research in developing new "technological means" to resolve contemporary issues, to support everyday life in urban environments [19] The need for PADR as a research method derives from the nature of urban informatics, which is situated in a socio-technical context. Therefore, PADR combines Action Research (AR) and DSR by adapting them to the cross-disciplinary needs and research context of urban informatics.

PADR incorporates different aspects of AR and DSR, and is constituted through five phases or activities: diagnosing, action planning, action taking design intervention (s), impact evaluation and learning and creation of actionable knowledge for the client, which in the context of urban informatics is the same as city planners, government, developers, local organizations and the public in general. Figure 3 depicts each and every phase of PADR.

PADR starts by activities for diagnosing and problem formulation. In the second phase, the authors state that it is important that the participants are involved as co-planners for taking action (e.g. the design of new technology). Activities such as design, development and evaluation of new technology shall be planned through increased participation for a realistic evaluation.

Fig. 3. Participatory action design research - a research method for urban informatics [19]

During the third phase, PADR is concerned with the actual design and development of the technology, as well as early testing. The phase involves participative design, prototyping and usability evaluation [27, 28]. However, Bilandzic and Venable [19] take distance from using ADR for prototype evaluation. Instead, they advocate for DSR-recommendations deriving from Baskerville et al. [29], who identify evaluation goals and how to achieve them using a combination of ex ante and ex post evaluations.

In the fourth phase of impact and evaluation, the overall goal is based on a collection of researchers, clients, and stakeholders collaboratively working together to define actions for design-interventions, which are then evaluated. Usability evaluation methods are borrowed from Human Computer Interaction (HCI) to provide insights to the HCI community about new artifacts and methods being used in the real world instead of an isolated laboratory.

In the fifth and final phase, participants are encouraged to collaboratively enable clients and stakeholders to carefully reflect upon valuable insights and learning from previous activities and phases. The authors stress that it is important that reflection and learning gets communicated to those involved in a PADR research project. They also suggest that such knowledge gets formulated and communicated as Urban Informatics Design Theories, as opposed to design theories in DSR [4–6].

In summary, Bilandzic and Venable's [19] method incorporates principles and concepts from a wide range of different research approaches such as Action Research, Design Science Research, Human Computer Interaction, Participatory Design and many more. The essence of PADR lies in adapting and offering an aggregated model, which applies streams of participatory action oriented methods for urban informatics. The method emphasizes the importance of involving and engaging relevant stakeholders through a participatory approach, where activities for design, development and evaluation is conducted collaboratively. However, reflection and learning is formalized as a last phase in the method, and not iteratively throughout the whole process of a PADR project.

3 PADRE (A Method for Participatory Action Design Research)

Inspired by works of Mullarkey and Hevner [18] and Bilandzic and Venable [19] and drawing on insights gathered from our own research project [11–13], and literature on PAR and PD [15–17, 27, 28], we will in the upcoming sections introduce PADRE, a method for Participatory Action Design Research.

3.1 The Basic Idea of PADRE

The idea of PADRE is to elaborate Sein et al's [10] ADR-method. PADRE stresses that reflection and learning can occur early on throughout the stages of problem formulation and BIE. Mullarkey and Hevner's [18] flexible model for entering action design research, also points at similar directions, incorporating reflection and learning at different levels of ADR activities (see Fig. 2). In line with Mullarkey and Hevner [18], we suggest that reflection and learning can be established early in an ADR project, providing an ADR-team iterative cycles of activities for planning, implementing, observing and reflecting for learning. PADRE is therefore inspired by principles deriving from PAR and PD, advocating for tight interaction between stakeholders and researchers, including and engaging the stakeholders throughout each and every stage in an ADR cycle. Such philosophical underpinning is already informed through the stages and principles of ADR. However, the ADR method doesn't provide an explicit notion on how to establish early iterative cycles of reflection and learning for each and every stage of the ADR-process. PADRE addresses such issue by incorporating principles from PAR and PD, which informs how to engage stakeholders and researchers into a reciprocal space for early iterative cycles of reflection and learning.

3.2 The Relation Between PADRE, PAR and PD

PADRE adopts, and is inspired by principles deriving from PAR and PD. The participatory nature of PADRE, suggests that it is important to build effective relations between stakeholders and researchers in an ADR project. Such relations shall be established early in a PADRE-project, based on a mutual understanding of the stakeholders' goals and motivations of solving crucial problems through an intervention. Early needs and requirements shall govern reciprocal dialogues between stakeholders and researchers. The dialogues are crucial for establishing mutual understanding through extensive forms of active participation throughout the whole process of formulating problems, to actually presenting and discussing action implications [16, 30].

We suggest that PAR and PD are relevant and sufficient in terms of establishing a "community perspective" between stakeholders and researchers, rather than a simple dichotomy that distinguishes them in terms of their specific roles in an ADR project. The community perspective goes in line with PADRE's notion of building a reciprocal space for early cycles of iterative reflection and learning between stakeholders and researchers. Furthermore, the community perspective offers a sense of mutual agreement between stakeholders and researchers, which affect the will of attitude and participation among the stakeholders in particular [15, 16]. Through such idea of establishing a community perspective, reflection and learning becomes crucial for stakeholders' and researchers' co-creation and sharing of learning outcomes in their community. For instance, researchers and stakeholders may iterate back and forth through mutual dialogues (e.g. through participative workshops), generating incremental suggestions for early prototyping and usability evaluation, which is then revised through an iterative manner into learning outcomes for a new cycle of iteration [27, 28]. The iterations are incrementally conducted until level of satisfaction and maturity of learning outcomes (e.g. formalized learning outcomes). Hence, depending on the nature of acquirement (e.g. problem formulation or solution search), the iterations may be one to many.

A further notion of systematizing the participatory philosophy of PADRE is illustrated in the next section. We will present the structure of PADRE, and illustrate the constitution of the structure through 4 key-components.

3.3   The Structure of PADRE

PADRE consists of four key-components together with comprising activities that inform each and every component. Figure 4 depicts and illustrates each and every component of PADRE.

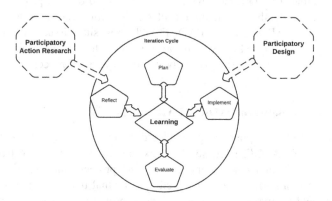

Fig. 4. The structure of PADRE

The first key-component is the component **Plan**. A PADRE project is initiated through planning activities for identifying needs and requirements that address knowledge requirement and need of artifact intervention. This initial stage is similar to the problem diagnosing and concept design stages in Mullarkey and Hevner's [18] extended ADR model, where planning to implement an early prototype of the artifact is possible for further decision-makings. During the planning stage, stakeholders are extensively encouraged to participate and contribute with representative input towards requirements and needs in terms of artifact features [17]. This early stage establishes a reciprocal space for interaction between stakeholders and researchers. The fundamental idea with such reciprocal space is based on an underlying participatory philosophy [30, 31], which aims to establish early reciprocal understanding towards identifying potential problems and solutions. Together, researchers and stakeholders create an atmosphere where participants are encouraged to engage themselves in relevant questions, which are addressed through each participant's base of knowledge and role (e.g. researcher, system developer, coordinator). Such reciprocal space may be established through early workshops (e.g. participative workshops) and training sessions together with stakeholders, providing mutual prerequisites for reflection and learning. During this stage a tight connection for co-creating an evolving research environment shall also be incorporated [31]. Finally, reflection and learning from the first stage results in early formulated needs, which are documented into the **Learning** nexus (positioned in the middle of Fig. 4) and addressed through implementation of an early prototype and system features.

The second key-component is the **Implement** component. Based on documented reflection and learning from the planning stage, the second component emphasizes PD-activities for implementing an early prototype together with prototype features that address formulated needs and requirements [27]. The prototype is, through the original ADR manner, implemented in the actual organization that it is going to be used in [10]. Stakeholders such as end-users and practitioners are, through guidance by the researchers, provided with early increments of the artifact for enhanced usability evaluation [28]. The implementation phase results into learning outcomes about the quality and usability of the early prototype features, together with how well they address stakeholders' early needs and requirements. Stakeholders establish an experience through interacting and testing the early prototype, which generates learning about the different functions of the prototype. In line with the PD-philosophy, learning gets transformed into insights about experienced moments with the prototype, which provides stakeholders more knowledge towards coordinating artifact roles (e.g. which stakeholder does what with the artifact) and revised functionality specification [27, 28]. The learning outcomes from implementing an early version of the documented plan, is documented into the **Learning** nexus and addressed further through evaluation.

The third key-component is the **Evaluate** component. Learning outcomes from the implementation component are documented and evaluated continuously through participative observations together with involved stakeholders. In line with PAR and PD, stakeholders are encouraged to learn how prototype features are used through observation and interaction [15, 16, 27, 28]. They interact with the features through participative activities such as regular meetings, workshops and training sessions, where they report what they want to refine in terms of prototype design and functionality. Hence, the stakeholders' and researchers' observations, leads to a mutual form of guided emergence, where participants of the workshops/sessions collaborate towards a refined version of the prototype. The learning outcomes from evaluating the implemented prototype, is documented into the **Learning** nexus and addressed further through collective reflections between the researchers and stakeholders.

The fourth and final key-component is the **Reflection** component. During the reflection stage, researchers and stakeholders present results and discuss proposed decisions for further action implications [16, 30]. Reflection is based on concrete experiences from the previous phases, emphasizing stakeholders' and researchers' learning outcomes from conducted workshops and training sessions. Each and every involved stakeholder is, together with the researchers, involved in a collaborative activity, providing each other general and/or specific input on further processing. Thus, in the end of the first iteration cycle, experienced knowledge is formulated as efficient learning outcomes for the second planned iteration cycle. It is during this stage, which the researchers and stakeholders decide whether the activities have generated satisfactory results for further endeavours. If the level of satisfactory is decided to be viable, then the preliminary plan gets revised and a new cycle of implementation, evaluation and reflection gets initiated. However, if the level of satisfactory is not decided to be viable, the PADRE-group identifies which activities to revisit. Such idea follows the philosophy of PAR, where decision-making becomes a collective choice between researchers and stakeholders [15, 16, 31]. Finally, the PADRE-groups' reflection outcomes gets documented into the **Learning** nexus and addressed for formalizing, documenting and communicating the learning outcomes.

The **Learning** nexus serve as a repository, or treasure chest of knowledge, which is filled with accumulated knowledge from planning, implementing etc. Hence, learning is embedded as an outcome and not as a separate stage of activities. Learning gets established through performance of planning, implementing, evaluating and reflection. Therefore, it is essential to document learning in various forms of findings (e.g. specified needs and requirements, identified artifact features) and at various levels of the PADRE-process (e.g. first iteration, second iteration) [15, 16, 27, 28]. Finally, the learning nexus is considered being established in the intersection of the PADRE-components (shown in Fig. 5).

Figure 5 depicts the interrelation between key-components of PADRE and the Learning nexus. We identify learning in the intersection between PADRE's 4 key-components and address it as a nexus because it serves as an embedded repository of knowledge for both researchers and stakeholders involved in a PADRE-project. The content of the learning nexus can both be used for initial inquiries (e.g. problem formulation) and/or final satisfactory results. Hence, if an iteration cycle has generated satisfying results for further activities, the learning outcomes may be formalized, documented and communicated in an appropriate form. The medium of appropriation is chosen depending on what the community of researchers and stakeholders believe is appropriate. For example, if the learning outcomes are only relevant for implementing an early version of the artifact, then the researchers may formalize their findings as design implications. But if the learning outcomes are a product of several cycles of iterations, then maybe the artifact is fully usable, and the researchers may decide to formalize learning outcomes into governing design theories.

We will in the next section, through a narrative manner, demonstrate how we have used PADRE in our intervention project [11–13]. We will emphasize the operationalization of PADRE's key-components, and illustrate their utility.

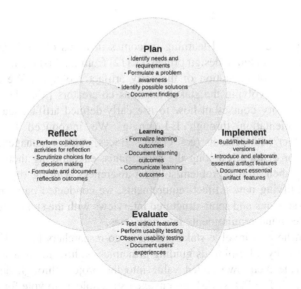

Fig. 5. The interrelation between key-components of PADRE and the learning nexus

4 Demonstrating PADRE

In this section, we demonstrate how we have used PADRE in a recent intervention project. The intervention project was initiated in December 2013 and was accomplished in mid 2015. A comprehensive project description has already been reported (11), but overall, the project was comprised by activities for building, intervening and evaluating an IT-artifact for conducting and distributing civic orientation through E-Learning [12–14].

The IT-artifact for civic orientation consists of features for informing newcomers about how the society works in terms of laws and regulation, democracy, societal norms and values etc. The IT-artifact also consists of features for organizing, maintaining and distributing learning material [13]. The target group for learning civic orientation is immigrants entering Sweden (newcomers), but the target group for using the IT-artifact for conducting and distributing civic orientation is a constellation of teachers, administrators and coordinators at a municipality in Sweden.

Our roles as researchers have been to: (**1**) build, intervene, and introduce technology, which expands the method of distributing civic orientation throughout different counties in Sweden; (**2**) establish organizational and pedagogical strategies for distributing civic orientation through E-Learning. We will therefore for the sake of reliability and validity of PADRE, demonstrate how we have implemented PADRE. Relevant stakeholders such as teachers, administrators and coordinators, have all been included as participants throughout the cycles of our research. Hence, we will now step by step demonstrate how we have utilized the key-components of PADRE in our own research.

4.1   Plan

In the **planning** stage, we used learning outcomes in terms of early-defined design implications [11] and tentative design principles [12] from the first cycle to formulate a plan for a revised implementation of the early artifact prototype. We established a reciprocal space by involving the stakeholders as co-creators [30, 31]. We involved them in supplementary courses in how to use early-defined artifact features for distributing civic orientation through E-Learning. We introduced the concept of E-Learning together with IT-tools (e.g. cloud services, content management systems) that opened up for dialogues among the participants, encouraging them to express a notion regarding their initial problem/solution-awareness. During the phase of discussing and identifying new artifact-requirements, we conducted participant observations, workshop sessions and semi-structured interviews with the stakeholders, to adapt their original needs and requirements into new ones.

Literature on how to involve stakeholders as co-researchers [16, 31] reduced the level of ambiguity, by informing us guiding principles on how to engage stakeholders and let them create their own added value into the project through democratic PD workshops [27, 28]. The PD workshops engaged stakeholders to vote for their top five most-wanted features, by writing them down on post-its and then presenting them one by one for every workshop participant. The workshops resulted into a democratic decision, where the participants had to choose collectively which features they thought were most appropriate for further implementation. Learning outcomes from the planning stage were documented through protocolling.

4.2   Implement

Based on the results from the planning stage, we decided to explore a new direction by initiating a second phase of **implementation**. This time, the implementation phase was initiated by envisioning the stakeholders' collective decisions towards a revised plan for implementation. New artifact features for distributing online-courses in civic orientation were implemented, together with general artifact features and roles for administration. Artifact features addressing administrative activities such as producing, maintaining, updating and distributing learning material, were implemented for the administrators. New technology was introduced and a new cycle of learning the new technology (e.g. interface features) was initiated (Fig. 6).

We also implemented embedded versions of power point material for the teachers, which they use as didactic tools during the course of their teachings. Each and every power point represents a certain theme within the civic orientation program (e.g. democracy, norms and values). Each theme is distributed online, and informed to the students collectively (e.g. classroom teachings) and individually (e.g. E-Learning). The new prototype featured as both being a tool for teachings in the classroom, and a tool for distributing civic orientation through E-Learning. Learning outcomes from the implementation stage were documented through field-notes and video recordings.

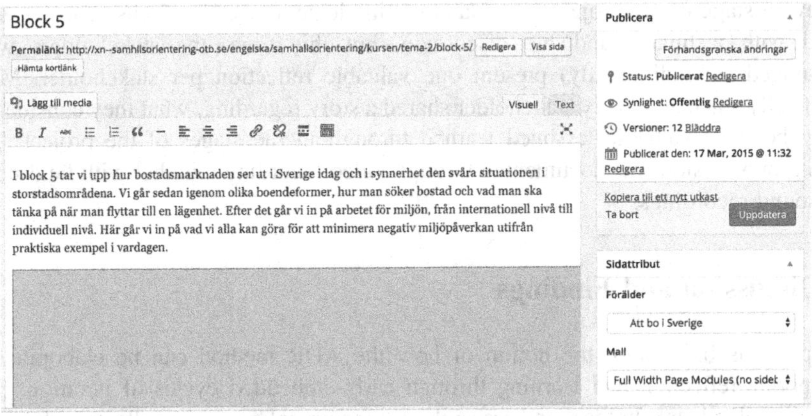

Fig. 6. Admin-features for online-distributed civic orientation

4.3 Evaluate

After implementing a new version of the IT-artifact, we **evaluated** the outcomes through usability testing and evaluation. We arranged a participative workshop together with the stakeholders. The theme for the workshop was to enhance the stakeholders' awareness towards becoming independent of us as researchers in the context using the artifact features. In other words, we conducted the workshop through a set of learning modules, providing them basic know-how towards how to use the different set of artifact features according to their revised needs and requirements (e.g. the revised plan). We introduced the revised version of the IT-artifact by arranging a set of tasks for each and every stakeholder. They got the chance to learn relevant aspects of the IT-artifact, according to their roles as stakeholders. For instance, administrators were provided with tasks relevant to their activities with producing, maintaining, updating and distributing learning material, while teachers were provided tasks relevant to their activities with informing civic orientation through E-Learning and classroom-teachings. Learning outcomes from the evaluation stage were documented through video recordings, sound recordings and field notes.

4.4 Reflect

The **reflection** stage was conducted through a focus group session together with the involved stakeholders. The focus group session was conducted 3 months after the IT-artifact had been implemented and evaluated. During the focus group session, the stakeholders where encouraged to answer questions coupled with their learning outcomes. For instance, the moderator of the session asked what the stakeholders have learned in terms of added values for their daily work with organizing, teaching and distributing civic orientation. The stakeholders shared their opinions through a roundtable discussion, where each and every stakeholder established a view about their individual learning outcomes and the impact of being involved as co-creators in each and every stage of the project (e.g. planning, implementing). The focus group session ended with a final roundtable discussion, but this time, the stakeholders were encouraged to (individually) present one valuable reflection per stakeholder. More specifically, each and every stakeholder shared a story regarding, what they considered, being the most valuable lessoned learned throughout the stages of the project. The focus group session was documented through video recording together with field-notes and sound recordings.

5 Discussion and Findings

Our paper is built upon the notion of how the ADR method can be elaborated to incorporate reflection and learning through early-embedded cycles of iteration, providing involved stakeholders and researchers a reciprocal space for reflection, learning and action. We drew inspiration from participatory research approaches such as PAR [16, 31] and PD [27, 28] and extensions of the ADR method [18, 19]. We summarize our contributions for this paper as follows: (1) empirical findings from actual ADR efforts have proven that the iterative, co-creative (participative) learning need to occur within each stage. PADRE incorporates learning as an embedded nexus within each and every cycle. Hence, learning is an integrated component of each stage, and not a separate stage; (2) empirical findings from conducting the second cycle generated an understanding towards how learning can inform the planning phase of an ADR-stage, and how it might in some cases inform a re-iteration of a current ADR-stage. 3) PADRE provides explicit steps for conducting an iterative, reflective, learning cycle that informs practice and research at each stage in the conduct of ADR.

Given the contributions above, our findings may merit and contribute to the evolution and elaboration of ADR, by integrating the structure of PADRE as embedded cycles (shown in Fig. 7).

Figure 7 depicts and illustrates how ADR can be elaborated through embedded versions of iteration cycles. The key-components **planning, evaluating, implementing** and **reflecting** adopts and provides ADR complementary activities, which emphasizes learning as an integrated nexus within each and every iteration cycle; learning is integrated and established through an iterative interaction between PADRE's key-components, and learning outcomes can be back-tracked across the ADR-stages.

A rationale for PADRE's structure within and across the ADR-stages is formulated as following: (1) **Planning** is designed for problem formulation, BIE-activities and formalization of learning, by adopting PAR through collective processes of self-investigation within the context of research and intervention [16]. A first plan can be revised depending on the level of satisfaction among researchers and stakeholders. The plan gets revised through iteration and collected knowledge within and across the ADR-stages. For example, an early designed prototype of the IT-artifact is implemented and observed in its actual context of use. Reflection and learning gathered from BIE-activities, is encapsulated in the learning repository, and used as insights for the new revised plan.

(2) **Implementing** is designed for presenting a structured problem formulation, implementing an early designed prototype or encapsulating design knowledge through

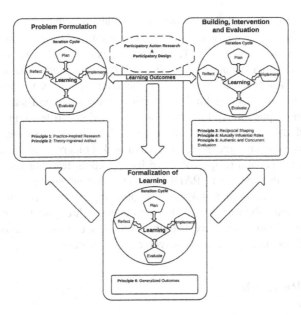

Fig. 7. PADRE implemented into ADR

design principles in a design theory. A first version of implementation guides the PADRE-team to work actively together. Throughout this activity, researchers are encouraged to increase the level of stakeholder empowerment and democratization through direct participation of stakeholders in system analysis and design work [27]. Outcomes from implementing a reciprocally shaped result (e.g. problem formulation, early prototype) are managed iteratively within and across each and every ADR-stage.

(3) Evaluating is designed based on the outcomes from ADR-stages, providing the reflecting phase input on lessons-learned and learning outcomes in general. Learning about how to revise an initial problem formulation or designed prototype, is established through the involvement of a broad set of sources for input (e.g. focus groups), rather than a small number of stakeholder representatives. Observational outcomes serve as means for reflection upon previous key-components (e.g. planning and implementing).

(4) Reflection is the key-activity that creates transparency for initiating a new round of iteration by settling accomplished tasks into relation with newly identified challenges and issues, which derive from previous key-components (planning, implementing and evaluating). Such insights can be early established through the first iteration cycle, but also flourish into more profound forms of reflection that emphasize outcomes from several cycles of iteration. Reflection fulfills the iteration cycle, but also initiates a new cycle of iteration depending on the level satisfaction with accomplishing tasks within and across the ADR-stages.

As we have stressed before, our own experiences with utilizing the rationale of PADRE in an ADR-cycle, demonstrated how to establish a reciprocal space for reflection, learning and action iteratively (when needed). Such reciprocal space, nurtures a sense of community feeling among the researchers and stakeholders, where they reciprocally can structure and share knowledge and learning during and after a project. Thus, learning and knowledge is integrated into the rationale for PADRE through the learning nexus (shown in Fig. 7). The learning nexus is fed with knowledge and learning during and after the activities of PADRE (e.g. planning). The researchers and stakeholders can whenever they want, use the learning nexus to store knowledge and learning (e.g. documenting findings), retrieve knowledge and learning outcomes (e.g. early design implications), but also share knowledge and learning after a project (e.g. formalized design principles). We believe that, in order for such continuous learning process to occur, the researchers and stakeholders need to interact in an atmosphere that adopts and reciprocal space for reflection, learning and action taking. Hence, we believe that the use of PADRE can establish an early sense of community feeling among researchers and stakeholders, allowing them to reciprocally identify goals, problems and solutions, which they can address throughout an entire cycle of PADRE-activities. Doing so, early learning outcomes can be fed into the learning nexus, and used for further iterative evolvement in a project.

6   Further Research

Although we have demonstrated the reliability and validity of our suggested elaboration on the ADR-method, PADRE is still its innovative state of progression. In order to prove the full potential of PADRE, we believe that we need to test it on a class of problems, which we haven't addressed for this paper. Therefore, a next stage in the development of PADRE would be to do so, and provide a revised version of PADRE. Doing so, we would actually follow our own suggested principles of generating learning outcomes through iterated forms of cycles. Furthermore, we address the limitations of our work through potentials for further research. More specifically, we believe that our work is a result of accumulated knowledge, where ADR serve a foundation for relevant works of Mullarkey and Hevner [18] and Bilandzic and Venable [19], which in turn served as sources of inspiration for our work.

References

1. Hevner, A.R., March, S.T., Park, J.: Design science in information systems research. MIS Q. **28**(1), 75–105 (2004)
2. Indulska, M., Recker, J.C.: Design science in IS research: a literature analysis. In: ANU Workshop on Information Systems Foundation (2008)
3. Venable, J.R.: The role of theory and theorising in design science research. In: Design Science Research in Information Systems and Technology (2006)
4. Alturki, A., Gable, G.G.: Theorizing in design science research: an abstraction layers framework. In: Proceedings of PACIS (2014)
5. Gregor, S., Jones, D.: The anatomy of a design theory. J. Assoc. Inf. Syst. **8**, 312 (2007)
6. Kuechler, B., Vaishnavi, V.: On theory development in design science research: anatomy of a research project. Eur. J. Inf. Syst. **17**(5), 489–504 (2008)

7. Walls, J., Widmeyer, G.R., El Sawy, O.A.: Building an information system design theory for vigilant EIS. Inf. Syst. Res. **3**(1), 36–59 (1992)

8. March, S.T., Smith, G.F.: Design and natural science research on information technology (1995)

9. Markus, L.M., Majchrzak, A., Gasser, L.: A design theory for systems that support emergent knowledge processes. MIS Q. **26**(3), 179–212 (2002)

10. Sein, M.K., Henfridsson, O., Purao, S., Rossi, M., Lindgren, R.: Action design research. MIS Q. **35**(1), 37–56 (2011)

11. Haj-Bolouri, A., Flensburg, P., Bernhardsson, L., Winman, T., Svensson, L.: Designing a web-based education platform for swedish civic orientation. In Proceedings of World Conference on E-Learning in Corporate, Government, Healthcare and Higher Education (2014)

12. Haj-Bolouri, A., Svensson, L.: Designing for heterogeneous groups of end-users: towards a nascent design theory. In: Proceedings of World Conference on E-Learning in Corporate, Government, Healthcare and Higher Education (2014)

13. Haj-Bolouri, A., Bernhardsson, L., Bernhardsson, P.: CollaborGeneous: a framework of collaborative IT-tools for heterogeneous groups of learners. In: Donnellan, B., Helfert, M., Kenneally, J., VanderMeer, D., Rothenberger, M., Winter, R. (eds.). LNCS, vol. 9073, pp. 376–380. Springer, Heidelberg (2015)

14. Haj-Bolouri, A., Bernhardsson, L., Bernhardsson, P., Svensson, L.: An information systems design theory for adaptable e-learning. In: 49th Proceedings on Hawaii International Conference on System Sciences (2016)

15. Swantz, M.L.: Participatory action research as practice. The Sage Handbook of Action Research: Participative Inquiry and Practice, pp. 31–48. Sage, London (2008)

16. Rahman, A.: Some trends in the praxis of participatory action research. In: The Sage Handbook of Action Research. Sage, London (2008)

17. Pretty, J., Gujit, I., Thompson, J., Scones, I.: Participatory Learning and Action: A Trainer's Guide. IIED, London (1995)

18. Mullarkey, M.T., Hevner, A.R.: Entering action design research. In: Donnellan, B., Helfert, M., Kenneally, J., VanderMeer, D., Rothenberger, M., Winter, R. (eds.). LNCS, vol. 9073, pp. 121–134. Springer, Heidelberg (2015)

19. Bilandzic, M., Venable, J.: Towards a participatory action design research: adapting action research and design science research methods for urban informatics. J. Community Inform. (2011)

20. Coenen, T., Mostmans, L., Naessens, K.: MuseUs: case study of a pervasive cultural heritage serious game. ACM J (2013)

21. Tate, M., Furtmueller, E.: Service development as action design research: reporting on a servitized e-recruiting portal. In: SIGSVC Workshop, International Conference on Information Systems (2012)

22. Rosson, M.B., Carroll, J.M.: Developing an online community for women in computer and information sciences: a design rationale analysis. Trans. HCI **5**, 6–27 (2013)

23. Lempinen, K., Tuunainen, V.K.: Redesigning the supplier reporting process and system in public procurement: case Hansel. Int. J. Organ. Eng. **1**, 331–346 (2011)

24. Maccani, G., Donnellan, B., Helfert, M.: Action design research in practice: the case of smart cities. In: Tremblay, M.C., VanderMeer, D., Rothenberger, M., Gupta, A., Yoon, V. (eds.) DESRIST 2014. LNCS, vol. 8463, pp. 132–147. Springer, Heidelberg (2014)

25. Sjöström, J.: Designing Information Systems: A Pragmatic Account. Uppsala University, Uppsala (2010)

26. Peffers, K., Tuunanen, T., Rothenberger, M.A., Chatterjee, S.: Design science research methodology for information systems research. J. Manag. Inf. Syst. **24**, 45–77 (2008)

27. Kensing, F.: Methods and Practices in Participatory Design. IT University Press, Copenhagen (2003)
28. Schuler, D., Namioka, A.: Participatory Design: Principles and Practices. Erlbaum, Hillsdale (1993)
29. Baskerville, R., Pries-Heje, J., Venable, J.: A risk management framework for design science research. In: 44th Hawaii International Conference on System Science, Kauai, Hawaii, USA (2011)
30. Whyte, W.H.: The Social Life of Small Urban Spaces. The Conservation Foundation (1980)
31. Argyris, C., Schön, D.A.: Participatory action research and action science compared: a commentary. Am. Behav. Sci. **32**(5), 612–623 (1989)

Making *Use* of Design Principles

Leona Chandra Kruse[1], Stefan Seidel[1(✉)], and Sandeep Purao[2]

[1] University of Liechtenstein, Vaduz, Liechtenstein
{leona.chandra,stefan.seidel}@uni.li
[2] Bentley University, Waltham, USA
spurao@bentley.edu

Abstract. This paper reports on the results of a study that investigates how design principles are used in design practice. Design principles have become the predominant way to capture abstract knowledge about the design of information systems (IS) artifacts—and as design science researchers, we expect that practitioners will use these outcomes of our work. Our empirical evidence is drawn from the analysis of spoken-out thought processes of designers as they attempted to use a certain set of design principles in a new context. Through our analysis, we identify five key categories conceptualizing the use of design principles: interpreting scope and content, matching with problem space, guesstimating missing information, projecting into solution space, and implanting into design process. We find that design principles do not shut down degrees of freedom, but rather, channel actions from the designer, who acts in a conscious, deliberative manner to creatively apply the design principles. Through our work, we contribute to (a) our understanding of how design principles are incorporated in design processes, and (b) the emergent stream of research about the formulation of design principles.

Keywords: Design principles · Prescriptive knowledge reuse · DSR and practice · Designer knowledge

1 Introduction

Contemporary research has argued that an appropriate outcome from design science efforts is knowledge in the form of 'design principles' [1, 2]. Design principles capture knowledge about the creation of other instances of artifacts belonging to the same class [2] and are derived as the researcher moves from the specific instance to the more generic level. An implicit assumption in this argument is that design principles are the right form of abstraction that would allow the community to accumulate knowledge that may then be useful to both, the next cycle of research as well as for design practice.

Unlike other modes of research (e.g., positivist or interpretive), design science inherently builds on the assumption that designing and intervening in authentic settings can generate new knowledge [2] that would be of benefit to the next generation of practitioners. The assumption essentially makes an end-run around the argument for 'making the research relevant' by tackling problems that practitioners have encountered or may encounter. The intent of the design science researcher is, then, unabashedly one

© Springer International Publishing Switzerland 2016
J. Parsons et al. (Eds.): DESRIST 2016, LNCS 9661, pp. 37–51, 2016.
DOI: 10.1007/978-3-319-39294-3_3

of generating knowledge that will aid the next generation of practitioners who may need to address similar problems [3].

As design science researchers, we expect that practitioners will then, use outcomes of our work. An implicit assumption we make here is that they will simply "follow the recipe" we give them. Unfortunately, much prior work tells us that such use (reuse) is not a natural adjunct to creative problem solving. Scholars describe phenomena such as "NIH" (not-invented-here) that have hampered use of prior knowledge in new situations [4]. The expectation that the design knowledge we generate and codify in the form of design principles "will simply be used in new situations" by the practitioners may, therefore, be naïve.

To understand whether and how practitioners will use design principles, a number of conditions need investigation. For example, there are several other forms of design knowledge, e.g., scenarios [5], patterns [6], or heuristics [7]. Each may be more or less useful depending upon the problem context [8]. The designer may bring little or substantial design experience or domain knowledge to the design situation, which will further influence how she will use prior design knowledge such as design principles. Insights from studies of designers and programmers tell us that the breakdowns [9] that occur in design efforts can trigger the search for such knowledge. Empirical studies of design [10, 11] also suggest that the messy nature of design processes can prevent the injection of external sources, including codified prior knowledge. And our understanding of design as a non-routine activity [12] warns us that design, particularly in complex settings, tends to be a situated activity [13] that must respect the knowledge brought to the endeavor by both, users and designers [14] who must then translate and integrate information from a number of sources, one of which happens to be the design principles. We thus ask:

How might (how do) designers use design principles (as a form of design knowledge) in new design contexts?

We believe that a number of designer behaviors are likely to manifest in such an examination. These include searching for sources of information [15], structuring the problem space [16], moving from the problem space to the solution space [16], evaluating the design alternatives, and so on. Each has been examined extensively in prior research. Our interest is *not* to examine these activities in themselves. Instead, our particular focus is on understanding how designers use design principles as they engage in the design process, which may include the above activities. In particular, we are interested in the processes of knowledge access, knowledge translation, and knowledge application that designers engage in—with a focus on design principles as the form of knowledge. Such knowledge is crucial as the design science research community attempts to develop a cumulative body of design knowledge.

We proceed as follows. In the next section, we describe how design knowledge is used in the practice of design, thereby focusing on relevant knowledge components and the understanding of design as a contextual activity. Next, we describe our research design. The analysis section ensues, and we conclude with a discussion of important implications for both research and practice and provide an outlook.

2 Using Design Knowledge in the Practice of Design

Experts and scholars argue and agree that design can never be decontextualized. Scholars in many research streams also agree, starting from Rittell and Weber [17], that design remains a wicked problem that starts with a user concern with no obvious answer, that is, it "is never a process that begins from scratch: to design is always to redesign. There is always something that exists first as a given, as an issue, as a problem" [18, p. 5]. The contextual nature of design poses a challenge for the creation and use of codified design knowledge (e.g., in the form of design principles), and thus for the development of a cumulative body of design knowledge created by design researchers. Codified design knowledge can be represented in various forms such as design patterns [e.g., 19, 20], technological rules [e.g., 21], analysis patterns [e.g., 22], and design principles [e.g., 2, 23]. In this paper, we focus on design principles, defined as "knowledge about creating other instances of artifacts that belong to the same class" [2, p. 39].

The definition suggests that design principles must be codified in some way and must be applicable to a class of problems. We may expect that information systems (IS) practitioners would use such design principles to produce reliable outcomes. On the other hand, the design of IT artifacts is thought to be ongoing and complex, shaped by their organizational context during development and use [2]. As a result, design principles must be understood in relation to the (often novel) contexts in which they are used. To understand how design knowledge is used in design practice and what makes design knowledge usable in practice, we thus need to get at the inherent tension between the formulation design principles that follows a nomothetic approach about how to design a class of things and their idiosyncratic use in highly contextual design practice. We can decompose this tension into two important aspects: (1) design is an activity that involves use of both codified and non-codified (un-codifiable) knowledge and (2) design is an activity that is repeatedly carried out across contexts and time to address similar, but still context-dependent and novel, problems.

2.1 Codified and Non-codified Knowledge in Design

Prior work highlights the epistemological differences in the spectrum of design knowledge, ranging from the more tangible or explicit knowledge to the more intangible or tacit [24–26]. Design Principles (in so far as they are considered a form of design knowledge) represent knowledge that is codified, explicit knowledge, readily accessible as prescriptive statements. Prior to the advances in design science research, such codified knowledge might have resulted from the externalization of tacit knowledge gained from design experience, derived from the combination of existent explicit design knowledge, or both. The design science research community is now engaged in explicating such principles from their efforts to generate IT artifacts in novel situations. Still, the caveats from prior work apply. Not everything can be explicated, "we can know more than we can tell" [27, p. 4], and "a wholly explicit knowledge is unthinkable" [p. 144]. This view suggests that there are limits on what can be expressed through design principles—and implicitly argues that not everything required for design practice can, or should, be explicated.

Using this position as a starting point, we may argue that when designers make use of design principles, they convert explicit knowledge (i.e., prescriptive statements that are shared in the form of design principles) into practice. This conversion is heavily influenced by designers' tacit knowledge base—both, about the new context as well as the class of problems for which the design principles have been explicated [28]. One approach to better understand the relationship between tacit and explicit knowledge is to use labels such as "know-how," "know-why," and "know-what" [29]. Although we know that these categories are not mutually exclusive, there are differences. Garud [29], elaborates these as follows: "in the context of technological systems, knowledge represents an understanding of the principles that underlie their functioning, processes employed to create them, and the uses that these technological systems serve" [p. 83]. Simply put, know-how is usually acquired through learning by doing, know-why through learning by studying, and know-what through learning by using. We suspect that these three categories come together as designers make use of design principles. We anticipate that understanding the interactions of these components in the process of design will, in turn, help us better understand what *should* (and more importantly, *should not*) be captured in design principles.

2.2 Idiosyncrasy and Generalization in Design

Although design is a contextual activity [e.g., 18, 30], design principles are about a class of problems [1] and are thus intended for application across contexts and across time. These contexts *are* different even though they might share certain boundary conditions. Design principles, thus, carry multiple possible meanings as they are interpreted differently in different contexts according to the need and purpose. This characteristic is crucial in understanding how design principles are used in different contexts. In essence, utilizing design principles means that designers must write their own version of those principles—the knowledge contained in these design principles is not "cast in concrete" [31, p. 289].

Understanding the use of design principles thus requires us to investigate the activities that occur when designers "write their own version" as they use design principles in various design contexts. This phenomenon is related to the degree of novelty as well as the complexity of the design situation in knowledge storage, retrieval, and transformation [32, 33]. So, in low complexity situations (such as deterministic change of non-human task through a more efficient algorithm) knowledge might simply be transferred, whereas higher level complexity situations (such that impact human tasks) might require that designers translate or transform knowledge [33]. In more novel situations, the focus shifts from one of efficiently using knowledge to one of effectively creating knowledge [32, p. 1192].

3 Research Approach

To explore how designers make use of design principles in the early phase of the process of designing artifacts, we captured and analyzed their thought processes during as they attempted to use a certain set of design principles in a new context. This allowed us to gain insights into how they *use* design principles during the process of design. Contrary to the common self-report method, which is dependent upon vagaries of recall and interpretation [34], we collected data while the designers were engaged in active use of design principles, i.e., as they attempted to design a representation of a proposed IS artifact. As the participants thought aloud, their words were recorded.

3.1 Collecting and Analyzing Think-Aloud Protocols

Think-aloud protocol analysis places an emphasis on "externalizing covert thinking without altering it" [34, p. 180]. This means that reactive thinking (describing and explaining—and therefore transforming—thoughts) is not encouraged. The method is based on the assumption that thinking is a sequential process and can therefore be represented as a sequence of thoughts [34, 35]. The closest connection between thinking and verbal reports (and therefore, the least altered externalized thinking) can be established by asking participants to think aloud while completing tasks [34]. This method of eliciting verbalized thoughts of designers while designing has been widely used in studies related to problem solving and cognitive analysis of design activity in various design fields, from architecture [e.g., 36, 37] to usability studies (for a comprehensive review see Cross [30, 37]). Table 1 summarizes key elements of the work we carried out to collect the think-aloud protocols.

Table 1. Collecting think-aloud protocols

Category	Description
Task	Designing a representation of a Clinical Decision Support System (CDSS)
Participants	Professional IT/IS designers, one participant for each session
Stimulus	A set of design principles for CDSS and a problem description
Instrument	Audio recorder, paper and pencil, printed instruction for participant (ensuring all participants receive the same instruction) that incorporates problem formulation and design principles
Duration	37 min (pilot), 35 min (participant P), and 31 min (participant Q), including training phase

The method we used aimed to elicit a verbal protocol [38] from each individual designer (i.e., excluding collaboration) as they made use of design principles in response to a problem scenario. Each session involved one participant and one researcher (in the case of our pilot, two), as described in Table 1. The data collection effort was divided into the four phases: preparation, training, design task, and debriefing. During the **preparation phase** each participant was formally asked for her/his consent to participate in this study. However, the researcher did not provide any information regarding the actual research objectives. The setting chosen for the experiment provided sufficient comfort and tranquility for the participant to feel at ease during the session, because it required them to think (talk) aloud. Participants were asked for their agreement to audio recording the session. Finally, participants were requested to give a brief description of their professional background, expertise, and experience in designing software or IS. In the **training phase** the participants were guided through a round of exercises for verbalizing their thoughts. When the researcher was satisfied with how the participant thought aloud, they moved to the **design task**. Here, the printed instruction including the problem formulation and the set of design principles were shared with the participants. The participants were also provided with a sketchbook and drawing/writing instruments. Before beginning the design task, participants were reminded to verbalize their thoughts, and encouraged to do so as a way of thinking instead of trying to describe or explain what they were doing, i.e., they were requested to focus on the design task itself. The researcher read the printed instructions and asked the participant to read both problem formulation and design principles aloud. A **debriefing phase** followed at the end of the design session. Participants were informed about the general aim of this study and were again asked for their continued consent, and further correspondence, should questions arise during analysis.

3.2 Design Principles and Scenario

The participants were provided with a scenario that was hypothetical, yet grounded in an authentic design science research project [39]. This ensured that the scenario was similar to what one might encounter in practice. They were also given a set of design principles. Table 2 provides an overview of the scenario and

Table 3 shows two example design principles along with a short description.

Table 2. Problem scenario for the design session

Marco is a lead software designer. His company has just acquired a contract to develop a piece of software that will support doctors who deal with deciding patient treatment at the local Cancer Care Center (CCC). The patient treatment decision is difficult because it requires a combination of perspectives and expertise from a number of specialists. These specialists are able to meet only about once every month, because they travel from different locations. At CCC, their meetings tend to run for about 2 hours and at each meeting, they end up considering as many as 15 patients. The meetings are attended by about 10-12 specialists in different fields who discuss each case and deliberate to finalize the treatment for each patient before moving to the next patient. These decisions can be very critical because they have consequences that may be irreversible.

Table 3. Design principles

Number of design principles	9
Two examples shown	
Principle 3: make available and visible case-relevant knowledge requested	Pre-populate case-relevant knowledge instead of relying on search-on-demand
Principle 8: preserve group memory	Record deliberations and decisions for each case

3.3   Participants

We collected data from three participants, all IT/IS designers with more than ten years of experience. The session with the first participant served as a pilot session and we thus excluded the resulting protocol from our analysis. Still, the pilot session assisted us in improving the clarity of instructions and the readability of both problem formulation and design principles. All sessions were conducted in German. The instructions, problem formulation, and design principles were made available in both German and English. The sessions were, however, conducted in German because we wished to allow the participants structure and describe their thoughts in the language they were most comfortable with, in spite of their proficiency in English.

The profile of the two participants (excluding the pilot) was as follows. The first participant (P) has a background in software design and engineering, but currently works as a business project manager in a large financial institution. P indicated the necessity to understand the logics of both business analysis and systems development in order to perform well in his function. More often than not, this participant must be able to translate the needs and implications from one side to another and vice versa. The second participant (Q) began his career in a software engineering company before eventually started up his own company in the same field. Being one of the leaders in the company, Q is also responsible for maintaining client relationships, and his expertise includes understanding client needs as well as explaining complex software systems in a simple yet intelligible manner.

3.4   Data Analysis

The recordings of participants' spoken thoughts were transcribed verbatim. Due to the exploratory nature of this study, we aimed to achieve the closest textual representation of the recorded audio—including indication of pause, stutter, murmur, and other unintelligible or incomplete words. Through our data analysis, we intended to explore the observed behaviors of designers as they tried to use design principles in a new, given context. In order to remain open, we thus coded the data in the spirit of open coding [40] to identify salient categories related to the use of design principles. We omitted those segments that were unrelated to making use of the design principles, for instance, training segments and instruction segments.

4   Findings

From our analysis, a number of categories emerged that highlight how designers use design principles. Table 4 provides an overview of these categories along with a brief description.

Next, we describe the categories and illustrate them with quotes from the data. Due to constraints on space, we provide only illustrative quotes. Additional details such as frequency or sequencing of our observations are not shown.

Table 4. How designers *use* design principles

Category	Description
Interpreting scope and content	Designers create meaning of, and reframe, the design principles against the given scenario and against their personal background
Matching with problem space	Designers match the design principles with the given application scenario
Guesstimating missing information	As designers experience incompleteness and degrees of freedom they make assumptions and draw analogies
Projecting into solution space	Designers translate design principles into more specific requirements of form, function, and usefulness
Implanting into design process	Designers attempt to embed design principles into a design/software development process

4.1   Interpreting Scope and Content

Our data suggests that designers interpret design principles and create meaning under consideration of the application context. That is, the data suggests that different designers apply the same design principle differently, even when given the same scenario. Participant P, for instance, said with regard to one of the principles:

> *...so that we can update the data again before the discussion... so timely beforehand still... That's what I think...that's what I make out of "plan for and ensure accurate and current content."*

When interpreting the same principle, participant Q mentioned:

> *Contents that are accurate and actual... that's... based on my experience always difficult, to maintain the data. It's a big topic. Here it can be done through... partly through... user guidance, so that the users tell us all kinds of data they need and so that the data can always be updated.*

In this statement it becomes also noticeable that in interpreting design principles, designers further draw on their personal background and experience. The interpretation of design principles is deliberative and conscious, and designers indeed write their own version of those principles. The need to interpret design principles also becomes evident in the language the designers used when thinking loudly, for instance, Participant P made repeated use of the phrase "it means...":

> *...it means, the templates and later the decisions... and everything must be an integral part...*

Collectively, these quotes suggest the following. As designers use the design principles, they exercise certain degrees of freedom. A generous interpretation of our data suggests that design principles do not prevent such degrees of freedom; instead, they channel the designers' creative actions towards a narrower band of creativity. This is further elaborated by the categories to which we turn next.

4.2   Matching with Problem Space

Designers match design principles with the problem space. This appears to involve two conscious acts. First, they weigh the design principles under consideration of their domain knowledge [41]. In doing so, they map the abstract form of the design principle against their understanding of the problem domain. Second, they attempt to match an implicitly instantiated form of the design principle against the specific situation at hand. Because design principles are an abstraction, this second act seems to require more effort. Consider, for example, the following statement from Q, that points to both:

> *... data security can be a discussion, since it's about medical data. [...] the problem lies a bit in the enterprise that manages it and where the data is stored, in which country.* (Q)

Here, Q points out that the system design needs to consider aspects of healthcare regulations in terms of legal requirements of the organization or country, thus clearly relating the discussion to his/her domain expertise. Participant P makes similar moves in noticing the time pressure while discussing and making decisions about each patient when matching that aspect of the problem space against another design principle:

> *It means someone must prepare the case-relevant knowledge...what I'd now implicitly assume is...that each of the cases comes from each of the experts, probably it's still...prepared by each of their employees. Otherwise you can never ever discuss everything in five to ten minutes.* (P)

However, we observed fewer traces in the data showing such engagement from the participants—in our case, expert designers—with the problem space than with the solution space. This observation is consistent with some of the findings of novice versus expert studies [e.g., 42] and relative focus of designers in both problem and design spaces [43].

4.3   Guesstimating Missing Information

The developers we studied perceived the design principles as lacking detail and providing certain degrees of freedom. This behavior thus logically follows from the interpretation of scope and content. As designers guesstimate this missing information, design principles appear to 'come alive.' In effect, the designers write their own version of those principles closely matched against the situation under consideration. In other words, guesstimating becomes an important process where designers act creatively within the boundaries provided by the design principles. For instance, participant P noted:

> *... but many details are still open, which I must then still pick up.*

and

> *I need then more detailed information so that I can design the system completely and eventually I will have to go one step back...*

It thus becomes noticeable that, in order to design an actual system, more information is required than is provided by the design principles. It is perhaps not surprising that designers have to make assumptions if the design principles are the only formal source of reference. Participant P said:

> ...what I'd now implicitly assume is...that each of the cases comes from each of the experts, probably it's still...prepared by each of their employees. Otherwise you can never ever discuss everything in five to ten minutes. (P)

P also noted:

> what's not stated in any design principle here...but I take it for granted, that one can't simply access the patient data at any time, but they are released...just in time before the discussion... those are private anyway...

The participant thus uses examples or assumptions from his professional experience (i.e., drawing on design and domain knowledge) and injects those into the description of the artifact/solution domain. Finally, it was expressed that the same design principle may have different meanings, from the participant's point of view:

> it means that...well this principle may also mean that we... it can have double meanings... on the one hand it means that one completely allows the access to... (P)

This conscious effort continues on the part of the designers. Not only do they interpret the design principles and deal with the lack of detail, but they also engage in translating the principles into concrete possibilities by considering the solution space.

4.4   Projecting into Solution Space

Both subjects showed a clear tendency to translate the design principles into what we might call "requirements," that is, physical and functional needs that a particular design, product, or process must be able to perform. This included both: (a) specific functions and their technical implementation details, and (b) envisioned user roles. At this, the degrees of freedom turned out to be important, as the participants identified various potential implementations, for instance:

> ...so it means everyone has a laptop or something like that, look at the date on his own, and for that the whole group an expert would...ok it's then... now I'd just say it like this...through...a... power point or similar presentation, where maybe keywords are presented and the facts revealed, and then each can still... (P)

This designer mentions the availability of a laptop computer or the use of Power Point as potential, appropriate means to allow for multiple presentation modalities (as stated in one of the principles). Not only did the participants speculate about potential implementations, but also about the quality of the system. For instance:

> It means also, that it needs to be easy to use, or that... that the UX...the user experience and design should be relatively simple, because the one it, yeah, broad things... or it has many different users... (Q)

Participant Q highlights the need to design a system that is easy to use [44] because its users will be doctors, who are non-IT experts. This was an interesting observation as none of the design principles expressly states the need to develop an easy-to-use system. Similarly, Q talks about "usability," while considering suggestions from another principle (in this case, "principle one"):

...principle one... so, that has much to do with usability, so a usability... problem... so that it becomes an integral part... it happens often that a user... or if the system should be user friendly...

4.5   Implanting into the Design Process

Both participants highlighted that design principles need to be embedded into a more comprehensive design process. The design process they were implicitly considering seemed to involve stages such as user observations, prototyping, and/or testing, for instance:

Afterwards we can actually start with a simple mock up or a click-prototype, that's how we call it, which has the real logic... or that can specify and demonstrate the user experience, how the sequence may look like with the mock up simply... or a few cases, those cases can be invented, and to review the workflow with some doctors. (Q).

Similarly, the same participant elaborates with regard to one of the principles, how users might be included in the design process:

Here it can be done through... partly through... user guidance, so that the users tell us all kinds of data they need and so that the data can always be updated... it can be done through a user guidance in asking questions.

These articulations appeared to indicate that the designers placed the design principles in a web of action that they considered appropriate to deal with the context—regardless of whether such guidance was available within the set of design principles.

5   Discussion and Implications

The data we have presented and the observations tied to this data suggest a number of possibilities. First, with regard to interpreting scope and content, our study raises important questions about whether and how boundary conditions of design principles may be specified. In our example case, the boundary conditions were provided by the scenario, but the design principles themselves did not contain any explicit boundary conditions. Prior literature on abstract design knowledge has highlighted the importance of boundary conditions, or scope, when developing such knowledge [3, 45]. Consequently, there is need to investigate if, and how, boundary conditions and scope might be considered in the development and formulation of design principles. Such knowledge becomes important as designers evaluate the applicability of design principles in specific contexts.

Second, matching the design principles with the problem space surfaces as an important, yet intricate, step in applying design principles. By their very nature, design principles are abstract. Matching them with the problem space requires the designer to act creatively by applying both her expertise and domain knowledge [41] in particular.

In our case, the participants were not experts in the field of healthcare, and did not have the opportunity to rely on such domain expertise. The design principles appeared to fill some of this lack of expertise by providing prescriptive guidelines, which the designers then seemed to weigh against their own knowledge-base.

Third, with regards to guesstimating, our study indicates that the formulation of design principles might lead to ambiguity and various degrees of freedom. Still, there are good reasons to argue that such freedom is required to allow for creativity and innovation in the design process. Design principles are not a simple set of instructions to be followed blindly. In fact, they do not contain procedural knowledge at such level of detail. To understand and enact design principles, designers must possess professional knowledge such as design skills and domain knowledge. It is our contention that it will be important to further investigate the appropriate levels of detail and abstraction that design principles must contain. These decisions would be important as the design science research community engages in the larger goal of (a) developing a cumulative, reusable body of knowledge without (b) compromising creativity and innovation.

Fourth, our analysis highlights that a key challenge is seen in translating design principles into more concrete requirements of form and function, as the participants in our sample struggled to understand 'what exactly' some of the design principles meant, and how they might be converted into something tangible like a concrete instantiation [46]. Coupled with the previous observation, this struggle points to the question of 'what exactly is enough' specification within a design principle.

Fifth, it became noticeable from the data we collected that designers naturally place the design principles into a design process. One promising approach to further study the use of design principles in practice might thus be through the lens of various software development approaches such as waterfall, spiral, or agile methods [47]. Further, it might be useful to differentiate between different types of design principles, for instance, design principles of form and function and design process principles [45], and expressly consider the stage at which the different design principles are intended to be useful. Such insights will further improve our understanding of how design principles should be specified.

Finally, we hope that our initial effort to understand how designers make use of design principles will be followed by comparative studies that include other forms or representations of design knowledge. Such efforts will contribute to the cumulative body of knowledge about the design of design principles, design knowledge reuse, and might have important implications for the overall design process.

6   Next Steps

This paper continues the ongoing discourse in DSR about studying designers' activity, i.e., "studying design" [48] or "ethnography to design" [49] as a mode of research. The study we have reported is, however, not yet another study of design processes. Instead, our effort is to consciously bring together the two streams of "doing design research" and "studying design" as argued in [42]. By doing so, we hope to make two contributions. The first is about the design processes themselves, based on our investigation of the (re) use of a new form of design knowledge (design principles). However, as pointed out earlier, our effort is not to examine the design process in and of itself—but rather, focus on how it incorporates design principles. This is our interest because we wish to implicitly test the assertion that design principles are an appropriate knowledge form that design science researchers should develop. The second contribution is to the growing body of writing about design principles. By understanding how future designers *use* design principles in actual design situations, we hope that we can feed back to design science researchers who can then use the lessons learned to formulate more effective and useful design principles. We hope that the work reported will start this dialog.

Acknowledgements. This research is funded by the Research Fund of the University of Liechtenstein (Forschungsförderungsfonds der Universität Liechtenstein).

References

1. Baskerville, R.P.H.: Explanatory design theory. J. Bus. Inf. Syst. Eng. **5**, 271–282 (2010)
2. Sein, M.K., Henfridsson, O., Purao, S., Rossi, M., Lindgren, R.: Action design research. Manag. Inf. Syst. Q. **35**, 37–56 (2011)
3. Gregor, S., Jones, D.: The anatomy of a design theory. J. Assoc. Inf. Syst. **8**, 313–335 (2007)
4. Katz, R., Allen, T.J.: Investigating the Not Invented Here (NIH) syndrome: a look at the performance, tenure, and communication patterns of 50 R&D project groups. R&D Manag. **12**, 7–20 (1982)
5. Carroll, J.M.: Scenario-based Design: Envisioning Work and Technology in System Development. Wiley, New York (1995)
6. Gamma, E.: Design Patterns: Elements of Reusable Object-Oriented Software. Pearson Education, India (1995)
7. Pearl, J.: Heuristics: Intelligent Search Strategies for Computer Problem Solving. Addison-Wesley, Boston (1984)
8. Purao, S., Storey, V.C., Han, T.: Improving analysis pattern reuse in conceptual design: augmenting automated processes with supervised learning. Inf. Syst. Res. **14**, 269–290 (2003)
9. Guindon, R., Krasner, H., Curtis, B.: Breakdowns and processes during the early activities of software design by professionals. In: Gary, M.O., Sylvia, S., Elliot, S. (eds.) Empirical Studies of Programmers: Second Workshop, pp. 65–82. Ablex Publishing Corp. (1987)
10. Gero, J.S., Kannengiesser, U., Pourmohamadi, M.: Commonalities across designing: Empirical results. In: Design Computing and Cognition 2012, pp. 265–281. Springer, Netherlands (2014)
11. Tang, H., Lee, Y., Gero, J.S.: Comparing collaborative co-located and distributed design processes in digital and traditional sketching environments: a protocol study using the function–behaviour–structure coding scheme. Des. Stud. **32**, 1–29 (2011)
12. March, S.T., Smith, G.F.: Design and natural science research on information technology. Decis. Support Syst. **15**, 251–266 (1995)
13. Riemer, K., Seidel, S.: Design and design research as contextual practice. Inf. Syst. e-Bus. Manag. **11**, 1–4 (2013)
14. Sanders, E.B.-N., Stappers, P.J.: Co-creation and the new landscapes of design. Co-design **4**, 5–18 (2008)

15. Cross, N., Christiaans, H., Dorst, K.: Design expertise amongst student designers. J. Art Des. Educ. **13**, 39–56 (1994)
16. Gero, J.S., Gero, J.S., Mc Neill, T.: An approach to the analysis of design protocols. Des. Stud. **19**, 21–61 (1998)
17. Rittel, H., Webber, M.M.: 2.3 planning problems are wicked. Polity **4**, 155–169 (1973)
18. Latour, B.: A cautious prometheus? A few steps toward a philosophy of design (with special attention to Sloterdijk, P.,). In: Proceedings of the 2008 Annual International Conference of the Design History Society, pp. 2–10 (2008)
19. Denning, P., Dargan, P.: Action-centered design. In: Bringing Design to Software, pp. 105–119 (1996)
20. Borchers, J.O.: A pattern approach to interaction design. AI & Soc. **15**, 359–376 (2001)
21. Van Aken, J.E.: Improving the Relevance of Management Research by Developing Tested and Grounded Technological Rules. Eindhoven Centre for Innovation Studies, Eindhoven (2001)
22. Fowler, M.: Accounting Patterns. Analysis Patterns: Reusable Object Models. Addison, Boston (2007)
23. Denning, P.J.: Great principles of computing. Commun. ACM **46**, 15–20 (2003)
24. Nonaka, I., Konno, N.: The concept of "ba": building a foundation for knowledge creation. Calif. Manag. Rev. **40**, 40–54 (1998)
25. Grant, R.M.: Toward a knowledge-based theory of the firm. Strateg. Manag. J. **17**, 109–122 (1996)
26. Nonaka, I., Toyama, R.: The knowledge-creating theory revisited: knowledge creation as a synthesizing process. Knowl. Manag. Res. Pract. **1**, 2–10 (2003)
27. Polanyi, M.: The logic of tacit inference. Philosophy **41**, 1–18 (1966)
28. Vitalari, N.P., Dickson, G.W.: Problem solving for effective systems analysis: an experimental exploration. Commun. ACM **26**, 948–956 (1983)
29. Garud, R.: On the distinction between know-how, know-why, and know-what. Adv. Strateg. Manag. **14**, 81–101 (1997)
30. Cross, N.: Designerly ways of knowing: design discipline versus design science. Des. Issues **17**, 49–55 (2001)
31. Romme, A.G.L., Endenburg, G.: Construction principles and design rules in the case of circular design. Organ. Sci. **17**, 287–297 (2006)
32. Carlile, P.R., Eric, S.R.: Into the black box: the knowledge transformation cycle. Manag. Sci. **49**, 1180–1195 (2003)
33. Carlile, P.R.: Transferring, translating, and transforming: an integrative framework for managing knowledge across boundaries. Organ. Sci. **15**, 555–568 (2004)
34. Ericsson, K.A., Simon, H.A.: How to study thinking in everyday life: contrasting think-aloud protocols with descriptions and explanations of thinking. Mind Cult. Act. **5**, 178–186 (1998)
35. Ericsson, K.A., Crutcher, R.J.: Introspection and verbal reports on cognitive processes—two approaches to the study of thinking: a response to Howe. New Ideas in Psychology **9**, 57–71 (1991)
36. Suwa, M., Tversky, B.: What do architects and students perceive in their design sketches? A protocol analysis. Des. Stud. **18**, 385–403 (1997)
37. Suwa, M., Purcell, T., Gero, J.: Macroscopic analysis of design processes based on a scheme for coding designers' cognitive actions. Des. Stud. **19**, 455–483 (1998)
38. Van Someren, M.W., Barnard, Y.F., Sandberg, J.A.: The Think Aloud Method: A Practical Guide to Modelling Cognitive Processes. Academic Press, London (1994)
39. Carmelo, G.: A practical approach to breast cancer knowledge management: a tumor board perspective (RTM). The University of Wisconsin (2010)

40. Strauss, A.L., Corbin, J.: Basics of Qualitative Research. Techniques and Procedures for Developing Grounded Theory. Sage, London, UK (1998)
41. Amabile, T.: Creativity in Context. Westview press, Boulder (1996)
42. Cross, N.: Expertise in design: an overview. Des. Stud. **25**, 427–441 (2004)
43. Purao, S., Rossi, M., Bush, A.: Towards an understanding of the use of problem and design spaces during object-oriented system development. Inf. Organ. **12**, 249–281 (2002)
44. Davis, F.D.: Perceived usefulness, perceived ease of use, and user acceptance of information technology. MIS Q. **13**, 319–340 (1989)
45. Walls, J.G., Widmeyer, G.R., El Sawy, O.A.: Building an information system design theory for vigilant EIS. Inf. Syst. Res. **3**, 36–59 (1992)
46. Gregor, S., Hevner, A.R.: Positioning and presenting design science research for maximum impact. MIS Q. **37**, 337–355 (2013)
47. Balaji, S., Murugaiyan, M.S.: Waterfall vs. V-model vs. agile: a comparative study on SDLC. Int. J. Inf. Technol. Bus. Manag. **2**, 26–30 (2012)
48. Purao, S., Baldwin, C.Y., Hevner, A., Storey, V.C., Pries-Heje, J., Smith, B., Zhu, Y.: The sciences of design: observations on an emerging field. In: Harvard Business School Finance Working Paper (2008)
49. Baskerville, R.L., Myers, M.D.: Design ethnography in information systems. Inf. Syst. J. **25**, 23–46 (2015)

Nascent Design Principles Enabling Digital Service Platforms

Hannes Göbel[(✉)] and Stefan Cronholm

University of Borås, IT-section, Borås, Sweden
{hannes.gobel,stefan.cronholm}@hb.se

Abstract. To facilitate innovation of value-enabling IT services in a service ecosystem, digital service platforms are needed. However, existing service platforms, neither fully inscribes premises of the service dominant logic, nor the principles of open innovation. Seldom are they digital. We argue that there is a lack of consolidated normative theory of how to design digital service innovation platforms. This is problematic, because it hampers actors in service ecosystems to combine and advance their capabilities. To this end, researchers and practitioners have jointly designed and evaluated a digital service platform using Action Design Research methodology. Accordingly, the overall purpose of this paper is to present intermediate results from the evaluation of the digital service platform and to contribute nascent *design principles* enabling researchers and practitioners to leverage other instances of purposive digital service platforms.

Keywords: Design principles · Service innovation · Action design research · Service platform · Service dominant logic · Open innovation

1 Introduction

The most important answer to the question of why anyone should embrace the concept of *service* is according to [1, p. 21] that *"service is the heart of value-creation, exchange, market, as well as [having] considerable implications for research, practice, societal well-being, and public policy"*. In addition, service is foundational to innovation [2, 3]. When combining *service* with Information Technology (IT), endless opportunities for IT service innovation emerge. IT enables organizations to innovate ubiquitous services that influence the way we structure society, live our lives and how companies design their business models. That is, it is not much of a stretch to argue that we are only in the beginning of the golden age of IT service innovation.

This paper is based on the idea that in order to achieve and facilitate innovation of value enabling services, Digital Service Platforms (DSP) are necessary. A common definition of a platform is *"...foundation upon which other firms can develop complementary products, technologies or services"* [6, p. 1400]. A general example of such platform is IOS. However, by adopting a service perspective on platforms, we define a DSP as a modular system that includes different components (resources) and facilitates the interaction of actors and resources (c.f. [3]). That is, we view a DSP as an artifact that facilitates and encourages actors (i.e. service providers and customer

J. Parsons et al. (Eds.): DESRIST 2016, LNCS 9661, pp. 52–67, 2016.
DOI: 10.1007/978-3-319-39294-3_4

organizations) in a service ecosystem to communicate, share capabilities and to co-create service innovations in order to boost value creation. We have not found existing exemplars of such a DSP. The need for DSPs is derived from both literature studies and empirical observations. From a research perspective, [3, p. 161] claim that actors in a service ecosystem *"find that service exchange is not very efficient without service platforms, which help to liquefy resources fostering value creation.* Moreover, several scholars suggest that dynamic platforms are needed to manage IT service innovation efforts [4–9]. That is, the significance of DSPs is increasing. From a practitioner's perspective, digital tools that are oriented to collaboration (e.g. a DSP) are important. Between 2003 and 2014 such tools have been located among the most significant IT investments, peaking in 2012 in 4th place [10]. Another argument for the need is according to [11, p. 5] that *"...managers, though motivated to perform and being aware of the links among service, competitive advantage, and firm performance, often fail to execute on service knowledge".* That is, academics have not sufficiently informed normative theory to support practitioners to implement and adapt to the new service paradigm [11].

A usable and normative approach to inform practitioners and researchers about DSPs is to present generic design principles (DP) as a solution to a shared problem (e.g. [12, 13]). We argue that purposive normative DPs for DSPs could leverage more and better value-enabling IT services, strengthen relationships and support practitioners to understand and manage service innovation. However, studies on the phenomenon remain scarce and insufficient [14], which means that practitioners still, lack the capabilities to build on related knowledge. Thus, the problem addressed is that there is a lack of generic DPs for DSPs facilitating IT service innovation. The overall research question reads: *How should digital service platforms facilitating service innovation in service ecosystems be designed?* In order to answer the research question, researchers and practitioners jointly agreed to design and evaluate a web-based solution (DSP) and consequently formulated solution objectives (SO) describing the overall requirements of the artifact. The first and overall SO of the DSP was that it should facilitate feasible and viable service innovation. To support the overall SO, additional SOs were set. The second SO set, was that the DSP should support co-creation between customers and suppliers in the service ecosystem. The argument for that was found in literature (c.f. [15, 2]) and was supported by practitioners. The third SO was to ensure effective and efficient problem identification as a base to co-create service innovations. The argument underlying the SO was that the resources of practitioners were often scarce and they could not afford to work in the wrong direction (i.e. with the wrong problem). The last SO, presented in this paper, was that the DSP must be easy to learn, use, and embed a "service innovation and value co-creation"-approach or "culture". The argument for that was that organizations in the research project traditionally did not have the routines to work with a systematic service innovation approach, which in the end, affected relationships and competitiveness negatively.

The structure of the remainder of this paper follows the generic template for design science research publications suggested by [20] and refined by [16]. In Sect. 2, we will briefly discuss the related work and the theoretical frameworks used as a base for DP grounding, as well as formulate initial design of the DSP. In Sect. 3, we describe the research design and methodology and in Sect. 4, our solution and nascent DPs are communicated. In Sect. 5, we present our evaluation of the DSP. We discuss the results in Sect. 6. Finally, in Sect. 7 we conclude our findings and reflect on implications and limitation while outlining future work.

2 Related Theories and Prior Work

We have based the formulation of the DPs presented in Sect. 4 on theoretical insights and practitioner's experiences of using the DSP in different service ecosystems. The DSP design has rested upon two kernel theories: service dominant (S-D) logic (c.f. [15]) and Open Innovation (OI) (c.f. [2, 17]). According to [18], a kernel theory is underlying a design theory while [19, p. 489] adds that kernel theories *"frequently are theories from other fields that intends to explain or predict a phenomena of interest"*. The argument to inscribe knowledge from S-D logic was that practitioners wanted to improve their existing service oriented approach and in addition researchers wanted to apply and evaluate the theory in practice. The argument for selecting OI was that OI contributes with innovation activities and provides with a somewhat different perspective on collaboration than S-D logic. In the following sub-sections, we briefly describe the kernel theories and related existing solutions that informed our initial DSP design. Such solutions were identified in our research project that aimed to improve organizations capabilities within IT Service Management (ITSM).

2.1 Service Dominant Logic, Service Ecosystems and Service Platforms

The distinct line that traditionally has been used to separate tangible products from intangible services began to blur when [15] summarized what nobody previous had summarized. Service is defined as *"the application of specialized competences (knowledge and skills) through deeds, processes, and performances for the benefit of another entity or the entity itself"* [15 p. 2]. Service is the process of enabling outcome as value and benefit while products are considered units of output. Hence, [4] asserts that S-D logic superordinate service to products (or goods) and [22, p. 217] argue *"service is increasingly recognized as the foundation of activities and value creation in the global economy"*. This means that S-D logic is grounded in collaborative processes including different actors; that challenges management at all levels to be service minded (ibid). S-D logic contains 11 foundational Premises (FP) some of which [23] consider axioms. We have viewed these FPs as important to consider when designing the DSP. Furthermore, the S-D logic implies that value is defined and co-created by several actors, always including the beneficiary of value, in a service ecosystem. An "ecosystem" in general alludes to the biology and ecology disciplines [24]. A central aspect of an ecosystem is according to [24] its ability to maintain its own inertia while adapting to "exogenous shocks". However, depending on the context, different researchers apply different views of the purpose of ecosystems. Within the technology context, ecosystems are often described as *product* platforms defined by core components produced by an owner of the platform and complements or "extensions", produced by autonomous companies on the periphery (ibid). This is in line with [25], who claim that technology platforms are composed by a set of components whose functionality can be extended. This approach supports development of *platform ecosystems* that encourage additional innovation by parties outside the firm [26]. However, we argue that this approach is directly related to the traditional G-D logic perspective, where services are viewed as "add ons to products", thus the view is product oriented. We claim that this approach hampers actors to jointly create value and in the long run reduces their competitiveness and ability to manage sustainable services. Instead, we have adopted an S-D logic perspective of ecosystems[1] and DSP (see Sect. 1).

2.2 Open Innovation

Innovation[2] in general and OI in particular, is a main driver for firms to grow and sustain a high level of profitability ([2, 17, 27–29]). The term "Open Innovation" was coined by [17, 30] defines OI as "a distributed innovation process based on purposively managed knowledge flows across organizational boundaries, using pecuniary and non-pecuniary mechanisms in line with the organization's business model". That is, definition describes how companies have shifted from a closed innovation process, within a single firm, towards a more open approach to innovation. Thus, a key to OI is to open up and cross previously solid organizational boundaries in order to enable innovations. As with service, innovation can be understood as a process consisting of several stages [32]. Although there are different ideas of what the process stages are, we choose to apply the already paved way of *process innovation* (c.f. [33]). Our argument to focus on those stages in the innovation process is that the DSP should facilitate service innovation and that service *per se* is a process. The stages for process innovation consists of five steps: identifying processes for innovation, identifying change enablers, developing a business vision and process objectives, understanding and measuring existing processes, and designing and building a prototype of the new process and organization (ibid). Some scholars' [e.g. 46, 47] view is that innovation emerges in a sequential linear fashion. Furthermore, [17] asserts that the innovation adoption process consists of two stages: initiation and implementation. We consider that the initiation stage is covered by the stages of [33] while the implementation stage is missing, which is why we added that stage to [33]. In addition to the very process of innovation, [17] defined 6 principles for OI; accepting that not all smart people were in-house; accepting external R&D can generate value; research not needing to originate internally in order to be profitable; internal and external ideas are essential to success; and buy other's IP when needed. Although, OI and general innovation theory can be

---

[1] We agree with [3, p 161] who define a service ecosystem as a *"relatively self-contained, self-adjusting system of mostly loosely coupled social and economic (resource-integrating) actors connected by shared institutional logics and mutual value creation through service exchange"*.

[2] We have embraced a broad definition of digital innovation, which is in line with [31] who describes an innovation as, "...an idea, practice, or project that is perceived as new by an individual or other unit of adoption". However, to be an IT service innovation we add that the innovation is enabling value and is composed of or enabled by IT.

used to accelerate and deepen services innovation, making innovation less costly, less risky, and faster [2], other claim that the relevance of open innovation to service innovation has not been researched correspondingly [e.g. [34]. This is in line with [35], who asserts that many firms still struggle to properly manage OI and that there is a need to study the phenomenon on an inter-organizational level. This need has inspired us to inscribe OI theory into the DSP.

2.3 Related Solutions Facilitating IT Service Innovation

The field that studies IT service innovation in practice is often referred to as ITSM. ITSM is customer oriented and relies on several well-defined processes in order to enable IT services to fulfill the needs and requirements in the service ecosystem. Processes such as service portfolio, business relationship, availability, change management, request fulfillment, and incident management are only a few examples of service processes[3] that exist to support *IT service providers* on different organizational levels such as strategic, tactical, and operative. We argue that such processes constitute important components of the final service, and that is why we have considered such processes when designing the DSP. ITSM encourages IT service innovation and [36, p. 6] describes that their framework *"provides guidance on managing the complexity related to changes to services and service management processes, preventing undesired consequences while allowing for innovation"*. Established frameworks such as ITIL [36], CMMI [37], ICM [38], and PIMM [39] exist on the market. However, these ITSM frameworks are not supported by DSPs and they do not explicitly support the very process of service innovation. Moreover, frameworks take into account neither the FPs described in S-D logic nor the principles of OI. This may be one reason for that framework owners explicitly focus and offer them to *IT-service providers*. Hence, we argue that existing frameworks do not fully recognize other actors in the service ecosystem as co-creators of service innovations. Furthermore, existing ITSM frameworks are sometimes considered complex and comprehensive, which is why they are inefficient to implement and use especially for small and medium sized enterprises (SMEs) [40]. Nevertheless, we view existing ITSM frameworks as important to consider when designing the DSP because they are based on best practice, include services, support innovation, and are established on the market. We have found a few digital attempts to facilitate service innovation: "Improve 1.0" [40], "OGC self-assessment tool for ITIL service support" [41], Service Desk Plus [42], and "Service Improvement Manager" [43]. However, these attempts are not explicitly developed from S-D logic or OI and they only target the service provider and thus exclude important contributions from customers. We do not claim that existing frameworks or digital tools are poor. However, we claim that they do not fully foster or facilitate service innovation within ITSM because they do not recognize diverse actors and resources within the service ecosystem. Hence, there is a great risk that the true value of the beneficiary is not identified and fulfilled. Nevertheless, digital DSP attempts teach us that *processes* are

---

[3] Note. There is a difference between *service process* and *service innovation process.*

of significance and should be in focus when designing DSPs. They also teach us that it is important to design DSPs that assess processes and to include functionality that facilitates the very innovation activities. These lessons are in line with the SOs that are described in Sect. 1. Therefore, we recognize these existing solutions as valuable sources to consider when designing the DSP.

3 Research Design and Methodology

In order to identify DPs for DSPs while solving the problem of the practitioners, we have adopted Action Design Research (ADR) [13]. One essential argument for choosing ADR is that the research method explicitly recognizes IT artifacts (e.g. DSPs) as shaped by a wide variety of stakeholders such as developers, investors and practitioners. Another argument for choosing ADR is that it emphasizes the organizational contexts, which also was a requirement for the participating partners in the study. In total, 19 organizations from public, private, and third sector have been involved in the design and/or evaluation of the DSP. To create possibilities to generalize the DP's we selected organizations: belonging to different sectors, were of different size (small, medium, and large), and that used different business models. The common denominator for the organizations was that they shared the same problem: they were lacking a DSP facilitating service innovation. The choices of the several diverse organizational partners were made because we wanted to secure a generic problem *and* a generic solution to the problem. Researchers and practitioners jointly and iteratively carried out the ADR research process that consists of four iterative stages: (1) problem formulation, (2) building, intervention and evaluation, (3) reflection and learning, and (4) formalization of learning. In the first stage, all practitioners and researchers agreed on the problem to solve, and on the SOs (see Sect. 1). In order to identify relevant existing meta requirements and meta design principles (MDP) to use in the initial design, we conducted a "state-of-the-art" assessment of related research in respect of OI and S-D logic. In addition, we investigated existing related platforms. In order to suggest design principles a set of meta-requirements (MR) should be derived from theory and best practices. MR describes the class of goals to which the theory applies [12]. The modifier "meta" is used to describe requirements for a class of problems rather than requirements of a single problem [12]. The second component is a meta-design describing a class of artifacts hypothesized to meet the meta-requirements [12]. In the second and third stage, researchers and practitioners jointly designed, evaluated, and reflected on the DSP. Based on MDPs, experience of practitioners and observations from using the DSP in real contexts, we suggested additional DPs that should be taken into account developing DSP instances. We tested and evaluated the DSP and DPs in three iterations. This was done in several organizations' ecosystems to ensure that the DPs were relevant to all organizations and thus met a certain degree of generality. In all tests, at least two actors (provider and customer organizations) participated. That is, these actors belonged to two different organizations, but to the same ecosystem. We have applied and tested the DSP in 14 of the 19 organizations. Moreover, we conducted interviews with practitioners in order to verify the value, utility, and efficiency of the DSP and inscribed DPs. Semi structural interviews with each organization in combination with group interviews (representatives from all organizations) were conducted [e.g. 44]. In order to do so, a "battery of questions" has been used on a number of pre-defined evaluation categories. These categories related to the DSP and were defined as: the rules inscribed in the platform, the working steps/procedure, the platform's relevance in relation to the organization's purpose, applicability in the context, understandability of content, grouping of content, and the effect of the DSP in action. Supplementary questions were asked, if necessary. Finally, we followed [16]'s suggestion to use the different forms of justification or groundings of DPs by [45] that help justify "theorized practical knowledge". The four grounding strategies are: value grounding (reference to an addressed goal), conceptual grounding (talking about the world/defining categories), explanatory grounding (justification for statements), and empirical grounding (in terms of instantiation and evaluation (ADR)).

4 Communication of Design Knowledge

4.1 Synthesized Design Principles

In Table 1, we have described how the meta-requirements were transformed to MDPs and their relation to kernel theories. In addition to MDPs we identified nascent DPs when designing and evaluating the DSP. In this section, we describe three DPs, following the structure proposed by [16]. The three DPs are: designing for dynamic processes uniting actors in service ecosystems; design to ensure an iterative co-innovation process; and, design for co-problematization. All DPs support the fulfillment of SO1 and at least one of the other SOs (see Sect. 1).

DP1: Designing for dynamic processes uniting actors in service ecosystems

Value Grounding: DP1 is specifically related to SO2 and SO4 because processes incorporated in the DSP allows for guidance yet in dynamic approach. The requirement this DP should help to fulfill was that actors needed guidance in order to co-create valuable service innovations. Current DSPs do not provide such guidance. Thus, we argue that ITSM processes should be adapted according to the FPs of S-D logic. That is, processes (as part of a service), should be the means to create a collaborative and interactive approach to facilitate service innovation. Moreover, they should constitute the interface that opens up previously closed organizational boundaries between actors. Another argument for requiring a process focus in the DSP was that service *per se* is a process consisting of several value enabling sub-processes [1].

Conceptual Grounding: Traditionally, practitioners have viewed existing processes to be mainly internal to a single organization, which delivered an *output*. This perspective is related to a product-oriented view of the world (c.f. [15, 17]). In contrast to this view, DP1 call on actors to design their service processes to *include* activities that traditionally has been related to external actors (Fig. 1).

Explanatory Grounding: We have shown that service innovation is very much related to processes, collaboration, and co-creation (see Sect. 2). A primary benefit of service platforms is that they leverage resource liquefaction and enhance resource density [3].

Table 1. Meta design principles derived from S-D (L)ogic and OI & existing solution (ES)

ID	Meta design principles	Source
MDP1	Design to ensure that service is the fundamental basis of exchange	S-D L
MDP2	Design to support rules/protocols of service exchange	S-D L
MDP3	Design to support value co-creation (always including the beneficiary)	S-D L OI
MDP4	Design for modular architecture	S-D
MDP5	Design for a shared world view	S-D L
MDP6	Design an architecture supporting participation to coordinate service exchange	S-D L OI
MDP7	Design to reduce cognitive distance amongst actors	S-D L
MDP8	Design for structural flexibility and integrity of loosely coupled actor network	S-D L
MDP9	Design for resource liquefaction	S-D L
MDP10	Design for enhancing the (process) transparency	S-D L
MDP11	Design for getting use of internal and external ideas.	OI
MDP12	Design to identify service processes for service innovation	OI
MDP13	Design to identify change enablers	OI
MDP14	Design to develop business vision and process objectives	OI
MDP15	Design to understand & measure existing processes	OI
MDP16	Design to build a prototype of the new process	OI
MDP17	Design to decide on and implement service innovations	OI
MDP18	Design for idea generation	ES
MDP19	Design for dynamic benchmarking and process assessment	ES
MDP20	Design for visualization	ES

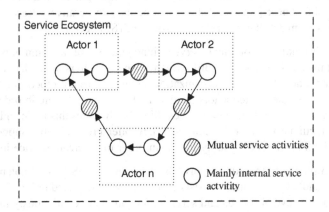

Fig. 1. Conceptual grounding model of processes uniting/bridging actors in service ecosystems

Thus, we argue that a DSP must make the capabilities of actors transparent and available to all relevant actors in the service ecosystem. Such capabilities are the very ITSM processes. Processes that support value creation and constitute the very value enabling service. By designing a DSP to open up previously, hidden service processes, we argue that it will serve actors to identify shared problems and to co-create service innovations. In this way, the DSP facilitates interaction between actors while it guides actors to focus on certain process aspects. The processes, jointly improved by actors, form a glue that tightens the relationship between actors and they integrate actors in a way that previously internal and closed processes did not. This is in line with the principles of S-D logic and IO claiming that actors should share its capabilities and open up boarders to co-create value.

Prescriptive Statement: DP1 could be inscribed in a DSP by a technical function that supports actors to select a number of service processes (e.g. "serviceified" ITIL processes) to use as a foundation for their innovation initiative. The specific processes should be designed as interfaces between actors in the service ecosystem by including activities related to more than one actor in the service ecosystem. To ensure that contextual characteristics are met, a functionality that enables actors to dynamically change existing services and add other processes should be implemented.

DP2: Design to ensure an iterative co-innovation process

Value Grounding: Practitioners perceive the field of ITSM as subject to rapid environmental changes (e.g. new actors, new technologies, new standards etc.). To this end, a continual innovation approach inscribed into the DSP was required. DP2 especially relates to SO2 and SO4 because it recognizes that partnership is not a one-time activity but something based on long-term trust and commitment (like a marriage). Thus, the iterative service innovation process should include actors directly related to the service in focus, in all activities.

Conceptual Grounding: MDP12-MDP17 are derived from [17, 33], while MDP18-MDP19 are derived from existing DSPs. Although, the innovation progress often is viewed as linear [e.g. 46, 47], it must be easy to iteratively learn and use the different stages to match the characteristics of the ITSM sector.

Explanatory Grounding: Continual service innovations are a commonly accepted approach within the ITSM sector [36], which means that hypothetically it should be possible to implement DP2 in the organizational contexts, as a protocol for actors, and in the DSP. Diverse distributed actors need shared institutional logic in order to create value [3]. Iterative service innovation stages (Fig. 2) advocates this logic and they form structures to facilitate resource integration. They offer protocols that support institutionalizing which actors could jointly follow in order to co-create service innovations.

Prescriptive Statement: In order to inscribe DP2 in the DSP, we implemented the concept of "round". One "round" consists of all the stages depicted in Fig. 2. Over time the actors conduct several rounds and service innovation are continuously improved in each round.

DP3: Design for co-problematization

Value Grounding: The requirement that DP3 aims to fulfill is that the actors (service providers and the customers) wanted to achieve an improved understanding of shared

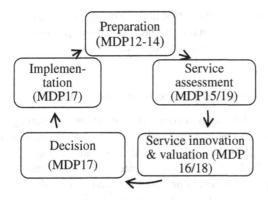

Fig. 2. Conceptual grounding model for DP2

problems in order to create efficient innovations. The argument was that shared problems should be solved together. DP3 is especially address SO2 and SO3 due to the fact that it supports the collaborative approach (e.g. S-D Logic and IO). Our analysis showed that individual actors often searched for and identified problems and challenges within their own organizational boundaries. This limited scope was not enough since the analysis revealed that identified problems often was caused by actions in another actor's organization. This limited scope also hampered a shared problem understanding amongst the actors involved in the service innovation process. The purpose of DP3 is to eliminate this problem.

Conceptual Grounding: The conceptual grounding model in Fig. 3 illustrates how different actors, be they organizations or technical databases or individual users, share their different views on problems in order to identify *generic* service problems.

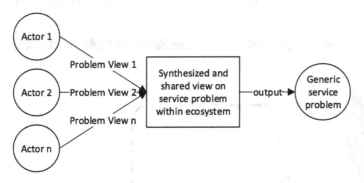

Fig. 3. Conceptual grounding model of DP3

Explanatory Grounding : DP3 interrelates with the S-D logic as well as with the OI theory because the kernel theories informed about how collaboration and co-creation are imperatives for service ([2, 15]). Hence, a shared view on underlying problems is necessary in order to leverage service innovation.

Prescriptive Statement: An action that hypothetically is applicable to implement DP3, is to develop technical functionality in the DSP allowing several actors assess service processes and compare the different assessment results.

4.2   The Service Innovation Process of the Solution

The DSP has emerged through several ADR iterations consisting of building, intervening, and evaluation. The current version of the DSP was composed in five phases (DP2). A key concept in the DSP was that a "round" linked the *service innovation process* in order to facilitate actors to co-create service innovation. The purpose of the first service innovation step was to prepare the round by including relevant actors in the service ecosystem and to *select* service processes as a base for service innovation. The DSP includes a set of pre-defined service processes (e.g. service-oriented ITSM processes) that could be changed dynamically to match the contextual needs in the service ecosystem. Each service process included in the DSP consisted of 17–25 statements guiding diverse actors in the service ecosystem to manage the service in an efficient way. The service processes were seen as interfaces bridging or uniting the actors (DP1). When a round had been prepared (service processes and actors had been selected), a URL directed to service assessment functionality was sent by email to selected actors. In the process assessment stage of the innovation process in DSP (DP3), employees (relevant roles) of the different organizations (e.g. a client and supplier) worked separately, to assess each statement. This act was performed by assessing each individual statement within each organization (this action did not span over organizational boundaries). Each organization selected and rated (c.f. [48]) how well the existing and implemented service process mapped the suggested activities in the DSP.

Next, actors jointly and in consensus selected and prioritized service deviations or gaps identified between actors to solve (Fig. 4). In the next stage implemented in the DSP,

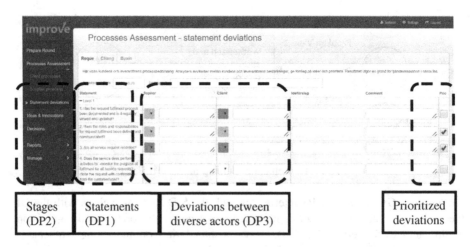

Fig. 4. Overview of DP1, DP2 and DP3 inscribed in the DSP instance

actors co-created tentative service innovations based on the service deviations/gaps identified. The DSP also allowed actors to evaluate identified service innovations to ensure that the most feasible solution to an identified problem was selected. Finally, actors jointly selected a solution (based on evaluation) and implemented it in the service ecosystem. The full iterative service innovation process (a round) was followed at least once a year with the same actors in order to compare results and analyze effects of implemented innovations over time.

5 Digital Service Platform Evaluation

The success of innovation is often defined as the organization's ability to exploit an innovation for its own performance improvement [e.g. 32]. In this section, the innovation referred to is the designed DSP. In order to present the evaluation result of DSP we have used the SOs.

SO1: Facilitate feasible and viable service innovation: The DSP has facilitated a situation where actors, in an efficient and effective way, are able to co-create valuable service innovations. Such service innovations could consist of simple changes in a single process activity, implementation of an entirely new process or a new IT-system. The DSP provided a rapid and feasible innovation process, which reduced the efforts spent, the cost of the innovation process, and the time to market. Based on the analysis of effects and interviews of practitioners, we claim that the DSP has contributed to feasible and viable service innovations.

SO2: Support co-creation between customers and suppliers in the service ecosystem: The inscribed co-creative approach in the DSP has been proven to work in different sectors including different ecosystems. That is, the co-creative approach has supported diverse actors to, in consensus, co-create valuable results in all stages of the innovation process and that is why we claim that S02 is fulfilled.

SO3: Ensure effective and efficient problem identification: The DSP support actors to focus on service related problems. This means that the DSP supports identification of shared problems that cross organizational boarders. Without the DSP, there is a risk that such problems would remain hidden in the service ecosystem and thus unsolved. Due to the guidance and support in the DSP, the communication between actors was done in a more focused and efficient way. Thus, we argue that SO3 is fulfilled.

SO4: Easy to learn, use, and embed a "service innovation and value co-creation"-approach/culture: In contrast to platforms that do not provide a digital support the actors considers the DSP easy to grasp and learn. The fulfilment of SO4 has been particularly valuable for SMEs since they often do not have the resources to learn or maintain expertise on service innovation knowledge. The DSP is also easy to use since no comprehensive manuals are needed to understand and follow the innovation process. Furthermore, the incorporated ITSM processes are considered as easy to understand. Finally, the practitioners argued that the DSP provided them with a process that formed a routine or protocol for the actors to co-create service innovations, which in turn improved the service culture in the organizations.

To summarize, we argue that the current version of the DSP is proven to be successful and we claim that all the SOs are fulfilled. However, the DSP still needs to be improved before it could be adopted as a business tool in a real empirical setting.

6 Discussion

In this study, we have observed that actors in service ecosystem, although aware of concepts of S-D logic and OI, often are working in silos, not effectively feeding each other with capabilities. This, we argue, has hampered actors to co-create valuable service innovations, which negatively affect organizational performance and in the end spill over to the entire service ecosystem. In order to reach feasible and effective service innovations we have shown that normative knowledge is needed. Hence, we have formulated MDPs and DPs by using kernel theories in combination with knowledge from practitioners. The first DP presented in this paper suggests that well-defined service processes form a normative part of the solution. That is, "true" service processes should unite different actors in the service ecosystem. In order to successfully unite actors, there is a need to make processes transparent through open up previous internal and closed processes. Moreover, processes need to include activities that traditionally have been performed outside the firm. This new approach foster a situation where improved communication, capability sharing, and relationships between actors leverage service innovation. Hence, a DSP facilitates a situation where actors can co-create service innovation. The second DP comprises that, in order to create service innovations, in a systematic way, an iterative innovation process should be followed (DP2), using pre-defined stages. The iterative and incremental nature of service innovation processes may complicate its alignment with innovation strategy and culture [49]. However, this assertion seems not be an issue when applying the process innovation stages of [33] and combining them with the implementation/adoption stage of [17] within ITSM. Instead, a structured, easy to implement, easy to use approach to systematic service innovation emerges if this principle is inscribed in a DSP. Finally, we have shown that when DP3 is incorporated in a DSP, the right problems are detected in an efficient way. In our research setting, actors traditionally searched for problems internally focusing on processes within organizational boundaries. That could lead to an actor putting effort into creating and implementing a service innovation that the true beneficiary (the customer) did not really need. Hence, a significant risk of increased costs emerges. In S-D logic, a key success factor is collaboration. We agree with that statement but in accordance with the aforementioned risk, we add that not only the creative phase of service innovation should be shared but also the problem identification phase should be performed in collaboration. This behavior will boost the efficiency of the service innovation process because the right problem is solved. Thus, an efficient DSP should consider functionality to inscribing DP3. According to [21, p. 46], "...*the more complex the system an innovation enters the more likely and severe those consequences will be*". IT service innovation and management is complex because it often includes several underlying processes (and an underlying IT product).

The bottom line is: in order to minimize risk and unintended consequences such as unnecessary cost, and to leverage valuable service innovation, actors need to collaborate and integrate their organizations. Our DSP facilitates a situation where actors are encouraged to collaborate, share capabilities and risks, and finally increase service innovation opportunities. To use the words of [3, p. 165] the platform "...*enable them to obtain a common perspective of their environment - that is, adopt a shared worldview -to ensure the ecosystem's survival.*" Our DSP also confirm the beliefs of [3], who argue that a service platform *may* lead to innovative, scalable solutions and that the primary objective for the platform would be to enhance opportunities for service innovation in the ecosystem.

7 Conclusion

Correctly designed, IT services enable value co-creation, increased sustainability, and tighten the relationship between actors in the service ecosystem. However, we have argued that there is a need for a DSP to facilitate the service innovation process. In this study, we have designed a purposive DSP by inscribing kernel theories (S-D logic and OI) and knowledge from practitioners. By evaluating the DSP in service ecosystems within the context of ITSM, we have been able to answer how DSP facilitating service innovation should be designed. The results presented are mainly three nascent DPs that have been shown to be useful and operational. Moreover, we have shown that existing theoretical statements in OI and S-D logic are possible to transform to DPs, and implement in a DSP applied within the ITSM field. By doing so we argue that we answer the call by [11] to generate normative knowledge. In this paper, the theoretical contribution consists of DPs and the contribution to the practice is the DSP. We claim the DPs to be valid and usable in order to design other similar instances of the solution class DSP. Considering that our DPs are inscribed and tested in different organizational settings, we argue they are generic within the ITSM context. A limitation of the study is that we have studied dyadic relationships within the service ecosystem (e.g. strengthened relationships between customer and supplier organizations). Future DSPs could be designed to also consider other actors. Finally, a limitation of this study is that we have focused solely on IT services in the ITSM field. That is, we cannot yet claim that the knowledge presented is applicable for DSPs facilitating innovation for other service types.

References

1. Vargo, S.L., Lusch, R.F.: Why service? J. Acad. Mark. Sci. **36**(1), 25–38 (2008)
2. Chesbrough, H.: Open Services Innovation: Rethinking Your Business to Grow and Compete in a New Era. Jossey-Bass, San Francisco (2011)
3. Lusch, R., Nambisan, S.: Service innovation: a service-dominant logic perspective. MIS Q. **39**(1), 155–176 (2015)
4. Henfridsson, O., Mathiassen, L., Svahn, F.: Managing technological change in the digital age: the role of architectural frames. J. Inf. Technol. **29**, 27–43 (2014)

5. Yoo, Y., Lyytinen, K., Boland, R., Berente, N., Gaskin, J., Schutz, D., Srinivasan, N.: The next wave of digital innovation: opportunities and challenges. In: A Report of a Research Workshop on Digital Challenges in Innovation Research (2010)
6. Yoo, Y., Boland, R.J., Lyytinen, K., Majchrzak, A.: Organizing for innovation in the digitized world. Organ. Sci. 23(5), 1398–1408 (2012)
7. Diener, K, and Piller, F.: Facets of open innovation: development of a conceptual framework. In: Open User Innovation Conference, Boston (2008)
8. Prahalad, C.K., Ramaswamy, V.: Co-creating unique value with customers. Strateg. Leadersh. 32(3), 4–9 (2004)
9. Nylén, D., Holmström, J.: Digital innovation strategy: a framework for diagnosing and improving digital product and service innovation. Bus. Horiz. 58(1), 57–67 (2015)
10. Kappelman, L., Johnson, V., McLean, E., Gerhart, N.: The 2014 SIM IT key issues and trends study. MIS Q. Exec. 13(4), 237–263 (2014)
11. Lusch, R.F., Vargo, S.L., O'Brien, M.: Competing through service: insights from service-dominant logic. J. Retail. 83(1), 2–18 (2007)
12. Walls, J.H., Widmeyer, G.R., El Sawy, O.A.: Building an information systems design theory for vigilant EIS. Inf. Syst. Res. 3(1), 36–59 (1992)
13. Sein, M., Henfridsson, O., Purao, S., Rossi, M., Lindgren, R.: Action design research. MIS Q. 35(1), 37–56 (2011)
14. Yoo, J. H.: Service platform strategy: social networking and mobile service platform perspectives. Doctoral dissertation, Massachusetts Institute of Technology (2011)
15. Vargo, S.L., Lusch, R.F.: Evolving to a new dominant logic for marketing. J. Mark. 68, 1–17 (2004)
16. Heinrich, P., Schwabe, G.: Communicating nascent design theories on innovative information systems through multi-grounded design principles. In: Tremblay, M.C., VanderMeer, D., Rothenberger, M., Gupta, A., Yoon, V. (eds.) DESRIST 2014. LNCS, vol. 8463, pp. 148–163. Springer, Heidelberg (2014)
17. Chesbrough, H.: Open Innovation: The New Imperative for Creating and Profiting from Technology. Harvard Business School Press, Boston, MA (2003)
18. Markus, M.L., Majchrzak, A., Gasser, L.: A design theory for systems that support emergent knowledge processes. MIS Q. 26(3), 179–212 (2002)
19. Kuechler, W., Vaishnavi, V.: On theory development in design science research anatomy of a research project. Eur. J. Inf. Syst. 17, 489–504 (2008)
20. Gregor, S., Hevner, A.R.: Positioning and presenting design science research for maximum impact. Manage. Inf. Syst. Q. 37, 337–355 (2013)
21. Merton, R.C.: Harvard Business Review 91(4), 48–56, 9p. 3, April 2013
22. Eaton, B., Elaluf-Calderwood, S., Sørensen, C., Yoo, Y.: Distributed tuning of boundary resources: the case of apple's iOS service system. MIS Q. 39(1), 217–243 (2015)
23. Vargo, S.L., Lusch, R.F.: Institutions and axioms An extension and update of service-dominant logic. J. Acad. Mark. Sci. 44, 5–23 (2015). Advance online
24. Wareham, J., Fox, P.B., Cano Giner, J.L.: Technology Ecosystem Governance. Sci. 25, 1195–1215 (2014). Articles in Advance
25. Boudreau, K.: Does opening a platform stimulate innovation? The effect on systemic and modular innovations. MIT Sloan Research paper No. 4611-05 (2007)
26. Ceccagnoli, M., Forma, C., Huang, P., Wu, D.J.: Cocreation of value in a platform ecosystem: the case of enterprise software. MIS Q. 36(1), 263–290 (2012)
27. Drucker, P.: The coming of the new organization. Harvard Bus. Rev. 66, 45–53 (1988)
28. Christensen, C.: The Innovators Dilemma. Harvard Bussiness Review, Boston, US (1997)
29. Thomke, S.: Enlightened experimentation - the new imperative for innovation. Harvard Bus. Rev. 79(2), 66–75 (2001)

30. Chesbrough, H., Bogers, M.: Explicating open innovation. In: Chesbrough, H., Vanhaverbeke, W., West, J. (eds.) New Frontiers in Open Innovation. Oxford University Press, Oxford (2014)
31. Rogers, E.M.: Diffusion of Innovations. Free Press, New York (2003)
32. Gopalakrishnan, S., Damanpour, F.: A review of innovation research in economics, sociology, and technology management. Omega 25(1), 15–28 (1997)
33. Davenport, T.: Process Innovation: Reengineering Work Through Information Technology. Harvard Business School, Boston (1993)
34. den Hertog, P., van der Aa, W., de Jong, M.W.: Capabilities for managing service innovation towards a conceptual framework. J. Serv. Manage. 21(4), 490–514 (2010)
35. Vanhaverbeke, W., Chesbrough, H., West, J.: Surfing the new wave of open innovation research. In: Chesbrough, H., Vanhaverbeke, W., West, J. (eds.) New Frontiers in Open Innovation. Oxford University Press, Oxford (2014)
36. Office of Government Commerce: ITIL Service Operation. The Stationary Office (2011)
37. CMMI Product Team: CMMI for Services Version 1.3, Carnegie Mellon. Software Engineering Institute, Pittsburgh, PA (2010)
38. Hoving, W., van Bon, J.: The ISM Method – Past, Present and Future of IT Service Management. The Stationary Office, London (2012)
39. Rostock, P.: En bok om IT Service Management. Stjärnförlag, Sundbyberg (2013)
40. Göbel, H.: IT Service management - design principles for IT service management, Licentiate thesis. University of Linköping, Linköping (2014)
41. ITSM Community.: OGC self-assessment tool for ITIL service support (2016). http://www.itsmcommunity.org/resources/tool/ogc_self_assessment_tool_for_itil_service_support/
42. Zoho Corp.: Service Desk Plus. https://www.manageengine.com/products/service-desk. Accessed 12 Feb 2016
43. Solisma, Service Improvement Tool. http://service-improvement.com/. Accessed 16 Feb 2014
44. Patton, M.Q.: Qualitative Evaluation and Research Methods, 2nd edn. Sage Publications, London (1990)
45. Goldkuhl, G.: Design theories in information systems - a need for multi-grounding. J. Inf. Technol. Theory Appl. JITTA 6, 59–72 (2004)
46. Robertson, A.: Innovation management. Manag. Decis. Monogr. 12, 6–16 (1974)
47. Zaltman, G., Duncan, R., Holbek, J.: Innovations and Organizations. Wiley, New York (1973)
48. Fowler, F.J.: Survey Research Methods. Sage Publications, Thousand Oaks, CA (2002)
49. Hipp, C., Grupp, H.: Innovation in the service sector: the demand for service-specific innovation measurement concepts and typologies. Res. Policy 34, 517–535 (2005)

Applying Agile Design Sprint Methods in Action Design Research: Prototyping a Health and Wellbeing Platform

W.J.W. Keijzer-Broers[(✉)] and M. de Reuver

Delft University of Technology, Delft, The Netherlands
{w.j.w.keijzer-broers,g.a.dereuver}@tudelft.nl

Abstract. In Action Design Research projects, researchers often face severe constraints in terms of budget and time within the practical setting. Therefore, we argue that ADR researchers may adopt efficient methods to guide their design strategy. While agile and sprint oriented design approaches are becoming common in the practitioner domain, they have not been integrated yet in Action Design research. In this paper we illustrate how a Design Sprint could jumpstart a design process in an ADR setting, fostering a low-fidelity prototype into a minimal viable product. We do so by describing an extensive case on a health and wellbeing platform for elderly people developed in a Living Lab setting. We extract lessons learned on how to apply design sprints in Action Design Research, which can be reused to guide other situated design projects with limited resources.

Keywords: Action design research · Agile · Smart living · Prototype · Health and wellbeing platform · Age-in-place · Design sprint

1 Introduction

Action Design Research (ADR) has been proposed by Sein et al. [1] as an approach to design IT artefacts in a problem-inspired and action-oriented setting. ADR combines action research (AR) and design research (DR) to generate prescriptive knowledge, is problem-driven and aims to build design principles based on iterative cycles. In doing so, the starting point of ADR is the practical problem in an organization, or a network of organizations, rather than a theoretical design problem [cf., 2]. While ADR provides a useful positioning of situated design projects, the approach still leaves a lot of freedom to the researcher, which design methods to use. In this paper, we focus on the specific class of ADR projects where researchers face severe constraints in terms of budget and time available in the practical setting. Such situations might especially be common in real-life settings where stakeholders participate in design efforts without external subsidies or funding. Due to limited resources we argue that ADR researchers may adopt efficient methods to guide their design strategy, without losing sight of the intended research goals. In order to track real-time problems during the design process and to allow rapid iterations, especially agile ways of working based on flexibility, adaptability and productivity [3] combined with User Experience (UX) design appear

© Springer International Publishing Switzerland 2016
J. Parsons et al. (Eds.): DESRIST 2016, LNCS 9661, pp. 68–80, 2016.
DOI: 10.1007/978-3-319-39294-3_5

promising in the practitioner domain. Both methods traditionally use different approaches for resource allocation [4] but integration of Agile and UX design methods is increasing in practice as it seems to produce better-designed products than versions designed using waterfall approaches [5, 6]. While agile and sprint oriented design approaches are becoming common in the practitioner domain, they have not been integrated yet in ADR approaches. Therefore, the research objective of this paper is to illustrate how to combine a design sprint method with Action Design Research. This by describing a design case of a health and wellbeing platform to support people age-in-place, which is developed in a Living Lab setting. Our case uses requirements and specifications developed in previous iterations as a starting point. The case is appropriate as it concerns a Living Lab with multiple stakeholders without external funding, implying that budget and time resources were severely limited.

After the description of the Action Design Research method (Sect. 2), a background on the case at hand is provided (Sect. 3). In Sect. 4 we enter the Building, Intervention and Evaluation phase. In Sect. 5 the design framework is described, subsequently followed by insights from the design sprint (Sect. 6). After the discussion in Sect. 7, we conclude our paper with lessons learned and future work (Sect. 8).

2   Action Design Research Method

For the design of the platform, we apply Action Design Research (ADR) [1] as an overarching method. ADR is problem-inspired and combines thinking with doing [7, 8]. ADR is an appropriate method as: (1) it combines action research (AR) and design research (DR) to generate prescriptive knowledge, (2) it is problem-driven, and (3) it aims to build design principles based on iterative cycles. Sein et al. [1] emphasized their model on the Design Science Research paradigm advanced by Venable [9]. The object of ADR is what Sein et al. [1] call an ensemble artifact, i.e., an artifact composed of technological and social elements. In our project, the artifact is an online match-making platform for health and wellbeing to support people age-in-place and the ADR team acts within a Living Lab setting. ADR differs from ethnography because the researchers intervene in the research context in situ. While ADR has received much attention since the breakthrough paper by Sein et al. [1], the method has not been fully explored in practice and there is a limited number of completed ADR cases in literature available [10]. Therefore, Iivari [2] explicitly encourages researchers to evaluate ADR in practice. To do so, our ADR case is based on primary data and comprises a cyclic process of design iterations (i.e., prototyping, testing, analyzing and refining) within a real-life setting. To reflect on the ADR process and to track the iterative design steps, the action design researcher kept an observation log on a daily basis (2013–2016) amounting up to 900 memos. Next to that, the logbook is used as a scientific record [11] establishing a chain of evidence, and therefore contains the decision steps and feedback loops related to the design process and the preliminary outcomes.

3 Case Description

Our case is situated in the domain of health and wellbeing in the Netherlands. As many other countries in Europe, the Dutch government is aiming at a better integration of health and social care not only to support older adults but also patients with chronic conditions in the community [12]. Although people prefer to stay at home as long as possible and deinstitutionalization is also based on the assumption that homecare services are less costly than institutional services, it also represents a major challenge, as increased support for homecare has to be provided somehow [13]. From 2015 onwards the responsibility and the execution of health care in the Netherlands is shifted towards the municipalities and therefore local authorities (i.e., municipalities) are: (1) responsible for supporting citizens so that they can participate in society, (2) free to decide for themselves how they meet these targets, and (3) accountable at a local level for their performance. On the other hand municipalities receive non-earmarked budgets, giving them strong incentives to contain costs and to improve cost-efficiency [14]. However, local governments are searching for solutions to mitigate the transition phase. Together with the support of a Dutch metropolitan city the research team established a Living Lab setting to explore the practicality of an online health and wellbeing platform, which could support elderly people to age-in-place.

In 2013 the first set of requirements for the platform were identified and the main purpose of the platform was defined as (1) an online community for contact, solutions, social wellbeing, interaction with the neighborhood and a digital marketplace for applications, (2) an information exchange platform, between providers and end-users (business to consumer), driven by the need for matchmaking between service providers and end-users, (3) a portal for bundled, services and solutions (business to consumer), driven by the one-stop-shop, philosophy for aging-in-place, where end-users can find relevant applications related to health and wellbeing, but also can create a personal profile, and (4) an intervention instrument for the local government (government to consumer) to get in contact with citizens about needs for services and questions about health care and legislations. Ultimately, such a platform should enable end-users to enhance self-management (i.e., independency) by the provision of relevant information and support in matchmaking between different stakeholder groups (i.e., consumers, providers and government). Eventually the platform has to enhance the quality of life of end-users.

In 2014 an initial set of Critical Design Issues (CDIs) for the platform is extracted from 59 interviews (i.e., strategic level stakeholders, affiliate level stakeholders and end-users). To elaborate on the main features, eight personas were introduced as vivid descriptions of the potential platform user [15]. The personas described potential users related to four different archetypes (i.e., elderly, informal caretakers, providers and representatives of a local government). During two focus group sessions the action design researcher evaluated if the personas, as a user-centered design tool, would lead to a better understanding of the end-user. Followed by two expert meetings to improve these personas and applied them as input for user stories and scenario descriptions. These design tools (i.e., personas, user stories and scenarios) are used to focus attention on problems and opportunities of a specific target audience.

4 Building, Intervention and Evaluation Phase

While the initial ADR phase (i.e., Problem Formulation) explored the generic scope and functional requirements for the platform, the next ADR phase (i.e., Building, Intervention and Evaluation) focused on the instantiation of the design in a municipal setting, and evaluated the platform in practice. To enter the stage of 'Building, Intervention and Evaluation (BIE)' we moved in 2015 from a pure academic environment to a Living Lab setting with a multi-disciplinary network of people and organizations. Our Living Lab can be described as a Quadruple Helix: an innovation co-operation between large and small-medium enterprises, the university, public organizations and end-users [16]. The focus of the Living Lab is to develop a service platform, which should not only create awareness among end-users about what services and technologies can help them, but also assist in matchmaking between (latent) needs and (yet unknown) services. Ultimately, such a platform should enable end-users to enhance self-management (i.e., independency) by the provision of relevant information and on the other hand support in matchmaking between different stakeholder groups (i.e., consumers, providers and government). Unfortunately, after a jumpstart executing the first two design iterations, we experienced a decreased energy level within the Living Lab setting. Because there is no subsidy or monetized compensation involved related to the stakeholders' effort, it was core to keep the participants motivated. After careful considerations about our constraints (i.e., time, money and energy level) versus the research goal, we decided to use a Design Sprint method [17–19] to speed up the prototype process, hoping that the design sprint workshop would give the Living Lab partners an energy boost.

5 Design Framework

To shape the design iterations within the BIE phase, we followed a specific method for Living Lab settings from Ståhlbröst and Holst [20] who emphasize five design iterations within a Living Lab setting (i.e., planning, concept design, prototype design, innovation design and commercialization). To execute these iterations we extracted not just two, like suggested in the framework of Da Silva [21], but even three teams from the Living Lab setting that worked in parallel on the design, development and evaluation of the platform. The Development team established a project plan, specified the critical design issues in a navigation plan and a high level architecture of the platform. The Design team designed mock-ups as basic input for the low-fidelity platform prototype and, translated the clickable model into a platform demo. The Research team identified related design issues by means of interviews, refined user stories and scenarios, facilitated workshops and evaluated the prototypes within multiple user tests. Although, agile development methods strive to deliver small sets of features with minimal design effort in short iterations, while UX design needs more time and considerable research effort, we adapted insights from both design methods [21, 22], and incorporated them in a design framework that was efficient for our project (see Fig. 1).

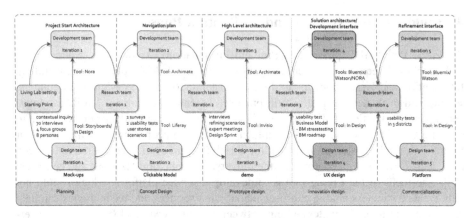

Fig. 1. Design cycle iterations: efforts from three ADR teams [21].

Meanwhile, input from potential end-users within the Living Lab (e.g., local government, service providers, informal caretakers and elderly) informed the research process. Having the end-user on-sight, made it possible to facilitate the user tests and allow the different teams to incorporate test results in subsequent design iterations.

As a starting point of the Living Lab setting previous research input (i.e., 70 interviews, contextual inquiry, results from four focus groups sessions and defined personas) [23] was already available to inspire the three ADR teams (i.e., Development, Design and Research team) at the same time. The preliminary research effort from the Research team could be regarded as **design iteration 0** [21]. In the **first design iteration** (i.e., the planning phase) the Development team focused on defining a project plan to guide the platform architecture, while the Design team worked on the first mock-ups of the platform. In the meantime the Research team developed user stories and scenarios based on the eight early-defined personas and refined the requirements as a result from previous conducted interviews and end-user surveys [24, 25]. In the **second design iteration** (i.e., concept design phase) the Development team worked on the initial version of the platform architecture, while the Design team translated the mock-ups into a clickable model (i.e., alpha version of the platform). Subsequently, the Research team refined the user stories/scenarios and evaluated the clickable model in two usability tests with potential end-users [26]. Based on the main features the alpha version of the platform captures basically three core functionalities: (1) a social environment for local activities and contacts, (2) a marketplace for smart living products and services with reviews, and (3) a health and wellbeing profile which can be extended with a personal Care Plan. The rationale behind the Care Plan is that people themselves can be the center of action-taking related to health and wellbeing, such as measuring, tracking, experimenting and engaging in interventions, treatments and activities. In the **third design iteration** (i.e., prototype design phase) the Development and Design team respectively refined the architecture and the clickable model and, subsequently, representatives of each ADR team were included in a three day Design Sprint workshop. As an output of the workshop the Design team delivered a demo of the platform. The demo is subsequently used for a usability test with elderly end-users, informal and professional caretakers, service-providers and representatives from the local government. In parallel the Research team arranged two business model workshops to be prepared for up scaling of the platform initiative. The outcomes of the third design iteration are being used for the **fourth design iteration** (i.e., design innovation phase), which is currently work in progress and focuses on the development of the minimal viable product (i.e., interface). **The fifth design iteration** (i.e., commercialization phase) is part of the future research agenda within the Living Lab setting.

6   Design Sprint Session

As mentioned before, the Design Sprint was part of the third design iteration (i.e., prototype design). Although there is no shortage of models, frameworks and methodologies to guide design thinking, limited resources challenged us to explore condensed design thinking methods like provided by IBM [17] and Google Venture [19] to shape our design sprint journey. Due to preliminary work in the first two design iterations the actual Design Sprint session could be limited to three days instead of the recommended five.

Before the design sprint was executed the workshop moderator (i.e., an experienced UX designer) formulated the design tasks and prepared six sprint stages (i.e., understand, define, diverge, decide, prototype and validate) as a guideline for the Design Sprint. In the meantime the workshop members (i.e., ADR researcher, UX designers and developers) reviewed related research input, which was stored at an online cloud tool.

The **first Design Sprint day** started with an overview of the workshop approach, followed by an in-depth interview with the problem owner (i.e., policy maker of the health and wellbeing domain of the metropolitan city). The rationale behind this interview was to verify if the initial idea about the platform was still valid, and if it fulfilled the basic needs of the local government to support people aging-in-place. Subsequently, the workshop participants compared these insights with the eight pre-defined personas before indicating persona Ria (see Fig. 2) as the key-user of the platform.

The rationale behind this is that persona Ria fits the user profile extracted from preliminary research efforts, because she is (1) an informal caretaker, (2) an intermediary for relatives, and (3) belongs to the young elderly group (age between 55–75 year). Persona Ria (55) is married, has a part time job as a caregiver, is devoting her time to take care of her parents and her children as well, and belongs to the so-called sandwich generation. According to Roots [27], adult children that are literally 'sandwiched' between their aging parents and their own maturing children (or even grandchildren) are, because of this burden, subjected to a great deal of stress. By defining what could unburden Ria, her persona description is extended with initial user stories (see Table 1).

User stories are written in the following format: As a<type of user>I want<some goal>so that<some reason>. This structure helps to really flesh out requirements and create a better understanding of the user [28].

Fig. 2. Caregiver Ria (one of eight predefined personas).

Table 1. User stories for persona Ria.

Requirements	Must-haves	Nice to haves
	As Ria an informal caretaker...	As Ria an informal caretaker
Functional	... I need to be able to support my parents so they can live independently as long as possible ... I need to find the right help at the right time to support my parents ... I need a monitor system to be notified when something is happening with my parents	... I want to post information in a diary and share this with my parents/relatives ... I want to stay in touch with my relatives about appointed and future tasks related to my parents ... I like to share a calendar with my relatives
User interaction	... I need a simple to use interface that encourages me to use an online system ...I need a online system that is trustworthy	... I want a helpline to support me with an online system ... I want to consult a review system for products and services
Social context	.... I need to have peace of mind related to the (health) condition of my parents .... I need help from my kids as a backup related to the use of an online system	.... I want to find likeminded people, to share ideas and problems

Based on previous research insights the following refined user stories have been created for Persona Ria, categorized as either functional, user interaction or contextual requirements [29].

Next to that, we approached the needs from both Ria as her parents from a preventive, urgent and after-care perspective to encounter end-user needs experienced in different situations. See Table 2.

Table 2. Needs from an end-user perspective.

Perspective	Needs elderly people	Needs informal caretaker
Preventive	What do we need to live in a comfortable way in our own home? Where can we find additional help if needed? Where can we find local activities which suit our interests?	How can I support/monitor my parents in a seamless way? How can I start a conversation with my parents about 'aging-in-place'? Where can I find local activities to suggest to my parents that will fit their interests and daily schedule?
Urgent	Who can help us in case of emergency?	How can I arrange practical help to support my parents in case of an emergency?
After care	What kind of additional help is available to recover/stay at home after an incident	How can I find trustworthy products and services to support my parents so that they can stay at home?

Based on the user stories and end-user needs the workshop participants discussed multiple scenarios, whereas one was chosen to guide the platform design:

What if Ria's mother Bep broke her hip? How can an online platform help Ria to make practical arrangements to ensure Bep can return home to her husband Jan instead of recovering in a rehabilitation center?

In the **second Design Sprint day** the scenario is extended with Ria's personal customer journey related to the arrangements she has to make in a certain timeframe after her mothers' fall incident. See Table 3.

After defining the customer journey the workshop participants made a competitive overview from existing health and wellbeing platforms to verify that 'the wheel was not invented elsewhere'. Subsequently, the participants sketched as many possible solutions that could support Ria with her customer journey, using different brainstorm techniques and diverge methods like mind maps, storyboards and 'crazy eights' (i.e., 5 min to create 8 sketches). This idea-generation phase, without regards for constraints and criticism, resulted in dozens of plausible platform ideas, which were accordingly categorized and extensively discussed. See Fig. 3.

At the end of the second day the participants voted for the three best ideas, and, at the start of the **Third Design Sprint day**, every participant had to pitch their most favorite idea. After the pitches the team discussed how to combine the most suitable ideas that could guide the platform design. Based on all input of the first two design sprint days the rest of the third day was used to shape and reshape the demo of the platform according to Bep's fall scenario and taking into account the pre-defined user-stories of persona Ria. See Fig. 4 for the first platform sketches. The Dutch platform demo can be consulted via: Zo-Dichtbij (translation of the title: *'as-close-as-possible'*).

Table 3. Arrangements Ria has to make, after her mothers'fall incident.

Timeframe	Arrangements after the fall incident
Directly	Collect insurance papers/medicines/identification/their doctor etc. Reassure Jan that everything will be all right with Bep Follow the ambulance to the hospital
Within 1-4 h	Inform close relatives Pick up toiletries for Bep Prepare questions for the surgeon Organize practical arrangements for Jan: groceries, meal, walk the dog
Within 24 h	Inform insurer/read insurance policy Contact helpdesk local government: demand for assistance Divide urgent tasks with close relatives: arrangements at home Schedule hospital visits Organize nursing aids: adjustable bed, walker/wheelchair etc.
Within one week	Find service provider for adjustments in the house: remove thresholds, renovate shower, install stair elevator etc. Divide daily tasks with close relatives/informal caretakers Think of a system to keep close relatives/informal caretakers informed about the situation (for instance a care plan). Find suitable activities for both parents that fit their interests and day schedule

Fig. 3. Overview (fragment) of used diverging techniques (e.g., mind maps and storyboards).

Fig. 4. First sketches of the platform demo Zo-Dichtbij (Dutch Market).

To ensure external validity in the third design iteration, the Research team used a couple of weeks to test the platform demo with 30 end-users (i.e., elderly, caretakers, providers and representatives of the local government). Our general motivation to include the end-user in the ADR process is the adaptability to new obstacles as soon as they pop up. Accordingly, the ADR research team adjusted the goal-setting procedures, confided to what the end-user states in the next design iteration. Furthermore, communication with our target groups is crucial to understand especially the abilities, morals and mindsets of elderly people. Overall the platform demo was positively evaluated and highly appreciated by the test group. Minor details were related to the use of colors, corps sizes, spelling mistakes and sequences of questions. Regarding extra functionalities interesting suggestions were made, like: anonymous use of the platform, chat possibilities with relatives, sharing diary with family, simultaneous use of the care plan, connection with social media for arranging local activities, frequent asked questions and adding checkboxes for social and medical arrangements. Next to that, some reviewers had additional questions about: the security of the care plan, privacy issues and if the 'guide' in the platform was intended to be a real person or a chat bot. Comments were gathered and the feedback was summarized in a revision table.

After internal discussions with the Living Lab participants, core adjustments were made in the platform demo as input for the fourth design iteration (i.e., innovation design) developing the minimal viable product. All suggested extra functionalities are added to the wish list.

7 Discussion

For the execution of the Building, Intervention and Evaluation (BIE) phase of our ADR project, we used insights from Da Silva [21] how to get 'the best' from two design worlds and integrate agile development with user experience practices. This is an initial attempt to combine UX and Agile design methods in a Living Lab setting and to foster collaboration between design teams (i.e., Development and UX Design) in an ongoing process. To guide the research process we incorporated the Research team in the design iteration cycles as well. During the whole research process we made sure the Research team kept one step ahead of the other teams by providing timely research input, so that the development and design team could focus on relatively small design tasks at the time, instead of designing the whole platform tool at once. However, improving an artifact does not come without risks or costs and in order to reduce this, the framework supports the idea that all the iterative design and evaluation steps are executed in a condensed form.

Therefore we consulted the Living Lab partners as efficient as possible, taking into account that we had to place the values of the stakeholders in the health and wellbeing domain into a real-life context. This context both stimulates and challenges research and development, as public authorities and end-users will not only participate in the Living Lab, but contribute to the whole innovation process as well.

In retrospect, combining UX design and the agile way of working within the Development team fitted well in the Living Lab setting, but it heavily relied on the ADR team members' ability to properly collaborate and to have an 'open mind' in the first place. This open mind proved to be crucial in the Design Sprint session, as well. Despite of the participants' background (i.e., development, UX design and research), we managed, within three days to develop a platform demo that justified previous research efforts. This could not have been done without the help of an experienced Design Sprint moderator. Nevertheless, the platform demo was a satisfying result from the Design Sprint, within a limited amount of time and restricted budget. Next to that, de sprint session generated also the predicted energy boost within the Living Lab. At least we had something tangible to show and discuss with the 'world', which was experienced as a valuable intermediate step to inspire the fourth design iteration.

Next to that, the demo made it easier for the ADR team to have thorough discussions about the platform idea in the market, not only with end-users (i.e., elderly, informal caretakers, providers and local governments) but also with potential (funding) partners. Since the Design Sprint session, the platform demo is successfully used as visual support during numerous 'pitches' with influential companies in the Netherlands to explore up scaling and valorization of the system.

8 Conclusion and Future Work

This paper provides an initial foray into integrating agile, sprint and user experience methods within an Action Design Research strategy. Based on an extensive and rich case of ADR we illustrated (1) how to combine agile and UX design approaches in a seamless way and, (2) how to apply design sprints as a condensed but sound design thinking method. The Design Sprint session is experienced as an enrichment of the third design iteration, because it forced the teams to refine earlier research outcomes and to make final decisions how to visualize the platform in a low-fidelity prototype, within a limited amount of time. Although, we only incorporated one scenario in the demo, extra scenarios from different perspectives are currently under review as part of the fourth design iteration: developing the interface. As a follow up, usability tests with different groups of informal caretakers, district nurses and potential end-users (age group 55–75) are foreseen, before implementing the minimal viable product in three districts of a Dutch metropolitan city.

The artefact can be seen as a groundbreaking concept for the smart living domain in the Netherlands, because it would be a first mover to combine and offer: (1) match-making between providers of smart living products and services and potential end-users (2) finding local activities (3) connecting with other people (e.g., family, caretakers) (4) information about aging-in-place and, (5) integration of successful, existing platforms in the health and wellbeing domain. Nevertheless, an important aspect for the success of the platform is the availability of resources within our Living Lab setting (i.e., intellectual, time and money). Limited resources required creativity and determination of the research team and this experience can guide other researchers dealing with similar design projects. The ADR method gave us the opportunity to get a close look at the complexity of the design process when multiple stakeholders with different value propositions are involved. Next to that, by maintaining a logbook the Action Design Researcher could track and trace the decision steps in the design process, to establish a chain of evidence and this improves transparency, validity and reliability of the research. Hence, researchers can use similar methods to create their own design science research studies.

References

1. Sein, M., et al.: Action design research. MIS Q. **35**(1), 37–56 (2011)
2. Iivari, J.: Distinguishing and contrasting two strategies for design science research. Eur. J. Inf. Syst. **24**(1), 107–115 (2015)
3. Schwaber, K.: Agile Project Management with Scrum. Microsoft Press, USA (2004)
4. Fox, D., Sillito, J., Maurer, F.: Agile methods and user-centered design: how these two methodologies are being successfully integrated in industry. In: AGILE, pp. 63–72. IEEE (2008)
5. Da Silva, T.S., et al.: User-centered design and agile methods: a systematic review. In: AGILE, pp. 77–86 (2011)
6. Sy, D.: Adapting usability investigations for agile user-centered design. J. Usability Stud. **2**(3), 112–132 (2007)
7. Markus, M.L., Majchrzak, A., Gasser, L.: A design theory for systems that support emergent knowledge processes. MIS Q. **26**(3), 179–212 (2002)
8. Kuechler, W., Vaishnavi, V.: On theory development in design science research: anatomy of a research project. Eur. J. Inf. Syst. **17**(5), 1–23 (2008)
9. Venable, J.: The role of theory and theorising in design science research. In: DESRIST, pp. 1–18 (2006)

10. Mullarkey, M.T., Hevner, A.R.: Entering Action Design Research. In: Donnellan, B., Helfert, M., Kenneally, J., VanderMeer, D., Rothenberger, M., Winter, R. (eds.) DESRIST 2015. LNCS, vol. 9073, pp. 121–134. Springer, Heidelberg (2015)
11. Alaszewski, A.: Using Diaries for Social Research. Sage, Beverly Hills (2006)
12. Rechel, B., et al.: Ageing in the European union. Lancet 381(9874), 1312–1322 (2013)
13. Jacobzone, S., Cambois, E., Robine, J.M.: The health of older persons in OECD countries: is it improving fast enough to compensate for population ageing? In: Labour Market and Social Policy Occasional Papers. OECD: Paris, pp. 149–190 (1999)
14. Schut, E., Sorbe, S., Høj, J.: Health care reform and long-term care in the Netherlands. In: OECD Economics Department Working Papers. OECD Publishing (2013)
15. Long, F.: Real or imaginary: The effectiveness of using personas in product design. In: Proceedings of the Irish Ergonomics Society Annual Conference, pp. 1–10 (2009)
16. Arnkil, R., et al.: *Exploring the quadruple helix* Outlining user-oriented innovation models. Report of Quadruple Helix Research for the CLIQ Project (2010)
17. IBM.: IBM Design Thinking. http://www.ibm.com/design/thinking/
18. Direkova, N.: Design sprint methods - Playbook for start up and designers. (2015)
19. Knapp, J., Zeratsky, J., Kowitz, B.: Sprint: how to Solve Big Problems and Test New Ideas in Just Five Days. Google Ventures (2016)
20. Ståhlbröst, A., Holst, M.: The Living Lab Methodology Handbook. Lulea University of Technology and CDT, SmartIES Project, a Transnational Nordic Smart City Living Lab Pilot (2012)
21. Da Silva, T.S., et al.: User experience design and Agile development: from theory to practice. J. Softw. Eng. Appl. 5(10), 743–751 (2012)
22. Preece, J., Sharp, H., Rogers, Y.: Interaction Design - Beyond Human-Computer Interaction. Wiley, New York (2015). vol. 11, 34
23. Keijzer-Broers, W., Nikayin, F., De Reuver, M.: Main Requirements of a Health and Wellbeing Platform: Findings From Four Focus Group Discussions. in ACIS. AUT Library, Auckland (2014)
24. Keijzer-Broers, W.J.W., de Reuver, G.A., Guldemond, N.A.: Designing a multi-sided health and wellbeing platform: results of a first design cycle. In: Bodine, C., Helal, S., Gu, T., Mokhtari, M. (eds.) ICOST 2014. LNCS, vol. 8456, pp. 3–12. Springer, Heidelberg (2015)
25. Keijzer-Broers, W., Florez Atehortua, L., De Reuver, M.: Prototyping a Health and Wellbeing Platform: an Action Design Research Approach. In: 49th Hawaii International Conference on System Sciences (HICSS). IEEE computer society, Kauai (2016)
26. Keijzer-Broers, W., et al.: Developing a health and wellbeing platform in a living lab setting: an action design research study. In: *DESRIST,* Dublin (2015)
27. Roots, C.R.: The Sandwich Generation: Adult Children Caring for Aging Parents. Routledge, Abingdon (2014)
28. Cohn, M.: User Stories Applied: For Agile Software Development. Addison-Wesley Professional, Boston (2004)
29. Verschuren, P., Hartog, R.: Evaluation in design-oriented research. Qual. Quant. 39(6), 733–762 (2005)

Exploring the Design, Use, and Outcomes of Process Guidance Systems - A Qualitative Field Study

Stefan Morana[1(✉)], Silvia Schacht[2], and Alexander Maedche[1,2]

[1] Institute of Information Systems and Marketing,
Karlsruhe Institute of Technology, Karlsruhe, Germany
`stefan.morana@kit.edu`
[2] Institute for Enterprise Systems, University of Mannheim,
Mannheim, Germany
`{silvia.schacht,alexander.maedche}@kit.edu`

Abstract. Organizations define processes specifying employees' daily work and require them to be process compliant in order to prevent expensive mistakes and ensure a high quality. Employees have difficulties in being process compliant, among other reasons, due to lacking process knowledge. Addressing this lack of process knowledge and the need to support employees' process execution, we investigate the process guidance concept. In this research, we present a process guidance system implemented in a case company and its evaluation in the form of a qualitative field study. The findings from the interviews and focus groups confirm the intended outcomes of process guidance on the users' process knowledge, performance, and process compliance. Moreover, we discuss in detail the outcomes of process guidance usage and identify opportunities for future research.

Keywords: Process guidance · Design principles · Qualitative field study

1 Introduction

Organizations define business processes to structure and specify their employees' daily work [1]. By implementing information systems (IS), organizations aim to support their employees with their process[1] execution. Conformance with the respective processes is defined as process compliance [2]. In contrast, failing to comply with the predefined processes will most likely result in a potential loss of resources, failures in the process execution, decrease of the process outcome's quality, and even legal penalties. In order to prevent these undesired consequences, organizations demand compliance with predefined processes. However, in practice, employees often have difficulties in executing processes according to the definitions due to various reasons. For instance, they might not be aware of certain details of the process definition or perceive a process compliant behavior as high effort [3]. Further, users might become frustrated during process execution when they face issues due to technical problems or lack of

---

[1] In this paper, we use the terms business process and process synonymously.

© Springer International Publishing Switzerland 2016
J. Parsons et al. (Eds.): DESRIST 2016, LNCS 9661, pp. 81–96, 2016.
DOI: 10.1007/978-3-319-39294-3_6

knowledge caused by poor training or their unwillingness to read instructions [4]. As a result, users are likely to choose less expensive strategies to fulfill their daily work and execute processes without considering the process specifications, leading to a loss of accuracy [5]. Such workarounds do not only negatively impact individuals' but also the organization's overall performance [6]. Thus, supporting employees' compliant process execution is relevant to the organization's success.

To date, some researchers (e.g. [7, 8]) implemented several tools that aim to support process compliance using the concept of process guidance. Some of the researchers [8, 9] evaluated the effects of such process guidance systems (PGS) on the users' satisfaction with the system and overall processing time in laboratory experiments. Although there are some artifacts supporting process compliance, the theoretical grounding and descriptions of the PGS design seem to be missing in current research. Aiming to design PGS that increase the users' process knowledge, execution performance, and compliance, we conducted a design science research (DSR) project [10] in cooperation with a case company. In doing so, we (i) identified gaps and requirements of PGS in order to (ii) derive appropriate design principles (DPs) grounded in existing research, and (iii) evaluate the resulting PGS artifact within a qualitative field study. Thereby, the following research question motivates our research:

How and why do process guidance systems influence users' process knowledge, execution performance, and process compliance?

This research contributes by evaluating the proposed PGS design and exploring the outcomes on the increase of users' process knowledge, execution performance, and compliance. The gathered design knowledge is of value for researchers and practitioners. Researchers can build on or extend the DPs to design their own artifacts to examine further outcomes of process guidance. As our study is conducted in a real-world setting, we follow the call by Peffers et al. [11] for more real-world evaluations of DSR artifacts. Moreover, we produce results having a high external validity [12] in a rigorous way by applying established research approaches in a field setting. At the same time, we derive design knowledge having a high practical relevance. Practitioners benefit from this knowledge, since we provide guidelines and examples on how to design a PGS for supporting users' process knowledge, execution performance, and compliance.

2   Related Work

We divide the related work on process guidance into two parts: **First**, in the context of decision-making and decision support, researchers intensively investigated the concept of guidance. In particular decisional guidance [13], explanations [14], and decision aids [15] were applied to various contexts and empirically evaluated multiple times. Within these studies, researchers examine considerable key factors when providing guidance. The type of guidance is one relevant factor for effective guidance and needs to be adapted to the complexity of the supported task. Within two laboratory experiments, Montazemi et al. [16], for example, demonstrate that suggestive guidance, which makes explicit recommendations, is more beneficial for tasks with low complexity.

In contrast, informative guidance that *"provides pertinent information that enlightens the decision maker's judgment without suggesting how he/she should act"* [16, p. 182] has a higher effect for highly complex tasks. As guidance also aims to support the users' task or context understanding, the degree of user participation is another relevant factor. When actively participating in the task execution, users will learn more effectively the task's underlying concepts [17] or contexts, which in turn will result, for example, in a higher decision quality, performance (effectiveness and efficiency), and satisfaction [18]. Researchers showed these outcomes of decisional guidance in laboratory settings [19, 20]. In particular, novice users will benefit from guidance, in the form of recommendations, when enriched with explanations. Thus, the expertise of the audience (novice vs. experts) should be incorporated in the design of guidance [21].

Second, some researchers applied the concept of process guidance to develop innovative artifacts and solve issues for specific contexts. Becker-Kornstaedt et al. [7], for example, applied the process guidance concept in the software development domain. The resulting artifact supports users with the system requirements analysis within a software development project. COPA [8] is another research prototype that applies the process guidance concept. Integrated into the users' email client, COPA automatically matches e-mails to processes, provides context-sensitive information, and enhances the e-mail with proactive annotations.

Summarizing, there are various evaluations of process guidance artifacts that demonstrate the effects on the users' performance, efficiency, and satisfaction. However, there is no report of the design of all the process guidance artifacts and the underlying theory for their design in current literature. Furthermore, although some researchers evaluate guidance artifacts, there is no research discussing the guidance provision outcomes on process compliance and subsequent design knowledge. Thus, the research on guidance in the context of decision-making and support provides important insights applicable for the process compliance context.

3   Design Science Research Project

Aiming to understand the phenomenon of process compliance, but also to create an artifact that solves the issues related to this phenomenon, our research follows the DSR approach [10] applying the suggestions by Kuechler and Vaishnavi [22]. We divide the overall DSR project into three subsequent design cycles, whereas this article reports the results of the third design cycle. In order to increase the relevance of the research, we selected an appropriate industry partner that also serves as the case company of our research project [23]. The case company is a global supplier, development, and service partner for customers in various sectors such as automotive, civil aviation, and mechanical engineering. In 2014, the case company employed 16.950 employees in over 45 sites in Europe and America and had sales of more than 2.1 billion €.

In the **first design cycle**, we explored the issues related to process compliance reported in existing literature and discussed within the case company. Therefore, we conducted a series of expert interviews in the case company and executed an extensive literature review on the guidance concept in IS research to identify meta-requirements (MRs) on PGS. The conducted expert interviews revealed that the employees have difficulties in executing processes according to their definitions and suffer from a lack of understanding of the underlying process models. In particular, one of the intervie-wees requested some *"...guidance, claiming the system which needs to be used in a particular business process step"* [3, p. 7]. Building on an extensive literature review on guidance in IS research, we propose the concept of process guidance and derive three theory-grounded DPs for PGS to support users' with increasing their process knowledge, their process execution performance, and, their process compliance:

> *DP1: Provide user-requested, predefined suggestive process guidance based on the monitoring and analysis of users' business context.*
>
> *DP2: Visualize lean and precise process guidance based on process specifications integrated in the users' work environment.*
>
> *DP3: Integrate detailed information about process specifications and required process resources into the provided guidance adapted to the user.*

Within the first design cycle, we qualitatively evaluated the derived DPs by conducting focus group workshops within our case company. The entire first design cycle, including the derivation of the theory-grounded DPs and their evaluation, is reported in [3].

In the **second design cycle**, we instantiated the DPs in a PGS artifact. As the second cycle aimed at demonstrating the effects of process guidance on novice users, the artifact was adapted to a laboratory experimental setting. In order to produce a quasi-real case situation, we selected the case company's ticketing process as the context for the experiment. Thus, we developed three simplified versions of the case company's applications used for the ticketing process. Each of the artifact implements various degrees of guidance by activating different DPs: (i) one PGS artifact imple-ments DP2 and DP3, (ii) one PGS artifact implements only DP2, and (iii) one PGS artifact implements none of the DPs, meaning that the artifact did not provide any guidance. In total, 118 graduate students from a German public university participated in the experiment equally distributed to the different artifacts. Within the experiment, the participants had to execute eight processes. The experiment revealed that novices benefit from process guidance and detailed information about the process steps, as they have little process knowledge. Providing process guidance supports novices to understand the process specification and increase their process execution performance. In addition, the visualization of process guidance (DP2) exploits its highest potential in combination with the provision of detailed information about the process steps (DP3). Thus, the results provide first indications on the impact of PGS on users' process knowledge and execution performance.

In the **third design cycle**, we aimed at evaluating and demonstrating the outcomes of the proposed DPs in a field study at our case company. Following the calls for more real-world evaluations of process compliance approaches by Becker et al. [24] and DSR artifacts by Peffers et al. [11], the DPs for PGS were evaluated in the case company to balance the rigor and the relevance of our research. We decided to observe the outcomes of the PGS design in the same context – the IT service ticketing process – as done in the experiment. The case company's IT governance team is responsible for the management of all IT related services. They defined four types of tickets with respect to the IT service management (ITSM) adapted from the ITIL framework [25]. For all ticket types, the organization defined distinct processes. To support the case company's ITSM team, a ticketing system implements all of the processes, and the users are required to use the system for their ITSM process execution. However, the IT governance head reports that especially the IT department employees have difficulties in a compliant execution of the ITSM processes and the usage of the ticketing system. Within two workshops, we presented the process guidance concept, the derived DPs, the existing prototypes, and discussed our findings with the ITSM team. Subsequently, the ITSM team presented the four ticket types and their underlying processes. Considering the ITSM context and the case company's ticketing system, we implemented a new PGS comprising the DPs. Figure 1 depicts a screenshot of the resulting ITSM ProcessGuide.

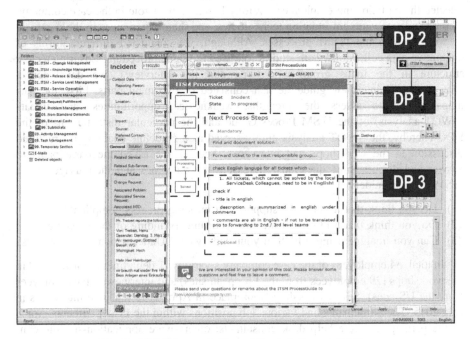

Fig. 1. ITSM ProcessGuide and the ticketing application

We integrated the PGS into the case company's ticketing system and the users can invoke it by clicking the button highlighted with DP1 in Fig. 1. Once clicked, the ITSM ProcessGuide starts and presents the process specification for the current process context of the user (DP1). The PGS depicts an overview of the ticketing process (DP2) and provides a list of the current process steps for the users (DP2). In addition, the system offers the users – if required – detailed explanations on each process steps (DP3). We evaluated the PGS artifact by conducting focus group workshops in a field study. Since researchers [26] criticize an evaluation of IS artifacts immediately after its introduction, we conducted the workshops several months after the go live of the PGS. Next, we present the field study methodology and the analysis of the results.

4 Qualitative Field Study

We decided to conduct a qualitative field study as we aimed to receive an in-depth understanding on when employees' use the PGS and under which conditions they perceive the guidance as supportive. Thus, we did not purely collect information on the users' opinion towards the PGS, but also examined the context of participants' various statements, which "*is best understood by talking to people*" [27, p. 5]. For the qualitative field study, we used two different methods, since some of the users are located in US sites and others in European sites of the case company. Due to the spatial proximity, we conducted a series of focus group workshops [28] with employees of the European sites and an interview series with employees of the American sites. We selected the participating employees carefully based on their role in the case company, their attitudes towards information technologies, and their experiences in the company as well as with the ITSM processes. Although, we conducted different forms of qualitative data collections, both studies followed the same procedure. Ensuring a clear structure in the focus group workshops and the interviews, we developed a semi-structured interview guideline that consisted of two main parts. First, the participants had to assess the strengths, weaknesses, opportunities, and threats (SWOT-analysis) of the ITSM ProcessGuide and the particular instantiations of the DPs. Thereby, the SWOT analysis purely served as a guideline enabling a structured discussion in the workshops and interviews. Second, we asked the participants to answer and discuss three questions addressing the outcomes and their usage of the ITSM ProcessGuide:

(1) Do you think that a PGS will support you in being process compliant?
(2) Do you think that a PGS will increase your understanding of the processes?
(3) Can you imagine using a PGS in your daily work? Under which circumstances?

In total, 34 employees of the case company's various IT departments participated in the workshops (29 employees from the European sites) and interviews (five employees from the US sites). Seven workshops took place in April 2015 and five interviews in July 2015. The participants had various job positions within the IT departments. Some of the participants were help desk consultants; others were application-specific consultants (from the CRM, DMS, and ERP teams). Furthermore, four team leaders, and two senior IT managers participated in the workshops and interviews. The selection of the participants from all hierarchical levels within the IT departments aimed to reveal a holistic view on the ITSM ProcessGuide's outcome with respect to the users' IT ticketing processes. Among all participants, 26 were male and eight were female having a mean age of 39.88 years (SD = 9.43). On average the participants had a total work experience of 14.40 years (SD = 8.38), worked on average 8.67 years (SD = 8.26) for the case company, and had an experience with the ticketing processes for 2.88 years (SD = 1.68). Especially, the experience with the ticketing processes requires a detailed discussion. On average, the participants from the European sites have an experience with the IT ticketing processes of 3.23 years (SD = 1.54), while the US colleagues have only an experience of 0.88 years (SD = 0.82). The differences of the experiences is due to the fact that the IT ticketing processes were recently rolled out to the US sites (together with the ITSM ProcessGuide) and, therefore, the experience with the IT ticketing processes is lower compared to the European colleagues. Please note, two of the participants from the US sites were involved in preparing the roll out of the IT ticketing processes and thus, have a higher experience than the other US participants.

Within the workshops, we encouraged the participants to discuss the topics openly, whereas, we asked the interviewees to think aloud. With the consent of all participants, we recorded the workshops and interviews. In addition, one of the authors took notes during the sessions. For the data analysis, two researchers transcribed and subsequently analyzed all recordings. Using ATLAS.ti – a software application for qualitative data analysis – the researchers identified statements the participants mentioned frequently and dominantly. Thus, the researchers followed an inductive coding approach [29]. At the beginning of the coding process, both researchers independently identified relevant text segments, marked them, and labeled them with an appropriate code. In total, one researcher identified 395 and the other 365 relevant text segments. Subsequently, both researchers compared and discussed the individual coded text segments and combined them into common quotes. Thereby, they defined a distinction between the two main parts of the interviews and the focus group workshops. The first part addressed the participants' assessment and perception of the PGS design. The researchers discussed and accordingly coded all quotes identified in this part. The second part addressed the participants' discussions and answers to the outcomes and usage of the PGS. Again, the researchers compared and discussed the identified quotes.

5   Results

As discussed previously, we selected the SWOT analysis method to frame the sessions for all invited employees. Thereby, the analysis addressed each DP individually and the ITSM ProcessGuide as an instantiation of the DPs. Analyzing the participants' feedback and consolidating the various statements, the researchers identified in total 66 quotes addressing the design and outcomes. The positive feedback dominated with 22 quotes on the strengths and 16 quotes on the opportunities related to the DPs and the PGS. Furthermore, the researchers coded 15 quotes on the weaknesses and 13 quotes on the threats. Overall, the participants appreciate the proposed PGS design and acknowledge its usefulness to support the ticketing processes. The results of the SWOT analysis are of interest as an indicator for the outcomes and usefulness of the ITSM ProcessGuide. In the following, we present the participants' assessments of the PGS design before discussing their feedback on the PGS use and its outcomes.

5.1   Assessment of the PGS Design

The **process visualization** and **process overview** within the PGS is a topic often discussed within the sessions. The participants intensively discussed the process depictions within the PGS and provided positive feedback as well as some points of improvements. In general, the PGS provides a *"useful overview on the process and* *states what to do"* and, therefore, the *"next steps are visible."* This process visualization is especially useful for users to get an *"overview of the process and the optimal process execution"* without overloading them mentally. The PGS also enables the users to identify their current position within the process. One participant highlights this feature of the PGS as it shows: *"where am I, and what needs to be done."* Despite the positive feedback on the process depiction in the ITSM ProcessGuide, some points of improvements also arose within the workshops and interviews. Due to the implementation of the PGS to guide the ticketing process, the process is primarily linear and thus, can be depicted in the PGS easily. However, the depiction of processes could become more difficult for processes that are more complex. Consequently, some participants mentioned issues with the current mode of process depiction. In particular, one participant stated that the current implementation of the ITSM ProcessGuide does not use established process modelling standards such as Business Process Modeling Notation (BPMN) or Event-driven Process Chains (EPC). However, the usage of such modelling notations is a double-edged sword. Whereas experienced users are able to understand these notation standards, inexperienced or unfamiliar users might by irritated or distracted by the specific symbols. Thus, the usage of a more abstract and general notation approach might be more beneficial, when the entire organization uses the PGS. Nevertheless, we recognized that the notation applied in the PGS requires more elaboration in future research.

The participants also intensively discussed the **process information** provided by the PGS. In order *"to ensure the acceptance of the PGS, short and precise process information should be provided,"* the process information should be *"compressed to the essential."* These statements reflect the sense and usefulness of the second DP, which claims that process guidance should be provided lean and precisely. Moreover, the less content the user needs to consume, the lower is the additional mental effort to process the information. However, the organization must ensure that the provided process information is up-to-date, reliable, and sufficient to comprehend the addressed process. In doing so, the PGS itself should be implemented in a way, that it could be used next to the corresponding application systems and *"you can see what the instruction is or what the guide is"* (see DP2). Fulfilling these requirements, the *"process information is easily available with the PGS."* Furthermore, participants recognized the benefit of properly designed process information as *"a user could trustworthy rely on the process information provided by the PGS, without searching for the content in the first place."* As the process guidance is provided based on the users' process context (see DP1), interminable searches for information as required in handbooks or traditional online help of the applications can be prevented. One participant also highlighted the advantage of the PGS over the documentation of processes in the form of a process handbook. Thus, the users can get a quick access to the required information when needed and the information is always up-to-date, when properly maintained. In addition to textual or visual formats of process guidance, the participants appreciated the provision of an access to process resources, such as documents, links to websites, or links to required application systems by the ITSM ProcessGuide (see DP3). According to the participants, this integration *"reduces time to search for such information."*

During the discussions on the ITSM ProcessGuide design, some participants also came up with suggestions for additional functionalities, which may improve the PGS.

Referring to the first DP, which claims to provide user-invoked process guidance, some participants discussed the possibility to **automatically invoke** the process guidance when the user errs in the process execution. Such a feature also enables the correction of users that are even more experienced or those users who think that they know the process. Capturing the users' context and automatically providing process guidance can prevent failures of which the users are not aware. One participant also requested the possibility to provide an **audio output** of the process guidance as an additional feature of the PGS. In general, most participants were satisfied with the format of process guidance and even spoke in high terms of the clear structure. According to these participants, the ITSM ProcessGuide provides a *"complete, but not too cluttered process overview."* However, some participants perceived an information overload due to the provided explanations. Thus, providing guidance in an audio format might be beneficial as it enables users to focus on their work and listen to the process guidance. Table 1 provides an overview of the identified topic clusters related to the PGS design and some exemplary quotes.

Table 1. Code clusters, codes and exemplary quotes addressing the PGS design

Code cluster	Exemplary codes	Exemplary quote
Process overview	• Depiction of processes • Increased process knowledge • Process context • Need for proper process specifications	*"I do like that it is minimal and small on the screen. [...] That is good that you have something side-by-side, where you can look at what the instruction is, or what the guide is and also look at what you question is. That's a real good strength, I would say"*
Process information	• Content of process guidance • Access to process resources • Availability of process information	*"The strength of the first [DP] is that it is easy to use and easy to get information on the process. Usually, these [information] are bulky PDFs and long – if there is something at all"*
Guidance format	• Audio output of guidance content • Information overload • Combined visual and textual format	*"I think, it would be an opportunity to add sound to the process guidance. So, in addition to the text, a spoken text would enable the user that he does not have to read the entire descriptions"*
Invocation	• Automatic invocation needed	*"User must click by himself. I think it would be good if it [process guidance] would be implemented as mouse-over for every field. For our CRM system, it is the same. No one clicks on the help. The people need to be encountered more intensively on the support"*

5.2   Assessment of Use and Outcomes of PGS

Subsequent to the discussion of the PGS design, the following sections summarize and discuss the participants' PGS usage and the PGS outcomes. Most participants mentioned the topic **PGS administration**. In several discussions, the participants cautioned against the effort required to maintain the processes provided by the PGS. In particular, when process specifications are changed, the participants expect a high effort to adjust the according process in the PGS. Without such adjustments, two participants indicated that there might be a gap between the process specification and its implementation in the PGS. Thus, the participants expect a high administration effort to adjust changing processes within the PGS and to keep the process descriptions and the related process guidance up-to-date. In line with this finding, the participants perceive outdated process information provided by the PGS as a major threat, which needs to be carefully considered as these *"process information are essential."* Moreover, providing wrong or outdated process information would limit the perceived benefit and thus, negatively affect the acceptance of the PGS. Consequently, the organization should have an interest in specifying their processes on the one hand, and to have the current process specifications stored in the PGS on the other hand in order to provide process guidance and to keep the PGS content up-to-date. There is the possibility to decrease the PGS administration effort by involving the end users, as they can provide feedback on the processes captured in the PGS and, therefore, can maintain the up-to-datedness of the process information and the according specifications. The participants of the workshops and interviews suggested that PGS users should be able to evaluate the provided process information and to identify possible weaknesses or improvements of the process specifications. Thus, by providing up-to-date process specifications within the PGS, the *"processes are more lived and used which should also result in an improvement."* In addition to feedback provided by the end users, the logging of the PGS usage frequency can also be an opportunity to identify processes or parts of processes where users require more support or the process specification requires an adjustment.

As a second outcome, the participants acknowledged a positive effect of the process depiction on the users' **process knowledge**. Due to the visualization of the process and the related steps, the users become aware of the entire process and, therefore, get to know the process in more detail. To date, this is not always the case in the case company. Thereby, the participants realized that properly depicted processes would also increase the users' process knowledge. As a consequence, an increased process knowledge *"give[s] the user the certainty"* about their process execution. Especially, when the process is not part of the users' routine work, process guidance can serve as a mnemonic device. Although the positive effects of PGS, with respect to increasing process knowledge, dominated the discussions, the groups also discussed some potential threats and weaknesses. As already highlighted in literature [30], some participants mentioned the risk that the mere guidance consumption does not necessarily lead to a learning of the processes or users thinking about their actions. Rather the system may induce the users to follow the provided guidelines mindlessly and thus, they rely on the process guidance without increasing their process knowledge. However, in general most participants perceive the provision of process guidance as a strength as the PGS increases the transparency, visibility, and awareness of organization's processes. One participant mentioned that the "*user will become aware that there is a process specification behind*" when receiving process guidance and seeing the process depiction and thus, the PGS can enable users "*to get to know the processes.*"

In order to increase the users' process knowledge, the participants often discussed **trainings** as one possibility. However, the discussions on trainings were very controversial. Some participants argued that process guidance could reduce the required training efforts, such as the actual training sessions and the time required for the trainings. Many participants perceive the provision of process guidance as an opportunity to supplement existing training activities or existing process documentations. In particular, new employees can benefit from process guidance as the participants perceived the PGS as a useful tool when starting in the job and novices want to get to know the processes. Other participants even had a more radical view on the value of process guidance. According to them, the provision of process guidance replaces the need to offer trainings on the process execution. However, not all participants share this radical view. Rather, many participants argued that process guidance is not able to replace trainings. In particular, the participants from the case company's US sites mentioned this argument very often. This can be traced back to the fact that the ticketing system, enriched with the ITSM ProcessGuide, is introduced with little and superficial trainings, and the employees had many difficulties in using the ticketing system itself. On the contrary, employees of the European sites already used the ticketing system for more than three years and only the PGS was new for them. In addition, the case company adapted the ticketing processes at the same time with the go-live of the ticketing system in the US. Based on the pros and cons to use a PGS as a form of training, some participants suggested to incorporate the PGS into the training sessions in order to show the employees, where they can find additional support in their daily work.

The positive influence of process guidance on users' process **acceptance** is another topic discussed within the focus groups and the interviews. When users perceive a benefit of the provided process guidance, they are more willing to accept and, subsequently, use the ticketing system and processes. This benefit is not only achieved by increasing the process knowledge or making the user aware of the process and its steps. Rather, the participants also realized a benefit due to the provision of process guidance based on an increase of their process execution effectiveness and efficiency. With respect to the effectiveness, the PGS enables a "*more effective working with the systems*" and an "*easier handling of the processes by the user.*" According the participants, the PGS could increase the process execution efficiency, as the user "*saves time.*" In addition, some participants acknowledged a high usability and ease of ITSM ProcessGuide use. Table 2 summarizes the exemplary codes and quotes addressing the PGS outcomes.

Subsequent to the discussions focusing on the PGS outcomes, we asked the participants to answer three open questions addressing the outcomes and use of the ITSM ProcessGuide. Discussing these questions, most of the participants agreed that the PGS **increases their process compliance** as it also **increases their process knowledge**. Especially, when no or only limited training is available for a certain process, a PGS can increase users' process knowledge and compliance. When the support bases on the

Table 2. Code clusters, codes, and exemplary quotes addressing the PGS outcomes and use

Code cluster	Exemplary codes	Exemplary quote
Administration	• Effort of changing the process in PGS • Actuality of process content • User involvement and feedback • Process specifications • Process change management	*"If the tool is not maintained, it does not provide an added value and thus, will not be accepted. The tool lives due to its content. Thus, the documentation needs to be complete"*
Performance	• Increased effectiveness and efficiency • Ease of use of PGS • Usability of PGS	*"The PGS saves time and provides some certainty to the end user. In addition it improves the work load of the ITSM team"*
Process knowledge	• No learning due to PGS • Learning and process compliance due to PGS • Process awareness/visibility	*"The usefulness of the system decreases the more a user uses the system, because the user builds up knowledge over time. The process guide is rather used to build up process knowledge"*
Training	• Supports missing or bad training • Does not replace training • Training of novices • Replaces training and reduces training effort	*"One opportunity of the tool is that it promotes the process understanding. I have used the tool to explain the American colleagues some fundamental things, to explain the processes and to create a rudimentary understanding. It is difficult to understand the process by only using the tool, but in order to explain the process,, the tool is very helpful"*
Process acceptance	• Increased acceptance • Decreased acceptance due to wrong content • Ignorance of PGS	*"A threat, I guess, would be that few of people are aware of it. Even if they are aware of it, it is easy to find, it is easy to use; people just don't want to use it. I guess this could be"*

process context, the participants perceived the PGS usage as even more beneficial. One participant mentioned that a PGS *"helps context-based, you learn to solve concrete problems through solving an actual problem. Especially when you are within a process execution."* In addition, one participant argued, *"users, which have done the processes always wrong, can be corrected with it"* by *"avoiding wrong process steps."* Using the PGS can support new employees in developing process knowledge and the training of new processes. One participant also mentioned that a PGS increases the process knowledge *"especially with the visualization and the flow of the process."* Nevertheless, as already discussed, many participants once more cautioned against a replacement of trainings by implementing a PGS. It only can serve as a support of trainings as the user should already possess a basic understanding of the processes. Thereby, the participants stressed again the importance of having current and up-to-date process specifications within the PGS in order to benefit from process guidance.

In general, all participants agreed to **use the PGS in their daily work** under certain conditions. As the reasonableness of being process compliant highly depends on various process characteristics, the participants argued that the effects of a PGS also depend on these characteristics. In particular, the process complexity has an impact on the usefulness of the PGS as highlighted by one participant with the following statement: "*the more complex the process, the more useful is the PGS*." Many participants agreed, that a PGS is not required for routine, but for non-routine work. Thereby, the PGS can provide "*certainty, when users are insecure what to do.*" Thus, employees can use the PGS "*for non-routine processes to quickly identify the required process steps*" and for exception handling. Reflecting the ITSM ProcessGuide as the current PGS instantiation within the IT organization, some participants suggested to make the entire organization more aware of the system and to promote its use. Adding to this, one participant argued that the PGS "*will be used, once it proves its value.*" Within the discussions, some participants also raised the idea to use the PGS to communicate process changes. One participant suggested using the PGS to check for changes within the process "*if I look at it every time to see if something changed.*"

6 Conclusion and Future Work

In this paper, we present the results of our DSR project's third design cycle on the PGS design. Within a qualitative field study, we assessed the PGS design and outcomes within several focus group workshops and interviews with 34 employees of the case company. The participants acknowledged that the PGS design in the form of the ITSM ProcessGuide is useful in their daily work and has a positive outcome on their process execution as well as process knowledge. Because the participants were able to get some experiences on the look and feel as well as the usage of the PGS, most of them argued to use the PGS primarily for increasing their knowledge about new processes and for the execution of non-routine processes. The workshop and interview analysis revealed several implications for the PGS design. **First**, various participants stressed that only up-to-date process specifications will create a benefit by the PGS. Thus, it is necessary to update the process information within the PGS immediately when a process is changed. As the processes are changed and adapted frequently in the case company, the participants also cautioned against the high effort related to the maintenance of the PGS' contents. With respect to the PGS design, in particular the third DP, it is important to enable users to maintain the process information easily. Moreover, in addition to the improvement of the PGS design addressing the easy maintenances; it is also important that the PGS and/or process owners are aware of their responsibilities. Once the organization changes a process, it should also implement the changes in the PGS immediately. **Second**, related to the first implication, the organization can use the PGS to communicate process changes to the user or to enable users to provide feedback on the processes and to improve the process specification with their expertise. Thus, the PGS design, especially the second and third DP, should be improved in order to highlight the changes in the depicted process information. In order to enable the users' feedback, we propose to extend the PGS design. We suggest adding a fourth DP addressing the process feedback functionality. Once the PGS design is implemented accordingly, again, the PGS and process owners are responsible to incorporate the users' feedback. **Third**, another opportunity could be the usage of an audio format for the provided process guidance in contrast to the current text and image-based guidance. Using an audio format could enable users to focus on their current task while receiving the explanations on what to do at the same time.

Although our research follows established guidelines, we want to discuss some limitations. **First**, our field study is a single case study and thus, might be limited in its generalizability. Addressing this limitation, we conducted the field study in an international company and balanced our data collection by inviting participants from European and US American sites with varying job and process experience. Due to the spatial availability of the European employees, we also have to acknowledge a slight imbalance between the two groups of participants. Nevertheless, we decided for this approach in order to collect various views on our PGS and its outcomes. However, more research in multiple companies having varying backgrounds and for different process contexts is necessary. **Second**, as in every qualitative research study, our interpretations of participants' statements could bias the data analysis. In order to mitigate this limitation, two researchers independently coded the interview and workshop transcripts and discussed the coding results. Although using quantitative data might result in more reliable results, we deliberately decided to conduct our field study as a qualitative study, in particular in the form of focus groups, because of two reasons. On the one hand, the application of a focus group approach is commonly used by many DSR researchers in order to evaluate the artifact [28]. On the other hand, the comments provided by the participants in such focus groups do not only result in feedback regarding the current version of the artifact, but also provides suggestions for future work and improvements of the artifact. In addition, there might be an undiscovered response bias due to the participants' feedback during the workshops and interviews. However, based on the overall statements done by the participants within the workshops and interviews, we perceive the participant selection as a balanced mixture between supporters and critics.

Our paper contributes to research and practice. **First**, we present our theory-grounded DPs and assess their validity by evaluating their instantiation in the form of the ITSM ProcessGuide. In doing so, we demonstrate that PGS, which are designed by considering our DPs, will support users with the required process knowledge during the actual process execution and will increase their process execution performance as well as process compliance. Researchers and practitioners interested in examining and applying the (process) guidance concept could apply our DPs as a baseline for their own studies. **Second**, the findings from our interviews and focus groups extend the body of knowledge on the design and outcomes of process guidance and guidance research in general. While there are some articles describing how to design a PGS, only few of them evaluated the outcomes of such systems. On the contrary, our research not only proposes theory-grounded DPs, but also instantiates the DPs and tests their outcomes in a qualitative field study. Thereby, the analysis revealed several positive outcomes of providing process guidance to users during their process execution. Moreover, the participants raised some issues with respect to the PGS usage that researchers should consider when providing guidance to users. Based on the field study, we also identified several implications for future research on the PGS design. **Third**, our research contributes to the DSR community by reporting the evaluation of an artifact in a field study. Following the call by Peffers et al. [11], our research demonstrates how DSR can be applied to enhance the theoretical knowledge of a topic of interest, while at the same time, addressing and solving a practical issue. For the field study, we supported the ticketing processes of our case company (as one possible process context), but the PGS design knowledge and our findings are applicable for other process contexts addressing ongoing challenges in organizations worldwide.

As a next step, we will address the participants' suggestions to improve the ITSM ProcessGuide. Subsequently, we aim to reveal additional findings on the effects of process guidance on the users' process knowledge, process execution performance, and process compliance in a longitudinal survey-based study. Moreover, the proposed DPs are applicable for other research contexts addressing the support with using IS and related activities. Researchers can apply the theory-grounded DPs as a baseline and extend the body of knowledge on (process) guidance research.

References

1. Davenport, T.H., Short, J.E.: The new industrial engineering: information technology and business process redesign. Sloan Manag. Rev. **31**, 1–31 (1990)
2. Schaefer, T., Fettke, P., Loos, P.: Control patterns - bridging the gap between is controls and BPM. In: ECIS 2013 Proceedings (2013)
3. Morana, S., Schacht, S., Scherp, A., et al.: Designing a process guidance system to support user's business process compliance. In: ICIS 2014 Proceedings (2014)
4. Ceaparu, I., Lazar, J., Bessiere, K., et al.: Determining causes and severity of end-user frustration. Int. J. Hum.-Comput. Interact. **17**, 333–356 (2004)
5. Singh, D.T.: Incorporating cognitive aids into decision support systems: the case of the strategy execution process. Decis. Support Syst. **24**, 145–163 (1998)
6. Rice, R.E., Cooper, S.D.: Organizations and Unusual Routines. A Systems Analysis of Dysfunctional Feedback Processes. Cambridge University Press, Cambridge, New York (2010)
7. Becker-Kornstaedt, U., Hamann, D., Kempkens, R., Rösch, P., Verlage, M., Webby, R., Zettel, J.: Support for the process engineer: the spearmint approach to software process definition and process guidance. In: Jarke, M., Oberweis, A. (eds.) CAiSE 1999. LNCS, vol. 1626, pp. 119–133. Springer, Heidelberg (1999)
8. Burkhart, T., Krumeich, J., Werth, D., et al.: Flexible support system for email-based processes: an empirical evaluation. Int. J. E-Bus. Dev. **2**, 77–85 (2012)
9. Krumeich, J., Werth, D., Loos, P.: Business process learning on the job: a design science oriented approach and its empirical evaluation. Knowl. Manag. E-Learn.: Int. J. **4**, 395–414 (2012)
10. Hevner, A., March, S., Park, J., et al.: Design science in information systems research. MIS Q. **28**, 75–105 (2004)
11. Peffers, K., Rothenberger, M., Tuunanen, T., Vaezi, R.: Design science research evaluation. In: Peffers, K., Rothenberger, M., Kuechler, B. (eds.) DESRIST 2012. LNCS, vol. 7286, pp. 398–410. Springer, Heidelberg (2012)

12. Bhattacherjee, A.: Social Science Research: Principles, Methods, and Practices. Textbooks Collection. Book 3. http://scholarcommons.usf.edu/oa_textbooks/
13. Silver, M.: Decisional guidance. Broadening the Scope. Adv. Manage. Inf. Syst. **6**, 90–119 (2006)
14. Gregor, S., Benbasat, I.: Explanations from intelligent systems: theoretical foundations and implications for practice. MIS Q. **23**, 497–530 (1999)
15. Arnold, V., Collier, P.A., Leech, S.A., et al.: Impact of intelligent decision aids on expert and novice decision-makers' judgments. Acc. Financ. **44**, 1–26 (2004)
16. Montazemi, A.R., Wang, F., Nainar, S.M.K., et al.: On the effectiveness of decisional guidance. Decis. Support Syst. **18**, 181–198 (1996)
17. Glover, S., Prawitt, D., Spilker, B.: The influence of decision aids on user behavior: implications for knowledge acquisition and inappropriate reliance. Organ. Behav. Hum. Decis. Process. **72**, 232–255 (1997)
18. Dhaliwal, J.S., Benbasat, I.: The use and effects of knowledge-based system explanations: theoretical foundations and a framework for empirical evaluation. Inf. Syst. Res. **7**, 342–362 (1996)
19. Limayem, M., DeSanctis, G.: Providing decisional guidance for multicriteria decision making in groups. Inf. Syst. Res. **11**, 386–401 (2000)
20. Shen, M., Carswell, M., Santhanam, R., et al.: Emergency management information systems: could decision makers be supported in choosing display formats? Decis. Support Syst. **52**, 318–330 (2012)
21. Arnold, V., Clark, N., Collier, P.A., et al.: The differential use and effect of knowledge-based system explanations in novice and expert judgment decisions. MIS Q. **30**, 79–97 (2006)
22. Kuechler, B., Vaishnavi, V.: Theory development in design science research: anatomy of a research project. Eur. J. Inf. Syst. **17**, 489–504 (2008)
23. Hevner, A.R.: A three cycle view of design science research. Scand. J. Inf. Syst. **19**, 87–92 (2007)
24. Becker, J., Delfmann, P., Eggert, M., et al.: Generalizability and applicability of model-based business process compliance-checking approaches – a state-of-the-art analysis and research roadmap. Bus. Res. **5**, 221–247 (2012)
25. Tan, W.G., Cater-Steel, A., Toleman, M.: Implementing IT service management: a case study focussing on critical success factors. J. Comput. Inf. Syst. **50**, 1–12 (2009)
26. Bhattacherjee, A.: Understanding information systems continuance: an expectation-confirmation model. MIS Q. **25**, 351–370 (2001)
27. Myers, M.D.: Qualitative Research in Business and Management. SAGE, Los Angeles (2009)
28. Tremblay, M.C., Hevner, A.R., Berndt, D.J.: The use of focus groups in design science research. In: Hevner, A., Chatterjee, S. (eds.) Design Research in Information Systems, 22, pp. 121–143. Springer, US, Boston, MA (2010)
29. Thomas, D.R.: A general inductive approach for analyzing qualitative evaluation data. Am. J. Eval. **27**, 237–246 (2006)
30. Steinbart, P.J., Accola, W.L.: The effects of explanation type and user involvement on learning from and satisfaction with expert systems. J. Inf. Syst. **8**, 1–17 (1994)

Bookkeeping for Informal Workers: Co-creating with Street Traders

Nasibu Mramba[1,2(✉)], Jesse Tulilahti[2], and Mikko Apiola[2]

[1] College of Business Education (CBE), Dodoma Campus, Dodoma, Tanzania
nasibu.mramba@cbe.ac.tz
[2] School of Computing, University of Eastern Finland, Joensuu, Finland
jtulila@cs.uef.fi, mikko.apiola@ieee.org

Abstract. Over 200 million street traders operate in Africa. Our previous research has identified a number of challenges of Tanzanian street traders and related technology innovation opportunities. One identified opportunity is technology to support keeping business records. In this study, an intercultural team of Finnish and Tanzanian technologists, researchers, and Tanzanian street traders was set up to create a bookkeeping application, contextualized for the needs of Tanzanian street traders. A research period, lasting four months, resulted in a successful first version of the application, ready for further DSR projects. In addition, first experiences about what works in co-creation in this cultural context and with this team setup were gained. These results are useful for managing related DSR projects in the future. This study shows the importance of launching similar DSR projects, and the high potential of DSR and co-creation in solving societal and economic challenges in developing countries with technology solutions.

Keywords: Developing countries · Tanzania · Informal work · Street trading · Street vending · Co-creating

1 Introduction

In many developing countries, a large part of work is informal. For example, in sub-Saharan Africa, an approximated 72 % of employment is informal [1], and consists of small and micro enterprises, self-employment, street trading, and small scale farming [2,3]. Informal workers are characterised more by survival rather than opportunity, and are typically outside of labor legislation or social protection [2,3]. In Dar es Salaam, which is the economic hub of Tanzania, street trading is the most common form of informal work [4].

A number of studies have been conducted about street trading (e.g. [2]). However, a limited number of studies have used design science research (DSR) [5,6] to address the challenges of street traders with technology innovation. To our knowledge, no previous DSR studies have targeted the street traders of Tanzania. Our previous research [4,7] used a mixed-methods approach in order

© Springer International Publishing Switzerland 2016
J. Parsons et al. (Eds.): DESRIST 2016, LNCS 9661, pp. 97–113, 2016.
DOI: 10.1007/978-3-319-39294-3_7

to understand the daily life and challenges of street traders, and to identify technology innovation opportunities to empower street traders.

In this research, a smartphone application to help street traders in bookkeeping was developed in an intercultural team that consisted of software developers, researchers, and a group of 15 street traders from Dodoma, Tanzania. This four month co-creation period took place in Dodoma, Tanzania, in Autumn 2015.

Research Question

Our previous research [4, 7] has pinpointed a number of potential areas for technology innovation to improve the business prospects of Tanzanian street traders, one of which is the need to improve records keeping capacity.

Well-kept business records enable entrepreneurs to plan, organize, make decisions, manage credit, and evaluate their business progress. Despite this importance, majorities of street traders in Dar es Salaam do not record their daily business transactions [4, 7]. Thus, the research question for this study was:

– *How can an intercultural team co-create a bookkeeping application that is contextualised for Tanzanian street traders by following the principles of DSR?*

2   Background

2.1   Street Trading

Informal business is the dominant mode of employment in the developing world, due to lack of production in the formal sector [1]. It is typical that informal workers do not register their businesses due to varying reasons, such as complex regulations and costs (see for example: [2, 10] in Mexico, and [4, 7] in Tanzania). Informal workers operate without business licence, do not pay tax or keep records, they are not covered by social security, and their business is characterised more by survival rather than opportunity [2, 4, 7, 10]. Main characteristics of street traders in Tanzania are summarised in Table 1.

Street traders sell different products including food products, ornaments, fruits, vegetables, clothes, stationeries, cosmetics, herbal medicines, soft drinks, and various other things. They can be found near highways, bus stands, mosques, churches, railway stations, marketplaces, schools, colleges, hospitals and in public gathering places. In 2007, an approximated 27% of the population of Dar es Salaam conducted street trading [7]. The current population of Dar es Salaam is 5.6 million, but accurate statistics about street trading is not available.

2.2   Technology for Informal Work

Despite the rapid expansion of mobile technology in Africa, only a limited number of applications are currently targeted for street traders. The most notable application is mobile money, which has revolutionised payments and access to credit

Table 1. Characteristics of Tanzanian street traders

Characteristic	Explanation	Ref.
Legal status	Informal	[8]
Evictions	Frequent evictions from cities	[4,7]
Business profile	Initial investment from 14.45€, to 1445€	[4,7]
	Daily profit between 2.5€ and 20€	
	Business hours from 6AM to 9PM	
Licence	No business licence. Unregistered business.	[8]
Access to credit	Weak	[4,7,8]
Impact to society	Only business opportunity for many poor and less educated	[9]
Significance	Significant impact to GDP and GND of developing countries	[9]
Education level	Low	[8]
Business skills	Weak skills in record keeping, pricing, customer management, inventory control, strategic planning and promotion	[4,7,8]

in Africa [11]. Communication through mobile phones via phone calls and short messages has also changed things. However, beyond the current applications, there are many possibilities for future technology innovation, which can significantly improve the street traders' business prospects [4,7] (see Table 2).

Table 2. Technology innovation possibilities arising from the needs, strengths, limitations, and types of work of street traders in Dar es Salaam, Tanzania [4].

Management	Marketing	Planning and bookkeeping
Customer profiling	Product database and catalog	*Bookkeeping*
Location-based matchmaking	Electronic Word of Mouth	Education (all business domains)
Traffic advisory	Advisory apps for formalising	Improved access to capital apps
Social networking	Wholesaler product availability	Management and planning apps
Customer-trader matchmaking	Trader-wholesaler availability	Counselling and healthcare apps
Order and delivery management	Storage optimisation	Digital storyboards, social media
Weather applications	Mobile money to replace cash	Advisory application

There is a growing, but still small trend of developing mobile applications for informal workers. Examples include online shopping [12,13], mobile procurement [14,15], applications for small scale farmers [16,17], records keeping, goal setting and planning applications [18,19], business education applications [20], financial literacy applications [21], tools for illiterate micro businesses [13], and educational applications for women entrepreneurs [20]. One study [18] proposes valuable ideas to allow flexible adjustment of applications to suit the needs of different contexts and informal worker groups.

None of the available existing applications were found to respond directly to the needs of Tanzanian street traders. First, most of the applications were found either too confusing for street traders, or not available in Swahili language. In addition, an important reason for starting this project was co-creation. Thus, the larger goal of this project, beyond a single bookkeeping application, was to lay grounds for future DSR activities. When the users are involved as equal members, they gain empowerment, and this is also a great way for the different project participants to learn to understand each other. Also, building our own application would allow easy addition of new functionality in the future. This would not necessarily be possible if an existing application was used.

Common challenges in co-design activities include *scepticism* about the motives of the DSR team, various *misconceptions* and *language issues*. What is obviously important, is *management aspects* in managing good relationships and trust between designers and participants, overcoming language barriers, rewarding participants, understanding beliefs, dealing with religious beliefs, dealing with financial challenges including rent, transportation, costs for translators and other support, and training costs. The *willingness of supporting organisations* is also crucial. Common recommendations include close interaction between designers, researchers, and project participants (see for example: [21]).

3   Research Design

The goal of DSR is to produce artefacts that can address real life business challenges [5]. Our previous research identified a range of ideas for technology innovation for Tanzanian street traders (see Table 2). From the list of ideas, records keeping was identified as an important challenge, which also matched with the available resources and skills for project implementation. Our background research found no existing applications to match the specific needs of street traders (see Sect. 2.2). Thus, this DSR project was motivated by the fact that street traders in Tanzania do not keep business records, which leads to weak business management, and improper decision making.

DSR projects typically start by providing requirements for research (e.g. what is the problem to be addressed with technology), and proceeds to design, construct, and evaluate suitable technological solutions [5]. A guiding framework for DSR projects [6, pp. 75–89] defines the typical stages of DSR projects as: problem explication, requirement definition, design and development, demonstration, and evaluation. Each of the stages makes use of a combination of research, design,

Table 3. Research design divided to DSR stages [6].

DSR stage	Activity	Outcomes and data	Section
Problem explication	*See Sect.* 2.2		
Requirement definition	Workshops 1, 2, 3	Requirements list Prototypes Observations Demographics	4.1
Design & development	Icon design App development	Icons Android app	4.2
Demo & evaluation	Field research App test period	Evaluation data Challenges list	4.3

and engineering strategies and methods including qualitative and quantitative research methods [6, pp. 75–89].

Table 3 lists the activities, outcomes and collected data of this DSR project per each stage of DSR as defined by [6]. First, *problem explication* was covered by our previous studies (see Sect. 2.2). Second, *requirement definition* stage involved three workshops, and resulted in requirements list, prototypes, qualitative observations, and demographics of participants. Third, *design and development* stage included icon designs and related icon testing, and development of the application. The results included a working application for Android platform, and a collection of icons. The *demo and evaluation* stage included field tests with mobile phones, application testing period, and resulted in evaluation data, and list of challenges for future development.

The results section is divided to sections that represent the stages of DSR as given in Table 3. Each section contains an explanation of the activities, outcomes, and analysis of the collected data. The project team consisted of one software developer, one researcher, a support team from CBE, Tanzania, and a group of 15 street traders that were recruited from Dodoma area.

4   Results

4.1   Requirement Definition

Workshops. The requirement definition phase started with preparing advertisements to call for potential street traders to participate in the project. The advertisements contained the name of the project, the condition for one to apply, how to apply, and the expected benefits. The advertisements were distributed in various streets in Dodoma town. In addition, CBE employees were informed to tell their friends, relatives, and family members about the project. A total of three workshops were arranged during the requirements definition phase.

1. Fourteen men and one woman participated in the first workshop. The street traders brought their products for sale with them. This workshop lasted for two hours, and was conducted at the facilities of CBE Dodoma Campus. In this workshop, the street traders were explained the aims of the project, what is expected of them, and what are the expected benefits. In addition, it was emphasised that the street traders had the right to either continue or quit from the project at any point, should they wish to do so. This was a very interactive workshop, and many questions were asked and answered. Demographic information was also collected from the participants. The male street traders were also encouraged to invite more female street traders to participate. After the introduction and get to know each other, a prototype of the application was introduced to the participants, and comments were asked. We received a number of questions and comments, such as "how will it work", "how we are going to use it", "what computations can the application make", and "what are the benefits of the application." The general atmosphere of the workshop was relaxed.

2. The second workshop was conducted with 12 lecturers from CBE who were teaching business related topics. This workshop lasted for two hours. The workshop took place at the CBE Dodoma Campus. The purpose of the workshop was to show the lecturers the current prototype, which was improved after the first workshop, and get their comments for further improvement. The majority of comments were in regards of making the prototype simpler, useful, and remembering to keep it in Swahili language. Also it was noted that it must include debts, and capital received. CBE lecturers appreciated the work done, and showed their determinations that the artefact can bring changes in street trade. This workshop was also important for building trust and in order to involve the CBE staff in the project. Based on the comments received, an improved prototype of the application was designed.

3. The third workshop included presenting a new prototype to the participating street traders. The meeting with street traders was conveyed in one of the classes at CBE Dodoma. In this meeting we had two new female street traders, and also we had one ICT lecturer from CBE joining in. One of the street traders commented that sometimes they fail to set a reasonable price for their products, hence requested the proposed mobile phone app to take into account that challenge. Discussion with individual street traders revealed that they need to see daily, weekly, and monthly profit in order to be able to make business decisions.

Demographics of Participants. The participating street traders ($n = 15$) had the following basic demographic characteristics. In regards of education, 14 of the participants were primary school leavers, who had failed to proceed to secondary education because of lack of school fees, and they had failed their end of primary school examinations. One participant was a college student, who was pursuing a degree in accounting. Two participants (not included in the 15 who participated) were found to be illiterate, and they dropped out. A lot of illiterate people are ashamed and may try to hide their illiteracy.

In regards of mobile phone usage, 14 had traditional mobile phones, and one had a smartphone. Three of the participants, excluding the one who owned one, had experience in smartphone usage. In the workshops, the ones who had experience in smartphones were instructed to assist those who had no previous experience. In regards of business experience, the participants had 1–3 years of experience from street trading with the exception of one participant, who had done street trading for ten years. Most participants explained that they do not conduct street trading from late November to early December, because they go to rural areas to help in farming activities. They explained to be out of street trading business approximately three weeks, annually.

In regards of the participants' expectations from this DSR project, the majority were sceptical, at start, if the mobile phones can help in their bookkeeping activities. Some of them thought that it will not work out. However, the researchers explained through examples such as mobile money, the possibilities that technology could have in the future. There were some misconceptions also in regards of "empowerment", which some participants thought was associated with money given to them or taken away from them. However, majority of the street traders reported to be happy to see what the team was aiming to do.

The common challenges encountered in street trading, as reported by the participants, were: lack of capital, low sales volumes, lack of business skills, and long walking hours. The street traders reported to operate within a capital ranging from 30 000TZS to 100 000TZS[1], which they reported as low for them to be able to buy products that they need. One participant commented *"Sometimes we finish a day without making any sale."* Street traders also mentioned lack of skills in business planning, record keeping, customer management, sales strategies, and how to access finance as barriers to success. Street traders explained to walk tens of kilometres per day in search of customers, without having information of the availability of customers.

List of Requirements. The requirement definition stage resulted in the following list of requirements for the app.

- Product database including stock per product
- Easy recording of sales and purchases
- Application works in Swahili
- Simple UI
- Suggesting an absolute minimum selling price
- Monitoring profits, losses, and expenses
- A week view, a month view, and a day view.

4.2   Design and Development

Icon Design and Tests. First, one workshop was arranged with street traders to design icons. The street traders were grouped in three groups. The researcher

---

[1] 100 000TZS equals roughly to 42€ (as of 26 January 2016).

Fig. 1. Designing icons

opened the session by explaining the purpose of the gathering. The groups started to brainstorm on icon designs that they would prefer for different functions in the application. A list of app functions was listed on the blackboard. Icons were drawn on the blackboard, and other street traders commented on the icon drawings. A total of nine icons were proposed at the end of the workshop. Figure 1 shows a photo from the icon designing workshops.

Second, an icon testing workshop was arranged. The tests were conducted by using mobile phones. An application was programmed that presented sets of icons for the street traders. For each functionality in the bookkeeping application, several icons were presented. The participants used the testing application to pick the one icon that they preferred for each functionality, or a question mark if none of them did. A total of eight different icon and word sets were presented. An example of a set of icons is presented in Fig. 1, which shows potential icons for ki-Swahili words Uza (sell), Nunua (buy), Matumizi (use), and Deni (debt).

Figure 2 presents a screenshot from testing icons with the testing application, with example results from eight icon tests in Table 4. The first row in Table 4 shows that four street traders selected the first icon (seen in Fig. 2) for the Sell-function of the bookkeeping application, none chose the second one, two chose the third one, and five participants chose a question mark (indicating that they did not prefer any of the presented example icons for Sell). The rest of the rows are similar, but for different functionalities. A total of eight different word and icon sets were tested by using the testing application.

A number of challenges were encountered during the icon tests. First, problems with the mobile phones occurred. These included power savings options, causing the screen to go to lock mode. In addition, failed swiping activities sometimes launched the camera, and on other occasions launched the music player. These incidents distracted the tests and probably caused some biases to the test results. Also, it was found that some of the tested icons were not understandable or they represented different meanings for the participants than intended. Thus, further icon design is necessary. However, the icon tests resulted in a list of icons to be used in the application, and that were preferred by the street traders.

Fig. 2. Icon testing application

Table 4. Test set results

Uza (Sell)	4	0	2	5
Nunua (Buy)	4	3	2	5
Matumizi (Use)	0	3	3	4
Deni (Debt)	1	0	4	6
Chakula (Food)	4	3	2	1
Nguo (Clothes)	5	4	1	1
Mtaji (Capital)	4	3	2	2
Vingine (Other)	2	1	3	5

Description of the Resulting Application. The aim was to design the application for maximum simplicity, but to include the basic defined requirements (see Sect. 4.1) in order to keep track of the product and money flows of the street traders. The following will give a general description of the flow of the application. When a trader gets more stock of a product (through growing, buying, or making) he or she either adds the product to the system if it does not exist in the system (Screen 6 in Fig. 3), or adds the amount to existing stock, including the expenses of obtaining the product. The item is stored in the database, and an absolute minimum selling price per unit is calculated. The minimum selling price is shown in the product overview (Screen 4 in Fig. 3).

When selling, a trader activates the sell function (Screen 7 in Fig. 3), the application suggests a selling price and shows how much profit that price will gain. The user can set the price and quantity manually, and the application will show the profit or loss. When the sales continue, the user can monitor the products progress of sales through the profits and losses diagram in the overview screen (Screen 4 in Fig. 3). A red line shows the costs, and the blue line shows the earnings. The user can switch between daily, weekly, and monthly views.

When the user increases the quantity of a product that is in the database, the application calculates a new absolute minimum selling price for the product. This also adds to the expenses. The functions include also removal of a product from the database. New expenses can be added from the expenses window (Matumizi), (Screen 3 in Fig. 3). Expenses are shown individually per product or per all products in a similar way as in the product overview screen. Expenses for individual products can be looked more closely, and new expenses can be added.

From the history screen (Screen 2 in Fig. 3) the user can see the overall financial situation. This includes list of sold products. This can be looked more closely and a graph will show total expenses in red and total earnings in blue. At the bottom screen the user is able to see the total expenses, earnings, and subtotals. There is also a trash bin (Takataka), consisting of removed products, sales, and expenses. Items in the trashcan can be recovered or ridded for good.

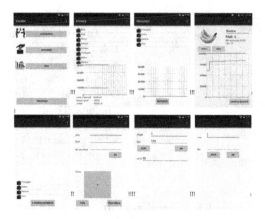

Fig. 3. User interface of the application. From left to right: main screen, history, expenses, overview, list of products, add product and photo, sell product, add expense (Color figure online)

Technical Description of Application. The application was developed using Android studio[2]. System models were created with Dia[3]. Android studio and Dia are both free software. User's data is stored in a SQL database using SQLite. Data is stored in three different tables and those are accessed through Cursor. Required data is collected from the database to an object using Cursor and modification of the data is done to the object. After modifications, the data is updated to the database. The application uses API Level 9 (Android 2.3). API Level 9 should work with 99.8 % of Android phones[4].

The application contains a total of 2100 lines of code. Phones for testing the application were selected by the following criteria. First, there should be a touchscreen, a camera, 700 MHz cpu, 256 MB RAM. Second, the phones should run on Android 2.3 or higher and price range should be from the lower end. Third, the phones should also be available to be bought from the local markets. With these criteria, Tecno Y3 was chosen. Techno Y3 phones have 1.0 GHz dual-core Cortex-A9, 4.0 in. touchscreen (480 × 800 pixels), 512 MB RAM, 2 MP front camera, A-GPS and they run Android 4.4 KitKat.

4.3   Demo and Evaluation

Training Workshop. A workshop was arranged up at CBE to teach street traders on how to use smartphones, and the developed application. The participants were grouped in groups of four. The street traders who had experience in using smartphones were faster to learn when compared with others. The session started by explaining the purpose of gathering together, and showing the basics

---

[2] http://developer.android.com/sdk/index.html.
[3] http://dia-installer.de.
[4] http://developer.android.com/intl/ru/about/dashboards/index.html.

of smartphones e.g. switching on and off, finding an app, sliding and charging. The following were the main activities in the meeting.

- Learn how to switch on and off, and using touchscreen
- Open and browse an app
- Posting sales, purchases, and expenses in the application.

Researchers passed through each group, instructing how to open the application, add stock, and post sales and expenses. After group instruction each street trader was given an opportunity to use the app himself for each step. The session lasted for two hours after which the traders tested the application on street.

Field Testing. The next day after the training workshop, mobile phones were handed over to street traders, who were requested to fill in an agreement form before taking the mobile phones. The purpose of having an agreement form was to ensure that traders will take care of the mobile phones and that they will use the application as instructed. A total of 15 phones were given out.

The street traders used the mobile phone app for two days. After this period, another workshop session was arranged where the street traders gathered to show the results of the two days period of using the app. It was found that 10 out of 15 street traders were able to add the transactions to the app correctly. The errors observed in this phase of evaluation included the following.

- Failures in differentiating purchases and sales when inserting transactions.
- Failures in locating units and values per product.
- Double insertions of the same transaction.

Evaluation Meetings. The second evaluation meeting lasted eight hours. Street traders were invited to do business within CBE compounds during the graduation ceremony of the college. It was a good opportunity for researchers and street traders to interact and learn from each other. In this meeting we observed all street traders using their app correctly. The new version of an app was updated on the street traders' mobiles phone in this day. The difference between the old and the new version was that in the new version the traders were able to see profit made daily, weekly, and monthly, and also the minimum selling price in which street traders shouldn't go below.

Another evaluation session took place three weeks after street traders started using mobile phone by using telephone interview. The focus was to know the usage progress. All street traders confirmed that now they can see the record of their sales, purchases, and expenses, however they didn't indicate how they are using it to make various business decisions. The challenges so far observed were the lack of power (charging), how to use the record to make various business decisions, uninstallation (unintended), and forgetting to record transactions.

Observed Challenges and Future Plans. First, it was found that for users who can't read or write, using the application is difficult. This is an important target group[5]. Future plans in regards of illiterate users include voice helper that reads out loud texts, as well as further development of icons. Users could use pictures and record names of the products instead of just writing. Second, it would be beneficial for the application to suggest locations and times of where to trade. Different products can be sold easier at some locations and time has also effect on that. Application could show the user at what time it could be beneficial to go selling goods and what time to do something else. Same applies to buying.

Third, data could be stored in a cloud. This would enable the collection of data from all users, and that data could be used to provide users with suggestions on where to sell, which product to sell, and when to sell. The data could be also used for a variety of business analytics research, and recommendation systems. Fourth, currently the application is programmed in Swahili language. Changing to English language is currently not implemented well. However, the technical architecture allows easy addition of languages. Fifth, a variety of options for expanding the application exist for future DSR projects.

5   Discussion

Research question *RQ*: asked, *"How can an intercultural team co-create a book-keeping application that is contextualised for Tanzanian street traders by following the principles of DSR?"* To answer this question, a team of software developers and researchers from Finland and Tanzania, and a group of Tanzanian street traders conducted co-creation activities that contributed to one full DSR cycle. Per each of the design stages, the following was found.

First, in regards of the *requirement definition* stage, a number of workshops were successfully arranged. These included prototyping, getting familiar with each other, building trust, and setting the grounds for co-operation between street traders, the project researchers and developers, and with the local collaborating university's staff (CBE). This stage resulted in a number of ideas, and a list of requirements for the application. General characteristics, and demographics of the participants also gave the background information for the use of application design. In addition to technical requirements, the requirement definition stage built trust and empowerment to the project team. This is a cornerstone of co-creation, which avoids dividing people between us and them, for example as users, software developers, clients, researchers, and designers. Instead, co-creation emphasises creating technologies together, with respect to different individuals' backgrounds.

Second, *design & development* continued the co-creation activities in the form of icon design, application development, and testing exercises. This stage resulted, through the design and programming of an Android application, in the first working version of a bookkeeping application that is contextualised

---

[5] Tanzania census survey of 2012 shows that 16.7 % of 15–35 year olds are illiterate.

for the Tanzanian street traders. A total of 2100 lines of code was written, and the first user interface was co-designed and successfully implemented. A number of usability challenges related to basic smartphone usage, as well as use of the designed application were found. These will help the future development of the application. Third, the *demo & evaluation* stage consisted of a training workshop, field testing, and evaluation meetings, continuing the trend of co-design within the project. A valuable set of observations from the application usage were being collected for future development of the application.

Challenges identified by previous studies (see Sect. 2.2), such as skepticism, misconceptions, importance of empowerment through co-design were confirmed by this study, as similar issues were observed. However, these were observed at a mild intensity, and none of them had a restricting impact on the implementation of this project.

To answer the research question, this study has shown that an intercultural co-creation team can be easily set up in an Tanzanian design milieu, even with relatively low resources, and a successful application for informal workers can be co-created in a good spirit, and doing that can be motivating to all participants. DSR proved to be an excellent framework for successfully implementing this project. DSR is widely used in Europe, USA, and Australia. However it has currently been applied relatively little in Africa [22]. We recommend a wider initiation of DSR to create local African technology solutions to African challenges.

5.1 Limitations

Evaluation of a DSR project should answer the question *"How well does the artefact solve the explicated problem and fulfil the defined requirements?"* [6, p. 146] In this project, the conducted evaluations remain somewhere in the between of *naturalistic evaluation* (artefact is evaluated in real practice), and *artificial evaluation* (artefact is evaluated in an artificial setting) [6, p. 147]. Some of the features were evaluated in a classroom-environment, while some functionality was evaluated while the end-users were conducting their actual business activities by using the artefact.

This project resulted in a first working prototype of a bookkeeping application, and a list of technical and usability related improvement suggestions that give a good basis for further development of the application. Equally important, this project resulted in understanding about potentially beneficial interactive design processes in this cultural context. Prior to implementing this project, little was known, for example, about the street traders' willingness to participate in a project of this kind, or what other unknown issues may restrict or enhance the implementation of this project.

In line with *critical realism* in design science [6, pp. 173–174], in this project we acknowledge the importance of investigating the structures in an environment that can support or counteract the effective use of the artefact. These can include technological as well as psychological and social factors, such as power games, resistance to change, and organisational cultures [6, p. 174]. By judging from the positive reception and successful implementation of this project, we gained a first, "scratch-of-the-surface"-level understanding of the underlying cultural and social issues related to application development and use. Further in-depth studies are, of course, required to gain a more comprehensive understanding of related complex social, organisational, and psychological issues.

Several factors do restrict the direct *applicability* of the designed artefact to street traders' business. First, most Tanzanian street traders do not, at the present moment, have smartphones, but they have USSD-capable "regular" mobile phones. Second, the developed application, although well functional, is still relatively simple, and there is no rigorous quantitative evaluation criteria, or mathematical analysis, that would "prove" the effectiveness of the application or the underlying design process employed. Thus, most of the evaluation results are qualitative. Qualitative results are rarely generalisable but provide insights and new ideas about previously unknown issues (see for example: [23]). These results provide an excellent basis for systematising this approach, and designing more rigorous quantitative evaluation criteria for future projects.

Moreover, designing applications for USSD[6], which is the current technological platform widely available for street traders, would be short-sighted. Smartphone ownership is increasing in emerging economies (see for example [24]), and it can be estimated that smartphones will be available to more and more informal workers, too[7]. As applications with proven business benefit become available, new business models can also emerge that allow mobile operators to rent smartphones to informal workers. New invoicing models may be connected to the usage of new business applications. We believe that implementing business applications for informal workers that are designed and evaluated by rigorous DSR methods, will only speed up this process, leading to significant gains in street traders' business, hopefully in the near future.

This project was implemented by relatively small resources. While the results are positive, we acknowledge that further DSR is required to develop the application further, and introduce larger scale usage tests. In addition, to reach the directly measurable benefits for the street traders, technology development and DSR should be brought closer together with other business, legal, and educational efforts to improve the street traders' business prospects. This and related projects provide exciting opportunities for local technology startups, too.

5.2 Future Work and Recommendations

We propose the initiation of software teams to work on a variety of topics, including applications for street traders. These teams can be initiated by companies, universities, or technology hubs. Co-design activities should also be brought into the information technology curriculums of HEIs in developing countries (see [25]). One important future direction is to support the formalisation process, and to add related taxpaying and bookkeeping functionalities.

---

[6] https://en.wikipedia.org/wiki/Unstructured_Supplementary_Service_Data.

[7] Statistics about smartphone ownership of street traders in Tanzania is not available.

Developing countries are not so much the focus of big software developers. The network of actors that enable the emergence of technology innovation, often referred as the innovation ecosystem, consists of universities, engineering colleges, business schools, entrepreneurs, startups, businesses, venture capitalists, business angels, industry-university R&D institutions, and business incubators [11,26]. In developing countries, informal technology hubs, often launched by young technology-aware people, are a new, growing player of the innovation ecosystem (see for example: [27]). In developing countries, the requirements for technology projects are often fuzzy, which highlights the need for research components in technology projects. Standard first-world software development models do not work well. In the near future, DSR can make a big contribution here.

6   Conclusions

Developing countries need to improve capacities in Science, Technology, Innovation, and R&D that contributes to human development. Small businesses need ways to generate more income. Technology can contribute to this, if implemented well. This requires the increment of DSR activities, and expansion of ICT4D research from evaluative research to DSR. Technology initiatives are not sufficient alone, but must be brought together with other legal, environmental, political, and economic efforts to improve business prospects of informal workers. This study has shown that DSR and co-creation are powerful tools that are fun to use, and they provide an endless number of exciting technology opportunities for joint DSR projects between technologists, researchers, designers, technology users, and people from different countries and cultures.

Acknowledgments. We want to thank the College of Business Education (CBE), Tanzania, for broad support of this project. We also want to thank the reviewers for providing valuable recommendations for improving this article. Finally, we want to thank the Finnish University Partnership for International Development (FinnCEAL) for partly funding the presentation of this paper in DESRIST2016.

References

1. Webb, J.W., Bruton, G.D., Tihanyi, L., Ireland, R.D.: Research on entrepreneurship in the informal economy: framing a research agenda. J. Bus. Ventur. **28**(5), 598–614 (2013)
2. Wongtada, N.: Street vending phenomena: a literature review and research agenda. Thunderbird Int. Bus. Rev. **56**(1), 55–75 (2014)
3. Böhme, M., Thiele, R.: Is the informal sector constrained from the demand side? Evidence for six West African capitals. World Dev. **40**(7), 1369–1381 (2012)
4. Mramba, N., Apiola, M., Kolog, E.A., Sutinen, E.: Technology for street traders in Tanzania: a design science research approach. To Appear in African Journal of Science, Technology, Innovation and Development (2016)
5. Hevner, A.: A three cycle view of design science research. Scand. J. Inf. Syst. **19**(2), 87–92 (2007)

6. Johannesson, P., Perjons, E.: An Introduction to Design Science. Springer, Switzerland (2014)
7. Mramba, N., Apiola, M., Sutinen, E., Msami, P., Klomsri, T., Haule, M.: Empowering street vendors through technology: an explorative study in Dar es Salaam, Tanzania. In: Proceedings 21st ICE/IEEE International Technology Management Conference, Belfast, Northern Ireland, 22–24 June 2015
8. Lyons, M.: Pro-poor business law? On MKURABITA and the legal empowerment of Tanzania's street vendors. Hague J. Rule Law 5(1), 74–95 (2013)
9. Lyons, M., Brown, A., Msoka, C.: Do micro enterprises benefit from the 'Doing Business' reforms? The case of street-vending in Tanzania. Urban Stud. 51(8), 1593–1612 (2014)
10. Bruhn, M.: A tale of Two Species: revisiting the effect of registration reform on informal business owners in Mexico. J. Dev. Econ. 103, 275–283 (2013)
11. Carmody, P.: A knowledge economy or an information society in Africa? Thintegration and the mobile phone revolution. Inf. Technol. Dev. 19(1), 24–39 (2013)
12. Talbot, M.J., Marsden, G.: SHOP-net: moving from paper to mobile. Reports of University of Cape Town, Department of Computer Science (2011). http://pubs. cs.uct.ac.za/archive/00000709/01/Talbot.pdf
13. Emmanuel, E.A., Muyingi, H.N.: A mobile commerce application for rural economy development: a case study for Dwesa. In: Proceedings of the 2010 Annual Research Conference of the South African Institute of Computer Scientists and Information Technologists, SAICSIT 2010, pp. 58–66. ACM, New York (2010)
14. Dorflinger, J., Friedland, C., Mengistu, M., Merz, C., Stadtrecher, S., Pabst, K., de Louw, R.: Mobile commerce in rural south africa: proof of concept of mobile solutions for the next billion mobile consumers. In: IEEE International Symposium on a World of Wireless, Mobile and Multimedia Networks Workshops, WoWMoM 2009, pp. 1–3, June 2009
15. Ntawanga, F., Coleman, A.: A lightweight mobile e-procurement solution for rural small scale traders implemented using a living lab approach. In: IST-Africa Conference (2015)
16. Misaki, E., Apiola, M., Gaiani, S.: Technology for agriculture: information channels for decision making in Chamwino, Tanzania. In: Proceedings 21st ICE/IEEE International Technology Management Conference, Belfast, Northern Ireland, 22–24 June 2015
17. Misaki, E., Apiola, M., Gaiani, S.: Technology for small scale farmers in Tanzania: a design science approach. To Appear in Electronic Journal of Information Systems in Developing Countries (2016)
18. Wasilewska, A., Wong, J.: Template mobile applications for social and educational development. In: International Multiconference on Computer Science and Information Technology, IMCSIT 2009, pp. 391–398, October 2009
19. Tohidi, M., Warr, A.: The bigger picture: the use of mobile photos in shopping. In: Kotzé, P., Lindgaard, G., Marsden, G., Wesson, J., Winckler, M. (eds.) INTERACT 2013, Part IV. LNCS, vol. 8120, pp. 764–771. Springer, Heidelberg (2013)
20. Giridher, T., Kim, R., Rai, D., Hanover, A., Yuan, J., Zarinni, F., Scharff, C., Wasilewska, A., Wong, J.: Mobile applications for informal economies. In: International Multiconference on Computer Science and Information Technology, IMCSIT 2009, pp. 345–352, October 2009
21. Sharma, A., Johri, A.: Learning and empowerment: designing a financial literacy tool to teach long-term investing to illiterate women in rural india. Learn. Cult. Soc. Interact. 3(1), 21–33 (2014)

22. Naidoo, R., Gerber, A., van der Merwe, A.: An exploratory survey of design science research amongst south african computing scholars. In: Proceedings of the South African Institute for Computer Scientists and Information Technologists Conference, SAICSIT 2012, pp. 335–342. ACM, New York (2012)

23. Creswell, J.W.: Research Design: Qualitative, Quantitative, and Mixed Methods Approaches, 4th edn. Sage Publications, California (2014)

24. Poushter, J.: Smartphone Ownership and Internet Usage Continues to Climb in Emerging Economies. Pew Research Center (2016). http://www.pewglobal.org/files/2016/02/pew_research_center_global_technology_report_final_february_22_2016.pdf

25. Apiola, M., Tedre, M.: New perspectives on the pedagogy of programming in a developing country context. Comput. Sci. Educ. **22**(03), 285–313 (2012)

26. Adesida, O., Karuri-Sebina, G.: Building innovation driven economies in Africa. Afr. J. Sci. Technol. Innov. Dev. **5**(1), 1–3 (2013)

27. Cunningham, P., Cunningham, M.: Report on innovation spaces and living labs in IST-partner countries. In: Cunningham, P., Cunningham, M. (eds.) IIMC International Information Management Corporation Ltd (IST-Africa Consortium) (2016)

Understanding the Everyday Designer in Organisations

Ciarán O'Leary[✉], Fred Mtenzi, and Claire McAvinia

Dublin Institute of Technology, Dublin, Ireland
{ciaran.oleary,fredrick.mtenzi,claire.mcavinia}@dit.ie

Abstract. This paper builds upon the existing concept of an *everyday designer* as a non-expert designer who carries out design activities using available resources in a given environment. It does so by examining the design activities undertaken by non-expert, informal, designers in organisations who make use of the formal and informal technology already in use in organisations while designing to direct, influence, change or transform the practices of people in the organisation. These people represent a cohort of designers who are given little attention in the literature on information systems, despite their central role in the formation of practice and enactment of technology in organisations. The paper describes the experiences of 18 everyday designers in an academic setting using three concepts: *everyday designer in an organisation, empathy through design* and *experiencing an awareness gap*. These concepts were constructed through the analysis of in-depth interviews with the participants. The paper concludes with a call for tool support for everyday designers in organisations to enable them to better understand the audience for whom they are designing and the role technology plays in the organisation.

Keywords: Design · Everyday design · Academic practice

1 Introduction

This paper builds upon the concept of an *everyday designer* as a non-expert designer who carries out design activities using available resources in a given environment [1–3]. This concept, previously applied to activities of daily living in the home, is used in this case to examine the activities of a diverse cohort of non-expert designers in an academic environment who undertake design activities for a given audience using the available technology. This role, which contrasts with expert designers on one side and end-users on the other side, is largely ignored in the Information Systems literature despite the fact that the design they undertake has a significant influence on the practices which are enacted in the organisation.

The everyday designer in this context is not usually a designer *of* technology. Rather, the everyday designer is usually a designer *with* technology. The outcome of their design efforts is a *practice*, sometimes a *new* practice, sometimes a *changed* practice, sometimes a *transformed* practice. A practice is a socially and materially constituted behaviour which is replicated over space and time. It is comprised of multiple social and material elements, among which technology has received increased attention in recent decades. So-called *posthumanist* conceptions of practice

© Springer International Publishing Switzerland 2016
J. Parsons et al. (Eds.): DESRIST 2016, LNCS 9661, pp. 114–130, 2016.
DOI: 10.1007/978-3-319-39294-3_8

such as *actor-network theory* (ANT) [4, 5], *structuration theory*, [6, 7] *human-machine configurations* [8], *mangle of practice* [9], *technology-in-practice* [10] and *sociomaterial practices* [11–13] have looked beyond the human role in forming and configuring practice to analyse simultaneously the material or technological elements which form and configure practice.

Everyday designers have an opportunity to make use of technology as they carry out design, but this requires that they understand to some degree the technology which is already in use in the organisation, the ways that technology is used in the organisation, and the diversity which exists in the use of technology among individuals and groups in the organisation. Unlike expert designers (e.g. software engineers, interaction designers, information system designers), everyday designers tend not to be trained in design and consequently are unlikely to engage in the types of user and contextual research activities that are undertaken systematically by such experts. In the absence of rigorous research activities, everyday designers must find other ways to understand the people for whom they are designing and the social and material context within which they work.

This paper reports on a study which took place involving 18 non-expert designers in an academic environment, specifically focusing on the early stages of design where user and contextual research is typically undertaken [14, 15]. The research question (RQ) addressed by the study was as follows: *How do the non-expert designers participating in the study learn about the people for whom they design and the role technology plays in their practices?*

The aim of the study was to investigate the ways in which the participants developed their awareness, knowledge and mental models of the people for whom they are designing and the way in which those people use technology in their daily practices. The people for whom the participants were designing were academic staff (lecturers, professors) who were using technology in their own practices for, *inter alia, teaching, research, personal organisation, communication,* and *collaboration.* The roles occupied by the participants included *course leaders, group leaders, learning development, staff training, quality assurance, student administration* and *information services.* These non-expert designers work with academic staff on an ongoing basis (to varying degrees) to direct, influence, change, or transform practices such as *communication with students, sharing of knowledge, course development, technology enhanced learning,* and *collaboration among team members.*

The participants were purposefully selected based on their role in the organisation and their daily activities. They were interviewed in-depth, and their interviews were analysed using qualitative methods typically employed in grounded theory studies. The analysis resulted in the development of three core concepts: *everyday designer in an organisation, empathy through design* and *experiencing an awareness gap.* The first of these concepts captures the way in which the non-expert designer develops their identity as a designer or a problem solver and the way in which they appreciate their role in the organisation. The second concept, *empathy through design,* describes ways in which the everyday designer learns about the organisation, its technology and its people while they carry out design activities. This process results in diverse and incomplete mental models among everyday designers, in the context under investigation. The third concept, *experiencing an awareness gap*, shows how these everyday designers themselves experience a limit to their own knowledge of the organisation, its technology and its people. This gap restricts how the everyday designer can use technology in their design activities because in many cases the everyday designer is unsure of how technologies such as email, Internet, mobile technology, authoring tools, cloud environments and institutional systems are used in diverse ways by their audience - academic staff.

The study concludes with a recommendation for tools to support everyday designers in organisations to develop their knowledge and awareness of the people for whom they are designing and the way in which technology plays a role in the practices of those people. There is a gap in the provision of such tools because there has not traditionally been widespread recognition of everyday designers as designers, and consequently there has not been a need for design tools to support their activities. This outcome is important for the Design Science Research in Information Systems and Information Technology community because it directs focus towards a new cohort of designers and asks researchers to consider how their design roles impact on the enactment of technology in organisations. It is argued elsewhere that despite some notable exceptions [16], the Design Science Research (DSR) community does not pay close enough attention to the people responsible for enacting technology [17] This means that the DSR community lags behind the Human Computer Interaction [18] community and others which have positioned the human at the centre of the design process and developed ways to recognise and respond to diversity in the user population [19, 20]. The research described here seeks to address this issue by giving recognition to the *everyday designer in organisations* and calling for support for their design activity.

2   Related Literature

Wakkary [1] introduces the concept of an *everyday designer* as a type of non-expert designer who extends designs into new uses. The concept is focussed largely on the appropriation of resources in the home and the creative activities undertaken by individuals as part of their activities of daily living [2, 3]. This conception of design is similar to Orlikowski's *technology-in-practice* model in that it centres on the appropriation or enactment of technology by the end user. The use of the term *everyday* implies action by non-experts and on a small scale. This has a clear parallel with activities undertaken outside the home in organisations, where the *creative resources* available to the designer include the formal and informal technologies [24] available in that organisation.

Recognition of the everyday designer in an organisation as a designer requires a liberal interpretation of the term *design*. Such an interpretation aligns with the description put forth by Herb Simon in *The Sciences of the Artificial* [25], now widely recognised as the foundation document for Design Science Research in general. In that book, Simon challenged the view that design is exclusively an activity carried out by experts, arguing instead that "*everyone designs who devises courses of action aimed at changing existing situations into preferred ones*". Famed product designer Don Norman supports this view, arguing that "*We are all designers. We manipulate the environment, the better to serve our needs*" [26]. Ezio Manzini [27] argues from a social innovation perspective (interestingly, the theme of this conference) that the greatest challenges faced by society can only be addressed by *diffuse design*, whereby competent, non-expert designers are enabled to design solutions on a grand scale. Expert designers, in his view, must take on meta-level responsibilities where they commence the initiatives and provide the design tools that support diffuse design. These include the tools required to understand the goals and practices of the people for whom design is taking place and the nature of the sociotechnical worlds which they occupy.

The everyday designer is engaged in practice-oriented design rather than the design of technology. A practice, it is argued, cannot be designed directly but its components can be designed or configured to influence its dynamics. There are many views on the components of practice, with posthumanist accounts [4–13] recognising the contribution of material to the dynamics of practice. Reckwitz's description of practice incorporating reference to *things and their use* is widely cited:

> *"A routinized type of behaviour which consists of several elements interconnected to one other: forms of bodily activities, forms of mental activities, things and their use, a background knowledge in the form of understanding, know-how, states of emotions and motivational knowledge"* [28].

Things and their use represent the most accessible components of practice for designers. Kuijer [29], citing Shove [30] in discussing the role of the artifact designer in the creation of practice, argues that *"the idea that 'material artefacts configure (rather than simply meet) what consumers and users experience as needs and desires' implies that 'those who give them shape and form are perhaps uniquely implicated in the transformation and persistence of social practice'"*. Bjorn and Ostelund [31], in discussing sociomaterial practices, argue similarly that *"the sociomaterial designer can design an artifact but cannot design sociomaterial practices. Sociomaterial practices emerge in practice, and therefore, cannot be designed"*. The configuration of practice through material or technology has influenced design in information systems [13], human-computer interaction [32], and computer supported collaborative work [33, 34], but usually from the perspective of the expert designer (which the everyday designer is not) or participatory design [35] (which requires the active involvement of an expert designer). The role of the non-expert everyday designer is not dealt with in these fields.

The non-expert designers in this study occupy roles in an academic setting. They seek to direct, influence, change or transform what academic staff do in their daily practices, and they seek to use the technologies in use by academic staff to do so. They seek, for example, to use the Institutional Virtual Learning Environment to impact on teaching practices, or mobile devices to impact on collaboration practices, or cloud storage to impact on personal organisation practices. They do not design the technology itself but they do seek to design how it's configured, enacted or used by others.

3 Research Setting

This research is undertaken in a large Higher Education Institute (HEI) in Ireland. The Institute (*de facto* university) has approximately 20,000 students and 2,000 staff. Approximately 1,000 of the staff are academic staff, the remainder are non-academic staff who support the academic mission. The Institute is located on seven main sites across its host city with no central campus. It is due to merge with two other Institutes located in the suburban area outside the city. It has a comprehensive provision across the sciences, engineering, business and arts. While the Institute is primarily a teaching focussed institution, it has a significant research profile with many of its staff active in research centres and groups.

The HEI has invested heavily in the use of a Virtual Learning Environment (VLE) for the support of teaching, learning and assessment activity, which has been broadly but not universally adopted among academic staff. Staff make diverse use of social media and informal tools in their daily activity. Email is by some distance the most popularly used technology, though even that technology is enacted in a wide variety of ways by academic staff. Other than email, it is difficult to identify specific technologies which form a core part of the practices of all academic staff.

The everyday designers who were selected for this study occupy a range of different roles. All are involved in design which is intended to impact on the practices of academic staff, including teaching practice, research practice, personal organisation practice, collaboration practice and communication practice. Figure 1 below lists the 18 participants in this study.

Role	Count
Learning Technologist	4
Information Services	3
Learning Development	2
Course Leader	2
Staff Trainer	2
Human Resources	1
Internal Communication	1
Quality Assurance Officer	1
Research Group Leader	1
Student Administration	1
Total	**18**

Fig. 1. Profile of 18 every designers who participated in study

4   Methodology

Qualitative methods typically employed for grounded theory studies were employed for this research. Grounded theory seeks to make sense of a research setting and understand what *"research participant's lives are like"*, culminating in an *"abstract theoretical understanding of the studied experience"* [36]. Several versions of grounded theory co-exist due largely to a series of conflicts among the key practitioners [37] since the method was first introduced by Glaser and Strauss [38] in the 1960 s. Kathy Charmaz's version of grounded theory [36] is positioned as an interpretive, social contructivist approach which sees the role of the researcher as *constructing* rather than *discovering* the theory.

This is the approach adopted for this work, in recognition of the fact that the concepts presented were developed due to the researcher's interpretation of the processes observed and made evident through the interviews carried out.

The objective of this research is to describe the experience of the participants as designers, specifically focusing on how they gain an understanding of the people for whom they are designing and their use of technology. Aspects of the Charmaz approach adopted for this work include, open and focused coding of interview transcripts, constant comparison of emerging theory with data, development of concepts and categories and purposive, theoretical sampling. Charmaz sees *memoing* as a vital part of the theory development process, whereby the researcher writes about the emerging concepts and categories in the theory and in doing so develops the theoretical analysis and understanding of the research setting. This was extensively used for the conceptual development of this work.

Data was collected for this research through the use of semi-structured, ethnographic interviews [39]. Interviews serve as a useful method for this type of study because they enable the researcher to narrow the scope and focus of the study as the key concepts emerge. The first stage of our research involved the collection of data from three course team leaders. It became apparent from the analysis of these interviews that their design for colleagues is largely impacted by the design which is undertaken elsewhere among non-academic staff. This led to interviewing of four learning technologists who are directly involved with the Institutional Virtual Learning Environment (VLE). As some key theoretical categories were emerging, data was collected from Heads of Learning Development, staff training and academic quality assurance. Additional data was then collected for comparison from staff involved in design with technology, including information services and student administration (timetabling system). A representative of human resources was interviewed to explore certain concepts.

The outcome of this approach is set of three concepts which describe the experience of the participants in this setting: *everyday design in an organisation*, *empathy through design*, and *experiencing an awareness gap*. Each of these three concepts are described using conceptual diagrams and a brief description (due to available space) in the next three sections.

5 Everyday Designer in an Organisation

The everyday designers in the setting under investigation who participated in the study broadly divide between those involved in *tech-centric* roles and *non-tech-centric* roles. Regardless of role, everyday designers largely do not see themselves as *designers of technology*, In fact, some identify as technophobes. One participant, Michael (a pseudonym, like all other names used in this paper), in a learning support role, identified *"ways of doing it beyond technology"* – identifying himself as someone for whom technology may not play a part in design. Another who uses technology as part of design, Joan, nonetheless commented that *"technology isn't the end in itself"*. There is significant variation in technical competence and engagement among the cohort of everyday designers who participated in this study, as fits with even a superficial understanding of their roles, leading to different emphases on the social, material and technical elements of practice in their design processes (see Fig. 2).

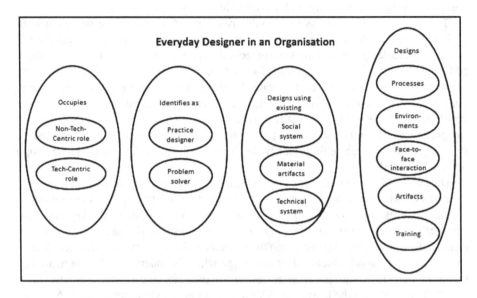

Fig. 2. The *everyday designer in an organisation* concept diagram

The degree to which everyday designers identify as practice designers is variable. For some everyday designers this dominates their understanding of their role – for example those involved in learning development and staff development roles. One participant, Rose – a quality assurance officer, described her objective as "*trying to encourage other staff members to adopt approaches that have worked for different people and to encourage sharing of best practice as well*". A similar point was captured by Eoin, from Information Services, who commented that "*So yes, I'd be trying to change the practices of staff and how they share content with each other and their students*". This contrasted with participants in the study who identified more as *problem solvers*. Dave, also from Information Services, described his activity as "*a lot of the times it is just solving problems rather than being a designer as such*", yet further analysis of this interview revealed circumstances where he sought to control or enhance the practices of academics with respect to their use of technology. In this example, he describes how he makes a decision regarding the practices academic staff enact when controlling their own technology:

> "*So, in that case you kind of, you gauge their level of IT skills and then our knowledge and then you generally give them administrative rights and say, you know, 'You can download this resource, this tool and then install it yourself.'*"

This is easily classed as a different type of design than, say, Gerard, who describes how his objective is to change the mindset of academic staff regarding their role in curriculum design and design of the learning experience:

"So it's trying to get them to see well you're designing your whole learning experience for your students and how do you want that learning experience to be designed, that's kind of a challenge."

The everyday designer may identify as either a *practice designer* or a *problem solver*. In either case, however, the objective is to impact on practice. The opportunity to do so can be undertaken through design of *social*, *material* or *technical* (as a sub-set of material) elements of practice. Indeed, some who had previously largely been involved in design of technical elements of practice observed how their role had evolved to engage with the social elements.

Susan, a learning technologist commented that her role had evolved in such a way that she was no longer involved in the development of artifacts which lecturers use in the classroom, but instead she and her colleagues were engaging with social elements of practice by *"changing our focus then more into supporting lectures doing these kinds of things"*. This theme of meta-design through social engagement recurred among other everyday designers, who saw themselves as designing an environment within which academic staff are better enabled to achieve their goals. Gerard, in a learning development role, described his role as one of *"consultant"*, whose objective was to change the mindset of academic staff. Michael, who has an objective of developing academic staff's engagement with learning technology describes how he and his colleagues *"still have been quite open to the notion of the organic growth of technology and individual"*, and see their role as providing a *"structure"* within which that takes place.

The everyday designers in this study seek to design practice with some focussing largely on the design of social elements and others on the design of material or technical elements. In order to enhance the use of technology in design, everyday designers need to gain a greater understanding of the role technology plays in the practices of academics. The informal process through which they currently achieve this, as discussed in the next section, is captured by the concept *empathy through design*.

6 Empathy Through Design

Users, even users in identical roles, are diverse. They often have different needs, goals, abilities, attitudes, aptitudes, fears, and relationships [20]. They often occupy quite different technical and material environments, even while in the same organisation, in particular in cases where they enact their personal choice of technologies in their practices. The interaction design community has adopted extensive user research methods in their own design processes in an attempt to capture diversity among the possible user community. The everyday designers in this study do *not* engage in extensive user research but instead acquire knowledge about their user population and their use of technology in practice through design. The concept *empathy through design* emerged from the analysis of the interviews with participants in this study, reflecting a co-construction process whereby everyday designers learn about their user population and construct mental models of their user population while designing either in real-time or asynchronously for them.

Figure 3 shows a separation between the *seeing* and *responding* processes engaged by everyday designers regarding the use of technology in the user population. *Seeing* captures the ways in which everyday designers see differences between people in their user audience. *Responding* captures the ways in which everyday designers incorporate what they see into the technical dimension of their design processes.

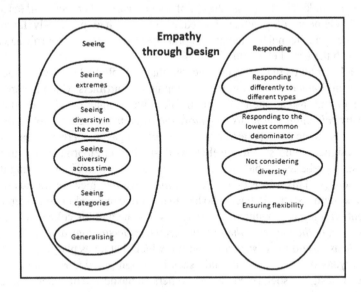

Fig. 3. The *EMPATHY through design* concept diagram

While it is typical for everyday designers to *see extremes*, everyday designers often also see *diversity in the centre*. Everyday designers have a relatively consistent understanding of novices and experts, with both terms or close synonyms being widely used in describing the user population. In describing one scenario involving users requesting control over their computer, Dave commented:

> *"But I have found that dealing with novice users, they don't tend to ask for it, it is really the people who are IT savvy, you know?"*

When asked to describe further what his understanding of a novice user is, he commented:

> *"Your email, your Word, your Excel, they log on to their PC and they access those tools and they wouldn't typically use anything outside of that."*

The sense of advanced users being people who can exercise greater autonomy both with their personal technology and the Institutional systems, is captured in the following response from Roberta, a learning technologist, in discussing the Institutional Virtual Learning Environment:

> *"Biggest difference I would find is that you'll have people who actually know what the tools are, so they come to you with a specific question about the tool itself and how they can use a tool."*

There is a shared sense of what to expect from novice and expert users, without necessarily knowing the specifics of their practices and their enactment of technology. The population in the centre, however, is less straightforward to characterise. John, a staff trainer, commented that:

"I think it is very hard to define an average user in terms of their skills."

and that while the extremes represent points on a spectrum where other users cover *"everything in between"*. Dave provided a specific sense of what he considers the evolution from novice to mid-range user to be, in terms of the development of the technical suite of tools used:

"They start broadening the amount of software that is on their system and there would be cloud applications, all these plug-ins and tools and they will start using them..."

The observation of diversity across time and the changing of classifications of users is a common theme, as is a tendency to generalise about academic staff, with reference to *"the vast majority"* by Gerard, for example. Age is widely used as a means to categorise people with assumptions of ability, motivation and interest associated differently with different age groups. Academic discipline is similarly referred to by certain everyday designers in terms of their mental model of academic staff.

The most common response to the mental models developed by everyday designers for academic staff is to *design for the lowest common denominator*. Paul, from student administration, gives a sense of what this means for his approach to design:

"That would be my lowest common denominator and then the people who aren't technologically savvy they have to be brought into it."

Paul recognises the need to design for the lowest common denominator as a limiting factor in design, and regrets that design targets this group to the cost of others:

"Do you know what unfortunately when you're designing the written type of material or the online material I think you're gearing it or you're aiming it towards the lower skilled end as a common denominator."

Another approach, most common in real-time design situations – for example, where a solution to a problem is designed while interacting with the person, is to tailor the response to the individual. This approach requires little in terms of a mental model because the response is tailored to the individual, but such an approach is not possible in non-real-time situations involving, say, the design of artifacts such as training materials. In certain cases, everyday designers seek to adopt a flexible strategy in the design of artifacts, responding to different groups, as described here by John:

"And the approach then is either dealing with it on a one-to-one basis or giving that alternative on an online course, you know, 'click here if you think you know how to', 'click here for the quick way' and 'click here if you need some more instruction.'"

The final strategy, as described by a Mary from the human resources team regarding the system and processes they develop, is to ignore diversity and engage with a generalised, often stereotyped understanding of the user population:

"I think we tend to work around what suits, maybe not us as HR, but what suits the situation or what suits the process that we are trying to develop. Because systems have limitations. But if the

system requires things to be done in a certain way we just need people to do things in a certain way."

Empathy through design describes five different ways in which the everyday designers in this study capture diversity among academic staff regarding their use of technology, and four ways in which this impacts upon their design for academic staff, using technology. The everyday designers' approach to designing using technology for academic staff is, however, limited by the degree to which their design experience has exposed them to knowledge of academic staff and their use of technology. The third core concept, related to this, which emerged from the analysis of interviews and which we explore in the next section is *experiencing an awareness gap.*

7   Experiencing an Awareness Gap

The everyday designers in this study do not carry out user research but instead develop their understanding of the user population by designing for them. This provides rich, authentic, experiential knowledge to the everyday designer, but it also limits their capacity to develop an awareness of the full range of users (see Fig. 4).

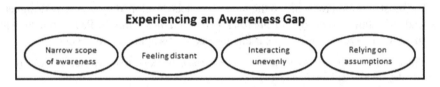

Fig. 4. The *experiencing an awareness gap* concept diagram

A number of reasons for this awareness gap emerged from the exploration of interview data. First among these reasons was the *narrow scope of awareness*. This refers to the knowledge which everyday designers generate of practices which are only directly relevant to the scope within which design is taking place. This may seem appropriate, but it means that designers for *teaching practices* are unaware of the practices engaged in by academic staff in areas such as *research, personal organisation, collaboration* and so on. This represents a missed opportunity for designers who may otherwise be enabled to leverage a successful practice from a different area to impact on the area within which they're designing. For example, consider Eoin's comment:

> *"I would be a bit grey in terms of how academics communicate with their students via email. It's not something I would know too much about."*

A second reason for everyday designers feeling an awareness gap is due to their feeling distant from the people for whom they are designing. Margaret, whose objective it is to design for the enhancement of teaching practices referred to this distance:

> *"I'm not great with technology myself but I don't have any judgement in my mind, because actually I don't know the staff well enough in general."*

John also referred to the disconnect between those who are responsible for design for academic staff, including software designers, and the academics themselves:

> "There is a huge disconnect between the designers of these software systems and the end user who expects an intuitive type of interaction with these things and they're just not that way, they're not designed that way."

A third reason for experiencing a gap is due to the uneven, non-systematic interaction with academic staff. This, obviously, is a consequence of everyday designers often interacting with those who are in most need of support, because direct support tends to play a large role in everyday design practice. Ruth, a learning technologist, commented on how the responsibility was on the staff to make contact:

> "No, they ring up and you try to solve the problem over the phone. Others will email you in; they mightn't have a contact number, so they just send them in, the help for them."

Finally, everyday designers may experience an awareness gap because they rely on assumptions about academic staff. Mary commented on how interaction with academic staff was not necessarily a requirement in order to design processes for them:

> "We don't actually interact with academic staff to ask them what would suit you, we just implement really"

The everyday designers in this study experience a gap between their awareness of how technology is being used, and how technology is actually being used. This is a gap that can be filled in a number of ways, one of which is through the provision of tools, the initial requirements for which are provided in the next section.

8   Tool Requirements

The Information Systems research community has been very fortunate in recent decades to benefit from high quality organisational ethnographies and case studies of the use of technology in organisations. These studies, however, have not been appropriately diluted and communicated to the people who will most benefit from the practical knowledge discovered. This paper presents a view that these people are the everyday designers in organisations – the people who seek to use the organisation's technology to direct, influence, change or transform the practices of others.

Based on the study conducted and the three concepts developed, a set of 10 requirements are presented for tools which will enable non-expert, everyday designers to gain an enhanced understanding of the people in their organisation and the way that technology is enacted in their practices.

*Tool Requirement 1. Tools should be **accessible** to everyday designers, enabling them to easily engage with the tool.*

The everyday designer in an organisation is a non-expert designer, in many cases not even identifying as a designer. He/she will often occupy non-technical roles and engage in design which they consider to be mundane. Tool users should not require knowledge of skills levels of an expert in order to use these design tools, since it is unlikely that they will seek to acquire these skills.

Tool Requirement 2. Tools should provide everyday designers with **comprehensive** *information about the organisation, including relevant aspects of the social, material and technical environment.*

The everyday designer in an organisation is a designer of practices, not a designer of technology. A practice is constituted of multiple elements, including social, material and technical elements. The context provided by these elements are important to ensure that the everyday designer understands how and why practices take place within the organisation, including practices involving the enactment of technologies.

Tool Requirement 3. Tools should be **reusable** *for multiple projects, not requiring significant redevelopment or reconfiguration for new projects.*

Design projects often commence with the development and configuration of tools to match the requirements for the project. This configuration can occupy a significant amount of time and often require expertise on behalf of the designer. In the absence of such expertise, tools for everyday design should be reusable with minimal changes across multiple, small scale and diverse projects.

Tool Requirement 4. Tools should be **reflective** *of the diversity in the organisation, exposing everyday designers to types of people they may not otherwise be aware of.*

Everyday designers may have a limited knowledge of the people in the organisation and may be unaware of the true diversity that exists among people in terms of their use of technology, their goals and their other practices. Tools for everyday design should ensure that everyday designers are enabled to learn about this diversity.

Tool Requirement 5. Tools should enable **empathetic** *engagement between the everyday designer and the people in the organisation.*

Empathy is a key requirement for effective design, enabling designers to predict the effect of the design on future practice. Emapthy can be acquired by direct engagement with people, but can also be acquired through artificial means, as demonstrated by empathy with artificial characters in the entertainment sector. Everyday designers should be enabled to empathise with the diverse people in the organisation.

Tool Requirement 6. Tools should be **practical**, *exposing everyday designers to practices they may not otherwise have been aware of.*

Everyday designers in an organisation can make use of existing practices such as existing enactments of technology for the formation of new practices. Everyday designers should be enabled to identify with appropriate practices with which to work for the creation of new practices.

*Tool Requirement 7.   Tools should be **operable**, enabling everyday designers to act upon the knowledge gained about diversity, people and practices in their design activities.*

Once everyday designers gain exposure to the diversity, people and practices in their organisation, they must be enabled to carry out design activities which makes use of the knowledge gained.

*Tool Requirement 8.   Tools should be **stimulating**, encouraging creativity in design among everyday designers.*

Everyday designers should be enabled to engage creatively with the environment for which they are designing, exploiting the various resources available in the environment as creative resources for the creation of future practice.

*Tool Requirement 9.   Tools should be **credible**, ensuring that everyday designers believe that the information regarding diversity, people and practices is accurate.*

The development of the tool is an activity undertaken by an expert designer, following user research and inquiry into the environment. The process engaged in by the expert designer for the development of the tool, and the output from that process, should be credible to the everyday designer such that they believe the tool to present an accurate representation of the organisation's diversity, people and practices.

*Tool Requirement 10.   Tools should be **extensible**, ensuring that they can evolve over time as people and practices change in the organisation.*

It should be possible for the tool, incorporating the representation of the organisation, to evolve as the organisation, its people and its practices evolve.

Tools, in this context, are practical, usable artifacts which incorporate a representation of the organisation, its people and its practices (including the enactment of technology in the organisation). Various methods exist for the development of representations of people and practices [14, 15, 40] and for the presentation of such representation in artifactual form [41–44], albeit not specifically in the context of non-expert, everyday design. The requirements set out here seek to fill that gap and lead to the development of new tools to support the everyday designer in organisations.

9   Summary

Everyday design is an important concept for the Design Science Research in Information Systems and Information Technology community. The everyday designer shares some attributes with expert designers (involvement in design, intention to impact on practice) while also lacking other attributes (design training and expertise, identity as designer). Similarly, end users share some attributes with everyday designers (use systems developed by others) while lacking other attributes (directly impacting of practices of others). Everyday designers seek to use the formal and informal technologies in the organisation to impact upon practice, but may do so without knowledge of the diverse ways in which technology is used in the organisation and the ways in which technology could be used to direct, influence, change or transform practice. This research recommends the development of tools to address this gap.

References

1. Callon, M.: Some Elements of a Sociology of Translation: Domestication of the Scallops and the Fishermen. Power, Action and Belief: A New Sociology of Knowledge (1986)
2. Latour, B.: Reassembling the Social-An Introduction to Actor-Network-Theory. Oxford University Press, Oxford (2005)
3. Giddens, A.: The Constitution of Society: Outline of the Theory of Structuration (1986)
4. DeSanctis, G., Poole, M.S.: Capturing the complexity in advanced technology use: adaptive structuration theory. Organ. Sci. 5(2), 121–147 (1994)
5. Suchman, L.: Human-Machine Reconfigurations: Plans and Situated Actions, 2nd edn. Cambridge University Press, Cambridge (2006)
6. Pickering, A.: The Mangle of Practice: Time, Agency, and Science. University of Chicago, Chicago (2010)
7. Orlikowski, W.J.: Using technology and constituting structures: a practice lens for studying technology in organizations. In: Resources, Co-evolution and Artifacts. Springer (2000)
8. Cecez-Kecmanovic, D., Galliers, R.D., Henfridsson, O., Newell, S., Vidgen, R.: The sociomateriality of information systems: current status, future directions. MIS Q. 38, 809–830 (2014)
9. Leonardi, P.M.: Materiality, sociomateriality, and socio-technical systems: What do these terms mean? How are they different? Do we need them (2012)
10. Orlikowski, W.J.: Sociomaterial practices: exploring technology at work. Organ. Stud. 28(9), 1435–1448 (2007)
11. Sein, M.K., Henfridsson, O., Purao, S., Rossi, M., Lindgren, R.: Action design research. MIS Q. 35(1), 37–56 (2011)
12. Haj-Bolouri, A.: The notion of users in design science research. In: 38th Information Systems Research Seminar in Scandinavia (IRIS 38), Oulu, Finland, 9–12 August 2015
13. Harrison, S., Tatar, D., Sengers, P.: The three paradigms of HCI. In: Alt. Chi. Session at the SIGCHI Conference on Human Factors in Computing Systems (2007)
14. Bannon, L.: From human factors to human actors: The role of psychology and human-computer interaction studies in system design. Des. Work Coop. Des. Comput Syst. (1991)
15. Cooper, A.: The Inmates are Running the Asylum: Why High-Tech Products Drive us Crazy and How to Restore the Sanity, vol. 261. Sams, Indianapolis (1999)
16. Vaishnavi, V.K., Kuechler Jr., W.: Design Science Research Methods and Patterns: Innovating Information and Communication Technology. Auerbach Publications, Philadelphia (2007)
17. Hevner, A.R., March, S.T., Park, J., Ram, S.: Design science in information systems research. MIS Q. 28(1), 75–105 (2004)
18. Peffers, K., Tuunanen, T., Rothenberger, M.A., Chatterjee, S.: A design science research methodology for information systems research. J. Manag. Inf. Syst. 24, 45–77 (2007)
19. Simon, H.A.: The Sciences of the Artificial, vol. 136. MIT press, Cambridge (1969)
20. Norman, D.A.: Emotional Design: Why We Love (or Hate) Everyday Things (2005)
21. Manzini, E.: Design, When Everybody Designs: An Introduction to Design for Social Innovation. MIT Press, Cambridge (2015)

22. Reckwitz, A.: Toward a theory of social practices a development in culturalist theorizing. Eur. J. Soc. Theory **5**(2), 243–263 (2002)
23. Kuijer, L.: Implications of Social Practice Theory for Sustainable Design (2014)
24. Shove, E.: The Design of Everyday Life. Berg, Oxford (2007)
25. Bjørn, P., Østerlund, C.: Sociomateriality and design. In: Sociomaterial-Design (2014)
26. Kuutti, K., Bannon, L.J.: The turn to practice in HCI: towards a research agenda. In: Proceedings of the 32nd Annual ACM conference CHI, pp. 3543–3552 (2014)
27. Wulf, V., Rohde, M., Pipek, V., Stevens, G.: Engaging with practices: design case studies as a research framework in CSCW. In: CSCW 2011, pp. 505–512
28. Rohde, M., Stevens, G., Brödner, P., Wulf, V.: Towards a paradigmatic shift in IS: designing for social practice. In: DESRIST (2009)
29. Ehn, P.: Scandinavian design: on participation and skill. Particip. Des. Princ. (1993)
30. Cosgrave, R., Rísquez, A., Logan-Phelan, T., Farrelly, T., Costello, E., Palmer, M., McAvinia, C., Harding, N., Vaughan, N.: Usage and Uptake of Virtual Learning Environments in Ireland: Findings from a Multi Institutional Study. AISHE-J (2011)
31. McAvinia, C.: Investigating the adoption of a university virtual learning environment: an activity theoretic analysis. Unpublished Ph.D. thesis, University of Dublin, Dublin (2011)
32. O'Rourke, K.C., Rooney, P., Boylan, F.: What's the use of a VLE? Ir. J. Acad. Pract. **4**(1), 10 (2015)
33. Selim, H.M.: Critical success factors for e-learning acceptance: confirmatory factor models. Comput. Educ. **49**(2), 396–413 (2007)
34. Šumak, B., Heričko, M., Pušnik, M.: A meta-analysis of e-learning technology acceptance: the role of user types and e-learning technology types. Comput. Hum. Behav. **27**(6), 2067–2077 (2011)
35. Trowler, P.R., et al.: Academic Tribes and Territories. McGraw-Hill, New York (2001)
36. Johannesen, M., Erstad, O., Habib, L.: Virtual learning environments as sociomaterial agents in the network of teaching practice. Comput. Educ. **59**, 785–792 (2012)
37. Lechuga, V.M., Altbach, P.G.: The Changing Landscape of the Academic Profession: The Culture of Faculty at for-Profit Colleges and Universities. Routledge, New York (2006)
38. Debowski, S.: The New Academic: A Strategic Handbook: A Strategic Handbook. McGraw-Hill Education, Maidenhead (2012)
39. Whitchurch, C., Gordon, G.: Academic and Professional Identities in Higher Education: The Challenges of a Diversifying Workforce. Routledge, London (2009)
40. Gornall, L., Cook, C., Daunton, L.: Academic Working Lives: Experience Practice and Change. Bloomsbury Academic, London (2013)
41. Musselin, C.: The Transformation of Academic Work: Facts and Analysis. Research and Occasional Paper Series: CSHE. 4.07. Center for Studies in Higher Education (2007)
42. Charmaz, K.: Constructing Grounded Theory, 2nd edn. SAGE, Thousand Oaks (2013)
43. Ralph, N., Birks, M., Chapman, Y.: The methodological dynamism of grounded theory. Int. J. Qual. Methods **14**(4), 1–6 (2015). 1609406915611576
44. Glaser, B.G., Strauss, A.: The Discovery of Grounded Theory: Strategies for Qualitative Research. Transaction Publishers, Chicago (1967)
45. Hammersley, M.: Ethnography: Principles in Practice (2007)
46. Goldkuhl, G., Cronholm, S.: Adding theoretical grounding to grounded theory: toward multi-grounded theory. Int. J. Qual. Methods **9**(2), 187–205 (2010)
47. Thornberg, R.: Informed grounded theory. Scand. J. Educ. Res. **56**, 243–259 (2012)
48. Urquhart, C., Lehmann, H., Myers, M.D.: Putting the 'theory' back into grounded theory: guidelines for grounded theory studies in information systems. Inf. Syst. J. **20**, 357–381 (2010)

49. Matavire, R., Brown, I.: Profiling grounded theory approaches in information systems research†. Eur. J. Inf. Syst. **22**(1), 119–129 (2013)
50. Klein, H.K., Myers, M.D.: A set of principles for conducting and evaluating interpretive field studies in information systems. MIS Q. **23**, 67–93 (1999)
51. Orlikowski, W.J.: CASE tools as organizational change: investigating incremental and radical changes in systems development. MIS Q. **17**, 309–340 (1993)
52. Carroll, J.M.: Making Use: Scenario-Based Design of Human-Computer Interactions (2000)

Out of the Bottle: Design Principles for GENIE Tools (Group-Focused Engagement and Network Innovation Environment)

Magnus Rotvit Perlt Hansen[✉] and Jan Pries-Heje

Institute for People and Technology, Roskilde University, Roskilde, Denmark
{magnuha, janph}@ruc.dk

Abstract. This paper addresses the design problem of designing IS tools for supporting inter-organizational innovation network groups. Inter-organizational networks are groups of people with diverse backgrounds and interests. Innovation networks consist of rationalized structures and socially constructed processes that are ongoing over long periods of time and is thus a highly complex problem. We argue that in order to design such IS artifacts well, we need design principles for constructing future IS artifacts. From the experiences of designing and evaluating a Group-focused Engagement & Network Innovation Environment (GENIE) nexus tool based on design science research, we propose five general design principles that aid how to design and utilize such IS tools when one plays a role in a innovation network group either as a member, facilitator or network sponsor. Our contribution is a proposal of a GENIE design theory as the foundation for future development of IS artifacts.

Keywords: IS design theory · Design principles · Inter-organizational networks · Innovation

1 Introduction

"*Companies come to us and say: We believe there is a treasure buried somewhere around here. But we can't find it! We don't just want to copy and change something others have made available on the Internet. We want something* new", a manager told us at an interview in a 50-people software developer house.

This focus on something new - and not just copying something others have made - leads to the concept of *innovation*. An innovation is an idea, practice, or object that is perceived as new, while diffusion of innovation is the process by which an innovation is communicated through certain channels, over time, among the members of a social system [1]. Innovative IT can be of two main types. The primary innovation is technical, involving new technologies, products and services. The second type of innovation is administrative, involving procedures, policies and organizational forms that are either enabled by the new technology, or necessary to support new technology [2].

The last decade there has been a movement towards *Open Innovation* [3], arguing that companies are severely limited by their own internal resources. Hence to be innovative they need to involve outside resources; people as well as knowledge.

© Springer International Publishing Switzerland 2016
J. Parsons et al. (Eds.): DESRIST 2016, LNCS 9661, pp. 131–146, 2016.
DOI: 10.1007/978-3-319-39294-3_9

Chesbrough [3] states that even though new discoveries and scientific development creates unseen opportunities for innovation this may be the worst time to be innovative: *"Many leading companies are having a terrible time sustaining their internal R&D investments"* ([3] pp. xvii-xviii). This need for creating innovation can be seen as a change in organizational design thinking from 'machine age' to 'organic' thinking where pluralistic process collaboration and long-term thinking is valued higher than structural, monolithic thinking [4].

Thus, to be innovative and maintain their innovative ability, companies needs to look for knowledge and ideas externally, often with the help of other companies. This has led companies to participate in *inter-organizational innovation network groups*. Most research in this regard, however, has focused on reasons and strategies, or which technology that can support the groups virtually, taking either a business-centric or technology-centric perspective. We argue that we need to take the perspective of technology as a product and medium for facilitating social motion within the groups.

In the Danish Region of Thy (in Northern Jutland) a vast amount of companies participate in innovation network groups, though they still struggle with figuring out how to ensure that members obtain benefit from participation. Thus they contacted the authors of this paper. After checking that this problem was nots isolated to Thy but was faced in network groups everywhere, we identified the research question: *How can we design improvements for inter-organizational innovation network groups?*

To answer that question we have worked with the Company Forum in Thy (CF Thy, Danish: "Thy Erhvervsforum") and iteratively designed and evaluated tools to help improve network groups. After a number of iterations we ended up with a design of an IT artifact – the GENIE nexus – that answered our research question. However, we also generalized from our design process five design principles that together form an IS design theory for Group-focused Engagement & Network Innovation Environment tools (abbreviated GENIE).

The remainder of the paper is structured as follows. First, we provide an overview of relevant (to our problem) kernel theories. Next we discuss our research method and the setting in which we undertook the case study with CF Thy. Then the core of the paper derives the five design principles for how to make IS tools support improvement of groups of inter-organizational network innovation. We illustrate the design theory and the principles using our case. Finally, we discuss the contribution and further research within this area.

2   Theoretical Background – Kernel Theories Used

This section has four parts. First a background section on knowledge transfer and knowledge management. Then follows a section on innovation networks where knowledge is transferred for innovation. Then a section discussing design theories of IS and finally a section where we identify a number of issues – called disconnects – with existing theory that we believe our design science approach can improve on.

2.1 Knowledge

When companies meet in network groups they are looking for *knowledge* to be innovative. Knowledge is an innately human quality, residing in the living mind because a person must *"identify, interpret and internalize knowledge"* ([5] p. 2) to act in an on the world. Knowledge is high-value information combined with experience, context, interpretation, and reflection ready to be applied to decisions and actions [6].

Articulated knowledge is expressed in some written or spoken form. Tacit knowledge is itself non-verbalized, intuitive and unarticulated [7, 8].

What seems to be novel in studies of IT project knowledge management is that they to take a much broader view than the "old" discussions of tacit and explicit knowledge [9]. A working definition of this broader view of knowledge is *"information embedded in routines and processes which enable action"* ([10] pp. 83–105). An example of the application of this broader view is Kautz and Thaysen [11] who demonstrated how a simple IT-based tool used in a small IT-developing organization transcended simple information into actual meaning.

However, there is a strong contrast between emergent, social knowledge sharing and management of knowledge and its transfer externally and internally [9]. The main disconnect here is a lack of theoretical knowledge on successful management of emergent knowledge to design the *"...creation of a high-level artifact, able to express and manage existing or emerging knowledge"* ([12] p. 1131).

2.2 Inter-Organizational Innovation Networks

While most social engagements result in informal networked interaction, inter-organizational innovation networks are more formal and based on commonly held interests and goals bound together by the specific professional backgrounds of the participants in search of *"access to information, advice and influence, as well as resources held by others"* ([13] p. 951). Inter-organizational innovation business networks will often focus on developing new ideas, using either a process consultant as a facilitator or by organizing meetings without assistance [14].

Batonda and Perry [15] found that to explain the process of an inter-organizational network, one has to combine stage models and state models (opposed to a lifecycle model) because networks evolve in unpredictable and highly volatile states depending on the entry point, time and commitment that participants bring to the network.

As innovation networking approaches become more and more popular [16], we find a third type of organizational actor: an organization that aids with the facilitation of different strategic innovation network for the potential members of these networks. We define this type of organizational actor as an "orchestrator", indicating less control and more room for individual actors to shape the networks through structural dynamics rather than normal 'management' [17, 18].

High-level artifacts are needed to manage the emergent knowledge of innovation networks. While attempts have been made through creating e.g. 'technological hubs' [13], these have primarily been designed for virtual, social communities with technology as the medium for interaction between only the business network participants [19]. As such, we find a disconnect in the literature as a lack of perspective on all relevant actors, especially the orchestrating actor.

2.3 Design Theories of IS

Within the last 25 years a distinct class of design theory has been developed [20]. Design theories are believed to be prescriptive, practical, basis for action, principles-based, and have a dualist construct [20, 22], and, equally important, grounded in relevant "kernel theories" [21, 23]. Markus et al. [24] emphasized the role of design principles in their definition of design theory components: *"(1) a set of user requirements derived from kernel theory, (2) principles governing the development process, and (3) principles governing the design of a system (i.e., specifying and implementing its features)."* ([24] p. 182).

The main advantage of having design principles is to abstract from the situated implementation to something more generic and applicable; Gregor and Hevner [25] call this level 2 for "nascent theory". Hence, by identifying design principles one raises projectability [26] and thereby the usefulness in other domains.

We are currently in need of design principles for inter-organizational information systems that support network innovation groups. Earlier literature on the inter-organizational realm, e.g. electronic data interchange (EDI), has found that those systems are mainly acted on through socially agreed-upon rules [28], with several design principles to guide development of such technology [27]. The same cannot be said about design principles for technology focusing on supporting innovation networks. Examples that come close are those by Bragge et al. [29] who designed a facilitation process model for repeatable collaboration through brainstorming and filtering ideas, or that of Lea et al. [19] who provided design principles for social media use for social business networks and the importance of designing for active participation. For designing the innovation business network itself, Smart et al. [30] uncovered seven principles: design for a lifecycle, design for proactive management, design for emergence, design for diversity, design for high involvement, design for diffusion, and design for strategic innovation portfolio. Design principles to support the network group after initiation are scarce, though.

Thus where we see a *'disconnect'* of design theory is in identifying design principles that can support highly social and interactive networks and where technology is used both as a medium *and* as a product of knowledge in an ongoing process [31].

2.4 Selecting the Perspective of Design

We have now uncovered the following disconnects in existing theory: (a) a disconnect between balancing human interaction to support both emergent knowledge sharing and managed knowledge transfer, (b) a disconnect represented as a lack of taking the perspective of the specific actor known as the "orchestrator", (c) a disconnect from viewing technology as medium as well as product to uphold the networks, and (d) a disconnect of design principles for designing for successful facilitation after initiation. This last disconnect is the main rationale for our research question.

We attempt to reconnect these disconnects by taking a design science approach and create a high-level artifact of a system design that acknowledges the viewpoint that: *"To build sustainable communities, managers need to view technology as an enabler and focus the effort on taking a participatory and iterative approach to build a system that reflects the needs and values of stakeholders at all levels in the organization."* ([32], p. 20). The high-level IS artifact is supposed to be utilized by the network orchestrating organization to work as both product and medium in the network.

3 Methodology

As stated above we are taking a contextualized, interpretive case study approach [33–35] as the authors were not part of the case context but were outside observers and designers solving a problem for the case organization. Interpretive research attempts to understand phenomena through the meanings that people assign to them [36], and access to reality is through social constructions such as language, consciousness and shared meanings [34, 37].

Methods for dealing with design problems are plenty. Walls et al. [21] provide a design method for a meta-design that frames the design parameters so the design outcome is predictable to the extent of the level of the design theory detail. Hevner [38] observes a three-cycle view of DSR that relates the design activities (including a build-and-evaluate design cycle), and Peffers [39] offer a process framework for conducting DSR. However, we used the Design Theory Nexus developed by Pries-Heje and Baskerville [40] due to its unique ability in dealing with wicked design problems. They note five steps for nexus artifact design:

1. Survey existing literature and findings for different approaches available in the given area of innovation.
2. Analyze alternative approaches discovered in the first step. Identify conditions under which each approach works best.
3. Construct an artifact that can be used to indicate whether the conditions identified are to be found in the actual problem setting.
4. Design and develop a decision-making process for evaluation of which and whether conditions found above are present.
5. Integrate approaches, conditions, and the decision-making process into a tool (an artifact) to support the evaluation of how to deal with a wicked problem.

One can distinguish between a formative and a summative evaluation [41]. In the construction of the nexus artifact step 5, we performed a summative evaluation through qualitative interviews with active network group members and facilitators of networks. 2 focus group interviews were held with 5 and 4 participants respectively, each focus group lasting around 2 h. The purpose of the focus groups was for the members to discuss openly the characteristics of their own network groups and how this affected their participation and value.

Six semi-structured interviews were held with 5 facilitators (2 females, 3 males, one male facilitator was interviewed twice) lasting approximately 60 min per interview. We made sure that the facilitators were currently facilitating at least two network groups. The purpose was for the facilitators to evaluate the GENIE nexus for how the tool could add value to their own facilitation practices. We later discuss the challenges of evaluating artifacts that support open innovation value.

Data analysis followed the interpretive tradition [34]. Interviews were transcribed and notes were taken from the observed meetings. These data and documents were then coded and analyzed in accordance with Miles and Huberman [42]. The coding tactics focused on the conditions of the nexus identified in the literature, and by finding contradictions and variables related to each other. The design principles were derived from the analysis of the focus groups and then re-evaluated after the facilitator interviews. Identified codes were used to evaluate the type and amount of value as well as the usefulness of network groups and the structure and process of these.

3.1 Necessity of a GENIE Nexus

The Company Forum in Thy (CF Thy) is a network organization that creates, supports, coordinates and orchestrates more than 11 innovation networks consisting of various types and genres of companies, primarily small to medium enterprises. CF Thy's focus is primarily on expanding innovation locally to regionally to nationally on areas such as agriculture, settlements and construction, infrastructure and services, climate and energy. At the time of writing, CF Thy currently involve 285 small to medium businesses (SMEs) as members that are all engaged in one type of innovation network or another. These networks range from maritime business networks for the fishing industry to production networks learning how to use automation and robots. CF Thy hosts around 5–6 member conferences a year focusing on increasing funding, growth, exports for firms with social and professional activities for members with speakers, specialist themes regarding education, industry subjects.

In the first half of 2016 alone, 17 activities were hosted by CF Thy consisting of open, professional counselling, cafes for entrepreneurs, courses for entrepreneurs regarding starting up, customer relationship management, using big data, expanding via marketing, search engine optimization as well as online profiling.

As a part of project 'Network North-West', set out to map existing innovation network groups, a report was published in February 2015 focusing on the untapped potential of the existing networks and interests in networks that specifically noted that most firms in the local area participated in some kind of network and often feel that they benefited from participating in innovation network groups, though very few had an explicit networking strategy and very little knowledge was gained of how to facilitate the process of those innovation network groups. As such, CF Thy decided that they needed a tool to increase transparency how the existing innovation network groups in CF Thy were doing so that proper actions could be taken.

They lacked a formalized tool to indicate 'health' of the networks and assist their network facilitators in learning how to increase member satisfaction and report these findings back to the management of CF Thy. In short, the structure of the networks was in place, while the coordination mechanisms for knowledge creation and sharing were not formalized in a way that could support continuous improvement.

4 The GENIE Nexus and a GENIE IS Design Theory

In this section, we present the GENIE nexus artifact briefly and describe the design principles that prompted to build the nexus in the first place.

4.1 The GENIE Nexus Background

The GENIE nexus consisted of three main artifacts: (a) an innovation network state cycle model, (b) an innovation network charter and (c) an assessment nexus meant to evaluate the innovation network continuously. All artifacts were generic document prototypes that served as information containers that all main actors involved in the innovation network group had access to. The GENIE nexus as such was the first prototype design in formalizing an information system as technology medium and product. We denote it as an information system for the following reason: the nexus is a tool for organizational members to produce, consume and manipulate information to further the innovation work process across organizational boundaries. As such, the owner of the nexus is the orchestrating organization that facilitates the inter-organizational activities (in the case study; CF Thy) while members of the innovation group networks can be considered its users. A pictorial representation of the three artifacts and how they are connected can be seen in Fig. 1.

In Fig. 1 we first have the Innovation network State Cycle (ISC, following arrows from left to right): the purpose of the ISC was to contextualize the network group as an ongoing process by visualizing the current states of the network to the participants. The ISC was designed as an instantiation of the design principle of "design for a lifecycle" [30] and inspired by online communities' life cycles [43]. States were chosen as this has been shown to most properly depict networks [15]. The state cycle consisted of 4 main states of which the network could freely change between: initiation (of the idea), definition (of the group and purpose), action taking (planning, hosting activities and evaluating), and termination (assessing and finishing).

Second, in Fig. 1, we have the Innovation network charter (INC): the INC artifact was an editable and generic document meant to contain the formal information of the purpose of the innovation network group. The INC was a formal document to be filled out by the network group creators (either participants or facilitators) and describes the network group, the scope and deliveries of potential products, the expected outcome, critical success factors, presumptions and conditions for the group to exist, budget, risk assessment and the roles and responsibilities of the different participants.

Third, we have the Innovation assessment nexus (IAN): the IAN was an interactive artifact meant for the participants to capture their perceptual assessment of their designated innovation network group. The IAN was meant as an instantiation of the design principle of "design for proactive management" [30]. The artifact was survey-based

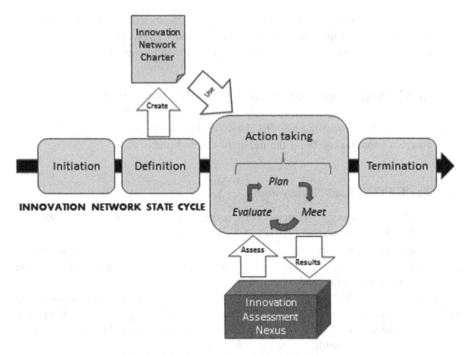

Fig. 1. The three artifacts in the GENIE nexus

with statements that correlated to a range of attributes of the innovation network group (size, purpose and success criteria, member composition, knowledge level and type, knowledge sharing and interaction, facilitation and leadership, and activities) that then were compared to 6 different innovation network group archetypes in a diagram (project network, network sprout, skill-based network, referral network, exchange of experience network, product innovation network). For each attribute that differed from the designated archetype, a prioritized gross list of actions was presented to suggest how to change the network group in the desired direction.

In use, the ISC was meant to be used by the facilitator with the members to determine the current state of the network group. If needed, the INC was then meant to be filled out together to create mutual understanding and meaning of the purpose of the network group and also to define what archetype the members would most likely want to resemble. The IAN was then meant to to be used formatively to assess the network and direct changes towards the desired archetype.

4.2   Principle 1: Design for Continuous Process Improvement Through the Use of Change Agents

For innovation networks to be innovative, they must be placed in the mindset of continuous improvement of the network group. From the beginning of the nexus design, it became clear that innovation network groups needed some sort of stimulus for them to move forward. As the main driver of a process in network groups are people, we noted that change agents had to be formally nominated to perform actions of continuous change. We deliberately use the term "change agents" because it designates a role that anyone can take (but will often be the formal facilitator of the network group) and the role implies that the network group will have to change. Change agent actions here were to provide dialogue and structure to the innovation network meetings and ensure that the social relations between the network members would provide constructive value. As such, we used principle 1 to identify and nominate the role of facilitator of the network groups as the main change agents. While the facilitators were clearly meant to interact with the network, the actual roles and actions that they were supposed to take as facilitators were less clear. Thus, by taking the design principle in use for the IS tool, it would have to indicate the specific role of who was in charge of changing the network group and that this needed to be done formatively as the innovation network moved through its different states.

Example of the design principle in use:

> The artifacts supported by this design principle were both the ISC and the IAN. In the case of the ISC the nomination of the facilitator role explicitly describes what the facilitator as a change agent is expected to do. Empirically, this was based on the perceptions of the facilitators themselves: *"I see a facilitator to be someone who influences a process." – FAC1*
>
> The IAN supported this principle by being a decision support tool used in the "activities" state of the ISC as a means of continuous assessment, rather than having implicit roles where the facilitator is merely a coordinator with no real impact.
>
> One example of this occurred when FAC1 identified a discrepancy between the overall formal purpose and the informal success criteria in one of his groups. He realized that the network had gradually shut itself more and more in and only held an implicit and informally enacted purpose through social meetings. He explicitly believed that the ISC could be used to reinvigorate the innovation network group.

4.3   Principle 2. Design for a Participatory Process

Introduction of new technologies requires participation [32]. Even though professional facilitation of networks is paid work, it is also to a large degree originated in a motivation for social engagement with the members of network. As such, it can be considered a voluntary action where much of the detailed work activities being performed by the facilitator go beyond what they are formally obligated to do. For example, one of the facilitators spent a high amount of time ensuring that her participants would remember the coming innovation network group meeting. Another facilitator initiated informal evaluations with the participants of their group every 6 months to get constructive details on what she could do better. The principle of designing the IS tool for a participatory process thus covers not only how the GENIE nexus will be used by the facilitator, but also how the GENIE will be used with the members of the innovation network. The idea here is that through asking questions and rating the answers, the participants of the innovation network groups will involve themselves and use the answers as reflection on how to improve the network, thus creating ownership.

Example of the design principle in use:

> The design principle was incorporated into the ISC as an activity that both facilitator and participants had to perform and discuss in the initiation and definition phase of the innovation network lifecycle. The facilitators strongly welcomed using the artifact because they had all experienced issues with proper expectations management with members. One of the facilitators noted that the toughest job was to contact members who did not fit in with the rest of group and believed that a formal ISC could assist with the justification of asking the participant to step down.
>
> The design principle of participating was also incorporated into the use of the IAN between facilitators and participants, as the best results were found to combine both parties' assessments. This was based on one of the facilitators who noted that she was less interested in what and how to do, and much more interested in using the IAN together with the members to facilitate constructive evaluation as she was wont to do in informal settings twice a year anyway.
>
> During evaluation, we found that despite the facilitators performing informal evaluations with the network members, the facilitators were still very interested in using an evaluation tool with the members to create new, constructive dialogue of how to improve the network. Several facilitators also pointed out that they were interested in using the tool in a meta-network with other facilitators.

4.4 Principle 3: Design for Supporting a Prioritized List of Recommendations Through Visible Attributes

Information systems consist of both structural elements (e.g. the specific technologies) and procedural elements (e.g. the process, flows and actions taken by human actors) that are interdependent of each other [44–46]. Seen from structuration theory, a network group is also bound together by structures supported by interaction between the human actors over time. It is up to the participants to socially construct meaning, norms and values, which can be highly subjective and implicit. This makes it difficult to manage, but also difficult to objectively define a method or task that is considered the overall best one. As a result, we identified importance of the design principle of designing for supporting a prioritized list of recommendations based on visible attributes. Visible attributes in this sense refer to what is considered commonly agreed upon, explicit attributes that the participants can use to identify their own network group. The design principle is that of a pragmatic nature treating the innovation network group both as an object and as a structure that is 'acted on' through actions of its members. The structures are upheld through actions but the structures of the network also shape the types of actions that the members and facilitators can take.

The importance of visualizing attributes was for the facilitator to see how his/her current network would score these measurements as indications of areas of potential challenges. As an example, a low scoring of knowledge sharing could indicate a lack of trust which would point to certain actions that the facilitator could take to enhance this aspect over time. However, as an innovation network group is often highly hetero-geneous, the design principle also explicitly notes that the list of suggested actions should be prioritized and selected by the facilitator and members themselves.

Example of the design principle in use:

> We incorporated the design principle into the IAN as structural attributes in the shape of purpose, size, member composition, and knowledge type. These were combined with individualized procedural and perceptual aspects in the shape of knowledge type, knowledge sharing, performed activities, and facilitator role. These attributes were all deemed as possible aspects of an innovation network group and were derived from both group participant interviews and facilitator interviews.
>
> We also incorporated the design principle into the IAN artifact as a decision support functionality through using information about the innovation network group to assess and provide suggestions for future actions that the facilitators could take. Specifically, the facilitators that we interviewed had a diverse interest in different types of decision support. For example, while FAC1 and FAC4 were interested in receiving suggestions for actions, FAC2 and FAC5 were less interested in actions and more focused on using the IAN as a tool for dialogue between themselves and the participants. FAC2 mainly argued for the IAN being used as a tool for dialogue because she had a large amount of professional experience as a facilitator. FAC1 and FAC4 were on the contrary less experienced and thus more interested in learning through using the IAN artifact. The common theme here was the fact that the motivation to improve and learn as a facilitator was intrinsic, and as such could not be reduced to following a to-do list. Rather, the list had to be presented as completely optional and prioritized according to what seemed relevant from the assessment.

4.5   Principle 4: Design for the Inclusion of Diverse Perceptions Through Contextual Ideal Types

An important finding of our research was the identification of the design principle of diverse perceptions of the type of the innovation network. This design principle is based on the finding that there are no objectively good or bad structures, processes or actions to take. This may be possible within certain specific organizational settings (where conformity of network group structures might be stronger desired based on the organization's set of norms) but in inter-organizational settings the diversity of interests coupled with the strict voluntary choice of participation make this impossible.

Instead, the design principle supports the idea of identifying ideal types of net-works, which the assessment can then be compared to. Each ideal type should then be identified with a dimensional tolerance of its measured attributes, indicating an ideal area where no problems seem to be present with the network group.

Example of the design principle in use:

> We incorporated this design principle specifically with the presentation of archetypes in the IAN artifact, combined with the purpose and success criteria of the ISC. It is thus possible to qualitatively deduce what ideal archetype the current innovation network group is striving towards based on the input of the ISC.
>
> Prior to evaluating the IAN we believed that certain dimensions of attributes would always be desirable, e.g. a high score of knowledge sharing or having the same facilitator role, always containing a specific and measureable purpose, or as high a number of participants as possible. However, during the evaluation, several facilitators mentioned that it was not always desirable to e.g. have a high level and type of knowledge or a high number of participants. For example, one of the network groups in question was focused on learning how to incorporate three-dimensional printing into their production work. Here, it was not relevant for the participants to work with high levels of knowledge, as they were more focused on learning and applying new skills to their own companies. Another example was a strategic management network that over the years had grown from many members who wanted to learn and share information to now a select few and inclusive dedicated members with very complex managerial challenges that they wanted concrete peer-to-peer feedback on.
>
> These examples illustrate that the inter-organizational context requires supporting the design of structures and processes in a relativistic (as opposed to objectivistic) light where the context and attributes of the innovation networks determine areas that might be challenging for the network.

4.6   Principle 5: Design for Situated Knowledge Transfer Through Diversity of Participants

What we end up with is a vast and complex size of different innovation network types that (often) all contain very different participants' backgrounds and interests. Ultimately this makes it impossible to plan ahead and design something with a known end product in mind. When designing, this problem is known to require 'situated design' meaning a design solution broad enough to handle contingencies while still letting the users focus on solving the present task that the design is meant for [47]. The design principle of designing for situated knowledge is meant to acknowledge the contextual backgrounds of the participants that enact the network, the type of network group, as well as the importance and difficulty of facilitating mutual understanding in this group of individuals. The design principle implies that actions that attempt to change the visible attributes in one area (most likely) will have an impact on changing some of the other attributes of the network.

It is important to point out that performing the actions will not guarantee better knowledge transfer. Rather, they are supposed to shape the conditions of how knowledge transfer and innovation takes place.

Example of the design principle in use:

> We incorporated the design principle into the specific recommendations of the prioritized list. One such example was for how to take advantage of the background of the participants of the network group. If for example the size of the network increased with a very heterogeneous group, one recommendation here was to split the participants into minor groups based on their interests, background and profession during the group meetings and finally synthesize the different perspectives in the end. Rather than having a multitude of vastly different points of views, this action would thus combine sharing knowledge in minor groups that would make it easier to overview later. However, the specific action could also be reversed if so desired to increase the heterogeneity of the group, e.g. if certain members kept interacting with each other, they could be placed into new groups with fewer common interests.
>
> Another example of actions that were designed for situated knowledge transfer was for contextualizing knowledge because it might be difficult to understand: here the specific recommendations were based on inviting bigger, and more well-known firms in as guests at the network group meetings. By experiencing how other, more successful firms adapted and implemented the knowledge, this would bridge issues with how to apply the knowledge gained. This was an often used tactic by FAC2 and FAC4 with their two skill-based networks. The opposite could also be done: making the participants present issues and concerns themselves and let them problem solve among themselves. FAC1 would often do this with his experience exchange network in order to increase trust and group coherency.

5 Discussion and Contribution of This Theory

Innovation requires knowledge and creativity not only from inside but also from outside. To obtain that many companies engage in inter-organizational network groups. We set out to answer how such network groups could be improved. Our solution was the GENIE nexus artifact and five design principles that together contributes a design theory for designing inter-organizational innovation network groups. In short we have contributed to IS design in the following two ways:

1. An IS design theory on the setting of inter-organizational collaboration.
2. Design principles for an IS artifact that can support social innovation group network processes.

These design principles we project can be useful for inter-organizational network groups in any domain where innovation and creativity is seen as important. The advantage of presenting our findings as principles and thereby going beyond the specific instance is exactly that it can easily be de-abstracted for use in other domains, Furthermore, the design principles derived move beyond design theory and principles already reported in literature, such as Smart et al. [30] who merely focused on the initiation of the networks.

The GENIE nexus artifact presented has been thoroughly evaluated in a number of diverse network types in Thy, in the northern part of Denmark, and was in these instances seen as a very valuable improvement. In fact, so valuable that the authors were asked train their network facilitators in the use of the GENIE nexus at the same time as this paper was published.

Evaluation of success is of course always a tricky thing. What may be considered a success from one point of view is not a success from another point of view. In this paper we take the actual and continued use as well as satisfaction with use as indicators of success. These success measures are inspired from the DeLone and McLean [48] model where exactly these two things (use and user satisfaction) are what derive the benefits of success.

Furthermore, there is a need for de-abstracting the design theory and the five principles into other contexts and instances. It is entirely possible that new dimensions could be revealed based on evaluating in different countries, such as countries with a more hierarchically-oriented power-distance such as Germany or France. Whereas in Denmark we have a very low power-distance [49]. Hence, this is one of the reasons for bringing our work to an international conference such as DESRIST.

References

1. Rogers, E.M.: Diffusion of Innovations. The Free Press, New York (2003)
2. Van de Ven, A., Poole, M.: Explaining development and change in organizations. Acad. Manag. Rev. **20**(3), 510–540 (1995)
3. Chesbrough, H.: Open Innovation: The New Imperative for Creating and Profiting from Technology. Harvard Business Press, Boston (2006)
4. McCann, J.E.: Design principles for an innovating company. Executive **5**(2), 76–93 (1991)
5. Myers, P.S.: Knowledge management and organizational design: an introduction. In: Myers, P.S. (ed.) Knowledge Management and Organizational Design, pp. 1–6. Butterworth-Heinemann, Boston (1996)
6. Davenport, T.H., De Long, D.W., Beers, M.C.: Successful knowledge management projects. Sloan Manag. Rev. **39**(2), 43–57 (1998)
7. Hedlund, G.: A model of knowledge management and the N-form corporation. Strateg. Manag. J. **15**(S2), 73–90 (1994)
8. Nonaka, L., Takeuchi, H., Umemoto, K.: A theory of organizational knowledge creation. Int. J. Technol. Manag. **11**(7–8), 833–845 (1996)
9. Schacht, S., Mädche, A.: How to prevent reinventing the wheel? – design principles for project knowledge management systems. In: Brocke, J., Hekkala, R., Ram, S., Rossi, M. (eds.) DESRIST 2013. LNCS, vol. 7939, pp. 1–17. Springer, Heidelberg (2013)
10. Baskerville, R., Dulipovici, A.: The theoretical foundations of knowledge management. Knowl. Manag. Res. Pract. **4**, 83–105 (2006)
11. Kautz, K., Thaysen, K.: Knowledge, learning and IT support in a small software company. J Knowl. Manag. **5**(4), 349–357 (2001)
12. Dekkers, R., Kühnle, H., Cheikhrouhou, N., Pouly, M., Huber, C., Beeler, J.: Lessons learned from the lifecycle management of collaborative enterprises networks: the case of swiss microtech. J. Manuf. Technol. Manag. **23**(8), 1129–1150 (2012)
13. Cantù, C., Ylimäki, J., Sirén, C.A., Nickell, D.: The role of knowledge intermediaries in co-managed innovations. J. Bus. Ind. Mark. **30**(8), 951–961 (2015)
14. McNaughton, R.B.M., Bell, J.: Competing from the periphery: export development through hard business network programmes. Ir. Mark. Rev. **14**(1), 43 (2001)

15. Batonda, G., Perry, C.: Approaches to relationship development processes in inter-firm networks. Eur. J. Mark. **37**(10), 1457–1484 (2003)
16. Dolińska, M.: Knowledge based development of innovative companies within the framework of innovation networks. Innovation **17**(3), 323–340 (2015)
17. Ritala, P., Hurmelinna-Laukkanen, P., Nätti, S.: Coordination in innovation-generating business networks-the case of finnish mobile TV development. J. Bus. Ind. Mark. **27**(4), 324–334 (2012)
18. Busquets, J.: Orchestrating smart business network dynamics for innovation. Eur. J. Inf. Syst. **19**(4), 481–493 (2010)
19. Lea, B.R., Yu, W.B., Maguluru, N., Nichols, M.: Enhancing business networks using social network based virtual communities. Ind. Manag. Data Syst. **106**(1), 121–138 (2006)
20. Gregor, S., Jones, D.: The anatomy of a design theory. J. Assoc. Inf. Syst. **8**(5), 312–335 (2007)
21. Walls, J.G., Widmeyer, G.R., El Sawy, O.A.: Building an information system design theory for vigilant EIS. Inf. Syst. Res. **3**(1), 36–59 (1992)
22. Baskerville, R., Pries-Heje, J.: Explanatory design theory. Bus. Inf. Syst. Eng. **2**(5), 271–282 (2010)
23. Goldkuhl, G.: Design theories in information systems-a need for multi-grounding. JITTA: J. Inf. Technol. Theor. Appl. **6**(2), 59 (2004)
24. Markus, M.L., Majchrzak, A., Gasser, L.: A design theory for systems that support emergent knowledge processes. MIS Q. **26**(3), 179–212 (2002)
25. Gregor, S., Hevner, A.R.: Positioning and presenting design science research for maximum impact. MIS Q. **37**(2), 337–355 (2013)
26. Baskerville, R., Pries-Heje, J.: Design theory projectability. In: Doolin, B., Lamprou, E., Mitev, N., McLeod, L. (eds.) Information Systems and Global Assemblages. (Re) Configuring Actors, Artefacts, Organizations. IFIP Advances in Information and Communication Technology, pp. 219–232. Springer, Berlin (2014)
27. Lempinen, H., Rossi, M., Tuunainen, V.K.: Design principles for inter-organizational systems development – case Hansel. In: Peffers, K., Rothenberger, M., Kuechler, B. (eds.) DESRIST 2012. LNCS, vol. 7286, pp. 52–65. Springer, Heidelberg (2012)
28. Alt, R., Klein, S.: Twenty years of electronic markets research - looking backwards towards the future. Electron. Markets **21**(1), 41–51 (2011)
29. Bragge, J., Tuunanen, T., Virtanen, V., Svahn, S.: Designing a repeatable collaboration method for setting up emerging value systems for new technology fields. JITTA: J. Inf. Technol. Theor. Appl. **12**(3), 27 (2011)
30. Smart, P., Bessant, J., Gupta, A.: Towards technological rules for designing innovation networks: a dynamic capabilities view. Int. J. Oper. Prod. Manag. **27**(10), 1069–1092 (2007)
31. Niehaves, B., Ortbach, K., Tavakoli, A.: On the Relationship between the IT artifact and design theory: the case of virtual social facilitation. In: Peffers, K., Rothenberger, M., Kuechler, B. (eds.) DESRIST 2012. LNCS, vol. 7286, pp. 354–370. Springer, Heidelberg (2012)
32. Dahl, A., Lawrence, J., Pierce, J.: Building an innovation community. Res. Technol. Manag. **54**(5), 19–27 (2011)
33. Pettigrew, A.M.: Longitudinal field research on change: theory and practice. Organ. Sci. 1 (3), 267–292 (1990)
34. Walsham, G.: Doing interpretive research. Eur. J. Inf. Syst. **15**(3), 320–330 (2006)
35. Yin, R.K.: Case study Research: Design and Methods, vol. 5. Sage publications, Beverley Hills (2009)
36. Myers, M.D., Avison, D.: An introduction to qualitative research in information systems. Qual. Res. Inf. Syst. **4**, 3–12 (2002)

37. Berger, P., Luckmann, T.: The social construction of knowledge: a treatise in the sociology of knowledge. Doubleday, New York (1966)
38. Hevner, A.R.: A three cycle view of design science research. Scandinavian J. Inf. Syst. **19** (2), 4 (2007)
39. Peffers, K.: Editorial: IS research using theory from elsewhere. J. Inf. Technol. Theor. Appl. (JITTA) **9**(2), 2 (2008)
40. Pries-Heje, J., Baskerville, R.: The design theory nexus. Mis Q. **32**(4), 731–755 (2008)
41. Venable, J., Pries-Heje, J., Baskerville, R.: FEDS: a framework for evaluation in design science research. Eur. J. Inf. Syst. (2014)
42. Miles, M.B., Huberman, A.M.: Qualitative data analysis: an expanded sourcebook. Sage Publications, Beverly Hills (1994)
43. Kraut, R.E., Resnick, P., Kiesler, S.: Evidence-Based Social Design: Mining the Social Sciences to Build Online Communities. MIT Press, Cambridge (2012)
44. Orlikowski, W.J.: Using technology and constituting structures: a practice lens for studying technology in organizations. Organ. Sci. **11**(4), 404–428 (2000)
45. DeSanctis, G., Poole, S.P.: Capturing the complexity in advanced technology use: adaptive structuration theory. Organ. Sci. **5**(2), 121–147 (1994)
46. Reimers, K., Johnston, R. B., Klein, S.: Theorizing evolution of inter-organizational information systems on long timescales. In: Proceedings of JAIS Theory Development Workshop (2008)
47. Simonsen, J., Svabo, C., Strandvad, S.M., Hansen, O.E., Samson, K., Hertzum, M.: Situated Design Methods. MIT Press, Cambridge (2014)
48. Delone, W.H., McLean, E.R.: The DeLone and McLean model of information systems success: a ten-year update. J. Manag. Inf. Syst. **19**(4), 9–30 (2003)
49. Franke, R.H., Hofstede, G., Bond, M.H.: Cultural roots of economic performance: a research notea. Strateg. Manag. J. **12**(S1), 165–173 (1991)

Conclusion to an Intelligent Agent as an Economic Insider Threat Solution: AIMIE

Betina Tagle[1]([✉]) and Henry Felch[2]

[1] Colorado Technical University, Colorado Springs, CO, USA
tinatagle2000@gmail.com
[2] University of Maine at Augusta, Augusta, ME, USA
henry.felch@maine.edu

Abstract. The design of solutions to problems in the information technology (IT) domain provides unique challenges. Many times the problem may not be solvable or presents phenomenological aspects. A well known IT problem is the insider threat. This unique threat is its position within the trusted boundary of an organization. They are behind the defenses put in place to keep the external attackers out. The insiders are those individuals that know the security processes and can easily circumvent these practices. Using Design Science research (DSR) allows for the exploration and iteration of possible solutions through design and scientific methods in parallel. This paper provides the findings of the intelligent agent research that was presented at the DESRIST 2015, where DSR created the Artificial Intelligent Memory Inference Engine (AIMIE). This research found that using already-in-place computing infrastructure for AIMIE's architecture and Emergent Intelligence creates an economic tool for insider threat detection.

Keywords: Insider threat · Linear genetic programming · Inference · Software agent · Learning

1 Introduction

The insider threat is a well-known security problem in the information technology (IT) domain. As was reported in Tagle and Felch (2015) employees commit more than 50 % of the security breaches, whether directly or indirectly, due to non-compliant behavior and the circumvention of security policies. The one activity that can possibly detect insiders is monitoring (Tagle and Felch 2015). This is because an insider must use a physical means to commit the breach as suggested by Blackwell (2009), but current tools and solutions are expensive and have been unsuccessful (Tagle and Felch 2015). The Artificial Intelligent Memory Inference Engine (AIMIE) is an intelligent agent, a tool, that can be used to monitor for possible insider activity in a Windows environment. AIMIE uses already in place computing infrastructure so she is inexpensive to operate. She was created as an IT artifact using DSR.

This paper presents the conclusion of AIMIE, the intelligent agent research that was previously expressed in the DESRIST 2015 conference paper, Exploring an agent as an economic insider threat, by Tagle and Felch in 2015. First the essence of AIMIE and

© Springer International Publishing Switzerland 2016
J. Parsons et al. (Eds.): DESRIST 2016, LNCS 9661, pp. 147–157, 2016.
DOI: 10.1007/978-3-319-39294-3_10

her goal is presented (Sect. 2). Next the creation of AIMIE using DSR is discussed (Sect. 3). Third the evaluation results of AIMIE is presented (Sect. 4). Lastly is the conclusion that includes future research intended (Sect. 5).

2   Essence of AIMIE

AIMIE is a software agent that uses the already in-place computing infrastructure of the .NET Framework of the Windows operating system (OS) environment, the Input/Output (I/O) that is inherent to the computing device, and LGP with C# programming to operate as an inexpensive tool for insider threat detection (Tagle and Felch 2015). The agent is context-driven and produces a Cognitive Unit of Programming Object Class (considered cognitive unit hereafter) as an instantiation of itself for processing audit log information. The cognitive units are the knowledge units AIMIE uses to process context through her three engines, the context, the inference, and the cognitive, as well as the objects with relational-type properties that can be manipulated by inferential mechanics. After the processing journey, AIMIE produces a response to her user interface (UI) with a simple alert message if insider activity is detected or not. To begin the cognitive units processing journey, AIMIE reads the audit logs of the computer she resides within and the protocol, or rule, that will tell her what she is to detect for that session.

2.1   Cognitive Unit

Once AIMIE reads the audit log, she translates each activity as a term that becomes an instance of context. This context is the virtual representation of the term and any associated properties of knowledge. The structure of this cognitive unit serves as both the container of knowledge, storable in memory, and an object of context and relational properties that can be manipulated by inferential mechanics in working memory (Tagle and Felch 2015). A cognitive unit acts as the container to the instance of context, and is processed through AIMIE's context, inference, and cognitive engine. This processing journey is to determine if the context represents, or is associated with, a possible activity by an insider (Tagle and Felch 2015). Figure 1, Cognitive Unit, is a picture of the cognitive unit, where object 1 is the asset, action is the activity, property is the policy, and object 2 is the user.

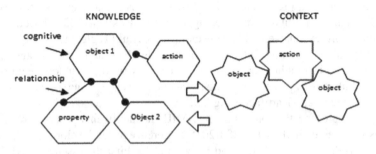

Fig. 1. Cognitive unit (Source: 5, p. 32).

2.2   Three Engines

AIMIE has three engines that the cognitive unit will travel through to process the context it contains, which are the context engine, inference engine, and cognitive engine. Figure 2, Context, inference, and cognitive engines of AIMIE, show the flow of the cognitive units.

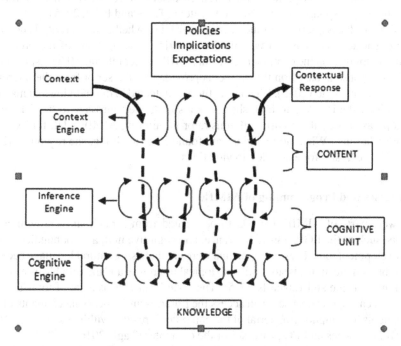

Fig. 2. Context, inference, and cognitive engines of AIMIE (Source: 5, p. 33).

The context engine assimilates the instance of context into a cognitive unit, which is arranged with the logical elements of inferential mechanics (Tagle and Felch 2015). The cognitive unit uses Extensible Markup Language (XML) as the storage for the hierarchical data and inferential mechanics within its structure, to access, search, sort, and process knowledge from the .NET Framework and XML formatted data in the cognitive engine (Tagle and Felch 2015).

The cognitive unit then travels to the inference engine where LGP and scripts, or protocols that are coded rules, are used to infer possible responses about the current context from AIMIE's experiences in processing prior context. At this point the cognitive unit is without the knowledge factors regarding the context, the information that can define the context in the cognitive unit it is processing (Tagle and Felch 2015).

The cognitive unit will then proceed to the cognitive engine to obtain the knowledge it needs to process the information further. In this engine the XML is used for context mapping, where the knowledge and context are mapped, as well as any context associations and properties (Tagle and Felch 2015). At this point knowledge is exchanged and stored between the cognitive unit and engine within its XML knowledge base for future use in associated experiences in context processing.

The cognitive unit will turn around and go back through the inference engine to process the new knowledge it obtained from the cognitive engine with inference. The last stop for the cognitive unit is the context engine that converts the inferred, processed, and assimilated knowledge into either new instances of cognitive units for further processing, or a response to the processed context (Tagle and Felch 2015).

AIMIE produces simple alert messages to her UI of whether the activity is possible insider threat activity or not (Tagle and Felch 2015). The outcome of the processed context is displayed on the computer screen in AIMIE's user interface (UI) display field. AIMIE's response is based on the protocols provided by the script from the inference engine (Tagle and Felch 2015). When an activity is detected in the audit log that matches the violations she is asked to find, she sends a simple alert message to her UI with a worded phrase set by the security administrator monitoring AIMIE's UI, for example 'known violations'. When no violations are found in an audit log, she responds with a worded phrase again, for example 'no violations'.

2.3   Classes and Programming of AIMIE

There were parts of AIMIE that had to be created from scratch since programming concepts, such as the LGP, logical inference, and cognitive unit, are not bundled with a code development tool. These components were created using natural language because it can be broken into units, is susceptible to logical inference, and measurable by a human programmer (Tagle and Edwards 2015). The code itself acts as a set of tools that the artifact can call upon because it can access the libraries and processing elements of the already in place computing material of the computer it resides within, such as the .NET Framework libraries and I/O processor of the computer (Tagle 2016).

AIMIE is an agent that processes knowledge so her very structure is knowledge-based, such as the cognitive units that carry the context for processing. AIMIE's components, such as her context, inference, and cognitive engines, do have a separate task to perform on the context. The cognitive unit creation of the context is in the context engine. The LGP processing on the context and the context's knowledge is in the inference engine. And, the knowledge gathering through XML by the context is in the cognitive engine. However, these tasks can depend on or feed another component in the steps of the processing journey. This means AIMIE can be programmed for ad hoc or recurring detection of threat activity. Figure 3, Class and programming structure of AIMIE, shows an overview of the classes within AIMIE's programming.

2.4   Goal

The goal is that AIMIE detects insider activities when they are performed and in undetectable areas of the computer, thereby decreasing the footprint available for the insider to hide. AIMIE uses concepts in artificial intelligence, machines cognition, and evolutionary computation in programming as a functional intelligent agent. It is not an agent that performs human functions, "but an entity with that amount of intelligence required

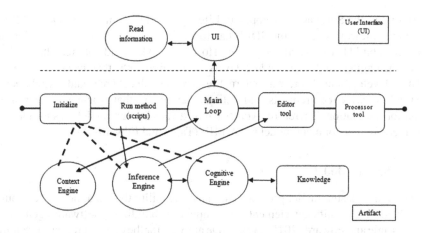

Fig. 3. Class and programming structure of AIMIE (Source: 5).

to perform its pre-described functions" (7, p. 6). The idea was to create an intelligent software agent that is inexpensive to use to monitor for possible insider threats, one that learns her environment for increased autonomous detection, and eventually programs her own knowledge base and environment.

3 Design Science Research (DSR) for AIMIE

The creation of AIMIE as an IT artifact using DSR was the research methodology's ability for iterations of solutions at each level of the agent. AIMIE as a whole agent, her components, or the concentration of the software functionality. It gives added knowledge of the whole research process not just applying the knowledge base to build AIMIE (Hevner and Chatterjee 2010). It is the platform to integrate external research and kernel knowledge, other scientific fields of Artificial Intelligence, Evolutionary Computation, Software Development, Cognition, and AI psychology for a science-driven design. Within DSR there are search patterns that guide what type of research iterations are conducted based on the need and outcome (Tichy 1998). For AIMIE's creation, the experiments and exploration pattern was chosen because it supports the need of creating a software agent from scratch (Vaishnavi and Kuechler 2015). This means that each component of AIMIE, down to the programmable object of coding would need to iterate through possible solutions for that one aspect. This is experimentation and exploration.

3.1 Software Development for AIMIE

AIMIE was a software artifact so an SDLC was used for its development. Here again, DSR gave the framework to generate experimentation and exploration of iterations and cycles of solutions that created and tested the software requirements and its alternates to create a suitable design (Simon 1996). The Rapid Application Development (RAD) with Iterative and Incremental development models (hereafter known as RAD-II) was chosen first as the Software Development Life Cycle (SDLC) model. Because AIMIE was being built from scratch, the SDLC had to use iterations at every aspect to find the right way to build her for each component. However, RAD-II did not meet the need for finding, managing, and tracking the layers of requirements that became a part of AIMIE's development. There was external research of subject areas and kernel knowledge used, software requirements, and testing requirements that produced further information for integration. Therefore, Arabesque Software Design model was established as an alternate development model for AIMIE (Tagle and Edwards 2015).

3.2   Arabesque Model

The Arabesque design model provided the same flexibility that an agile SDLC would, but included the significant elements that supported building a software agent from scratch (Tagle and Edwards 2015). Arabesque allowed for the external research, requirements, and testing to be managed and tracked by using its Three-Tree Hierarchy Requirements model (Tagle and Edwards 2015). It also meant that the software components could be developed separately during the same time period with the ability to associate the external research, requirements, and testing to any of the components (Tagle and Edwards 2015). Figure 4, Arabesque development of artifact, shows a visual of how development in Arabesque is flexible and research encompassing.

Using the Three-fold Tree Hierarchy Requirements model allows for the working use of DSR's Three-Cycle model of rigor, design, and relevance, that can establish validity and reliability of research through the development of the artifact (Hevner et al. 2004). Figure 5, Three-fold Tree Hierarchy Requirements, shows how the Arabesque manages and tracks the requirements gathering process during DSR.

The significance in using the Arabesque model is the ability for AIMIE to be evaluated based on the criteria and the requirements developed from scratch as she was created. The software requirements where needed to be a part of AIMIE from her inception to completion, meaning from the beginning of the research where the problem was defined. DSR supports not just building the software from scratch but the idea that started the research in the first place. Arabesque was an excellent design model while using DSR.

4   Evaluation of AIMIE

The Intelligent Agent, AIMIE, was evaluated in the DSR framework, where Venable (2006) suggested that to justify new knowledge the evaluation is key to DSR research. AIMIE had two objectives to meet. First, that she could detect possible insider activity threats (Tagle 2016). Second, that she does work with the inexpensive infrastructure she was built, for that was the basis of the research (Tagle 2016). Two test cases were used in the evaluation of AIMIE, USB use and use of a file in a restricted folder (Tagle 2016). The criteria for the software was that no error messages were seen during the evaluation of AIMIE (Tagle 2016). The components of AIMIE had to be developed and enhanced separately then integrated as a whole. To test inference and cognition for its

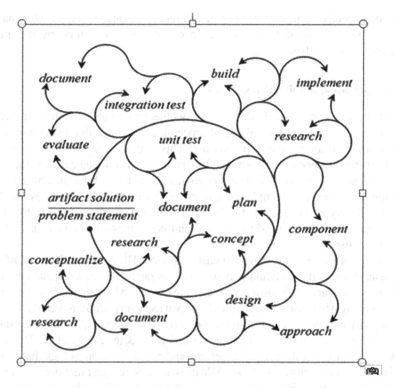

Fig. 4. Arabesque development of artifact (Source: 6, p. 2).

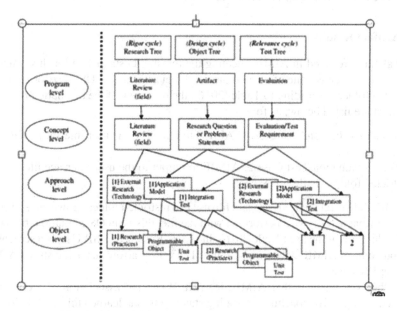

Fig. 5. Three-fold tree hierarchy requirements (Source: 5).

context the expected responses need to be returned, and this can occur when natural language is used as the testing medium since it can be understood by the human programmer (Tagle 2016).

4.1   Interpretation of Objectives

The inexpensive architecture of AIMIE is a key objective for this research. This architecture is meant as the programming and processing structures that are common to a computer, and that a software agent can use. This is the already in place computing material that can be a part of the agent's infrastructure, as mentioned earlier in the paper, the .NET Framework of the Windows OS environment, the I/O that is inherent to the computing device, and LGP with C# programming, as well as XML for processing .NET Framework library and inferential mechanic information (Tagle and Felch 2015). For insider tools to work, they need to be used, and being inexpensive provides a better availability of use.

The intent of the evaluation was to ensure that AIMIE could work as intended to detect an insider activity, particularly between the infrastructure of agent and computer. Therefore, two commonly known activities were chosen, where the USB test case was of the most interest because of its commonly known use with malicious activity. Because insider activity may be different from one organization to another, AIMIE is an intelligent agent that uses scripts, or programmed rules, as its detection baseline. The organizations would program the scripts to detect those activities in audit logs that it needs for its insider threat vector. Therefore, AIMIE is a software agent that does not require recurring updates found in many threat detection tools, such as the most commonly known one of signatures for anti-virus software.

4.2   Artifact Results

The evaluation resulted in AIMIE meeting the threshold established for this research, where she had to detect one of the two insider threat activities of USB use, or file use in a restricted folder. According to Tagle (2016), the overview of the evaluation results of the artifact are listed below, as follows:

- "Artifact Evaluation Test Case 1: AIMIE to output to the user interface USB use - pass;
- Artifact Evaluation Test Case 2: AIMIE to output to the user interface file use in a restricted folder - Fail with exceptions" (p. 81).

AIMIE did detect the USB use and file use in a restricted folder. However, she could not detect what activity was performed with the file, this is an OS limitation, but could read the duration of the use (Tagle 2016). In Fig. 6, Results of USB Use, is a screenshot of the outcome of AIMIE detecting USB use. The yellow arrow on the left shows AIMIE detecting USB use.

Another key result is that AIMIE learned. When the association of words were increased by repetitive coaching, repeating statements, she learned this association and used it the next time she processed context. In Fig. 6, above, the star shows the increase

Fig. 6. Results of USB use (Source: 5, p. 79).

in association being made, where the word known was replaced with identified to have her change her alert message. The lightning bolt shows AIMIE used the new word identified after she performed a processed. She learned through Emergent Intelligence, a theory where an agent's cognition grows as it performs its inferences (Wooldridge 2009).

4.3   Software Results

Observation of how the software performed during the evaluation of AIMIE was important to determine she worked as intended within the environment she was built. According to Tagle (2016), four major development milestones occurred during the design and creation of AIMIE, an intelligent software agent, as follows:

- the User Interface (UI) and architecture shell - the Windows Form application was chosen over the Windows Console to separate out the different functions into controls and because it is inherently active in the Windows OS;
- using static classes over static objects so each class has a scope that is global and this means only one static instance has to be made for a class;
- using a context-driven architecture over input-driven so a queue could hold context (cognitive units) until they were processed;
- the programmable unit of knowledge, the cognitive unit, is instantiated and not the whole artifact, which allows for efficiency.

The importance of these results is to see that a scientific-driven foundation during software development is needed when creating software from scratch. DSR allows for this, but more importantly is that the software development model use a design approach that accommodates experimentation.

5   Conclusion

The intelligent agent, AIMIE, successfully detected insider threats using already-in-place computing material as its infrastructure and Emergent Intelligence (Tagle 2016). The concluding implication is that it is an inexpensive tool that can monitor and identify possible insider threat activity. Again, the inexpensive architecture is the key to this research, where the idea was that the computer has infrastructure that is common and can be part of a software agent that provides a tool that anyone can use towards the detection of insider threats (Tagle 2016). AIMIE has an infrastructure that is a step to increasing the strategy to combat the problematic issue of the insider threat because she is inexpensive to use. AIMIE also is an agent that is already available for research into more deep monitoring of kernel-level system functions that occur during insider activity. Using an intelligent tool that can be programmed gives the ability to measure those areas of insider computing use that remain undetectable, difficult to each or associate activity to an occurrence of activity. Using DSR to create AIMIE allows for a design that increases her future capabilities, as well as gives quality knowledge for future research.

References

Blackwell, C.: Security architecture to protect against the insider threat from damage, fraud and theft. In: Proceedings of the 5th Annual Workshop on Cyber Security and Information Intelligence Research: Cyber Security and Information Intelligence Challenges and Strategies, p. 45. ACM, April 2009

Hevner, A., Chatterjee, S.: Design Research in Information Systems: Theory and Practice, vol. 22. Springer Science & Business Media, Heidelberg (2010)

Hevner, A.R., March, S.T., Park, J., Ram, S.: Design science in information systems research. MIS Q. **28**(1), 75–105 (2004)

Simon, H.A.: The Sciences of the Artificial, vol. 136. MIT Press, Cambridge (1996)

Tagle, B.J.: Exploring an intelligent agent with the cognitive units using interred-based rules and linear genetic programming as an economic insider threat monitoring solution using design science research. Unpublished doctoral dissertation, Colorado Technical University, Colorado (2016)

Tagle, B., Edwards, S.: Arabesque: software development process model for design science research (DRS Working Paper No. 513). Submitted to Conference the 50th Anniversary Design + Research + Society Conference, DRS 2016, Brighton, England, June 2016, pp. 27–30 (2015)

Tagle, B., Felch, H.: Exploring an agent as an economic insider threat solution. In: At the Vanguard of Design Science: First Impressions and Early Findings from Ongoing Research Research-in-Progress Papers and Poster Presentations from the 10th International Conference, DESRIST 2015, Dublin, Ireland, 20–22 May 2015

Tichy, W.F.: Should computer scientists experiment more? Computer **31**(5), 32–40 (1998)

Vaishnavi, V.K., Kuechler, W.: Design Science Research Methods and Patterns: Innovating Information and Communication Technology. CRC Press, Boca Raton (2015)

Venable, J.: The role of theory and theorising in design science research. In: Proceedings of the 1st International Conference on Design Science in Information Systems and Technology (DESRIST 2006), pp. 1–18, February 2006

Wooldridge, M.: An Introduction to Multi-agent Systems. Wiley, Hoboken (2009)

Prototype Design of a Healthcare-Analytics Pre-adoption Readiness Assessment (HAPRA) Instrument

Sathyanarayanan Venkatraman[✉], R.P. Sundarraj, and Anik Mukherjee

Department of Management Studies, IIT Madras, Sardar Patel Road,
Chennai 600036, Tamil Nadu, India
sathya.venkatraman68@gmail.com, rpsundarraj@iitm.ac.in,
anikit.jgec@gmail.com

Abstract. Healthcare organizations (HCO) adopt emerging technology solutions such as Healthcare Analytics (HA) to improve the quality and efficiency of their operations, patient care, and clinical decisions. While their intent is to adopt HA, many of them are unsure of their organizational readiness for that adoption. There is a paucity of research on HA pre-adoption readiness assessment techniques and tools, which can be leveraged by hospitals, to make well-informed decisions. In this paper, we fill this gap, by proposing a prototype design of an instrument based on the design science approach. We base the constructs used in our artifact on our findings from the multi-case study analysis of three hospitals, which we also discuss briefly. The key contribution of this research is the process that we followed in integrating the case study approach with DSRM in the area of HA adoption.

Keywords: Healthcare-analytics · Case study · DSRM · AHP · DEA · Assessment

1 Introduction

Across the world, hospitals are focused hard on improving their healthcare processes. In the US, between the year 2014–2024, the health expenses are projected to grow at the rate of 5.3 % CAGR [1]. HCOs increasingly consider the Healthcare information systems (HIS) and within that, specifically, healthcare analytics (HA) as a lever to curtail costs and improve service quality [2, 3]. HA applies descriptive, predictive and prescriptive models [4, 5], to enable fact-based decision-making for planning, management, measurement and learning [2]. Hospitals, today, are collecting vast amounts of data [6], and this offers organizations opportunities for HA-based innovations to their business processes and services.

Despite the well-recognized advantages of HA, currently, its adoption in hospitals worldwide is poor [7], owing to many challenges. First, hospital data has diverse characteristics [8] and is moreover, unstructured [6]. Second, despite regulatory and compliance requirements, the adoption rate of EMR (Electronic Medical Records) is still low across the world [9, 10], thereby restricting the scope for real-time analytics. Third, many executives are not sure about IT's potential to create value in the healthcare sector [11].

© Springer International Publishing Switzerland 2016
J. Parsons et al. (Eds.): DESRIST 2016, LNCS 9661, pp. 158–174, 2016.
DOI: 10.1007/978-3-319-39294-3_11

These challenges motivate the need for hospitals to understand their readiness levels for HA adoption. This paper presents a design of "Healthcare-Analytics Pre-Adoption Readiness Assessment (HAPRA) Instrument" aimed at supporting hospitals to make informed decisions on HA technology adoption. We follow the DSRM methodology in the process of developing the artifact. However, since the adoption of HA is at a nascent stage in the market, we start with a qualitative multi-case study, understanding and evaluating the real-life cases in the field and use the findings from our case studies in our design artifact. The core contribution of this research is the integration of case study approach with DSRM.

The paper is further organized as follows: Sect. 2 reviews the literature on the HA evaluation models; Sect. 3 provides the details on the DRSM approach that we followed in designing the instrument; Sect. 4 elaborates the design and development process of the artifact, including the details on multi-case study based qualitative study we undertook, which provided the basis for our design and the details the instrument that we developed; Sect. 5 highlights the implications of this research; and Sect. 6 summarizes and concludes.

2   Literature Survey

Past research on healthcare IT adoption primarily deals with (i) general study on adoption (ii) application of IS adoption models for HA, and (iii) development of new models.

- **General Study of Adoption:** Adler-Milstein and Jha [9] and Angst and Agarwal [12] study adoption of EMR for better decisions and outcomes. Bonney [13] explores the key benefits, challenges, and obstacles to incorporating the BI technology.
- **IS Models:** Some well known IS adoption models include TAM [14, 15], TOE [16] and D&M [17]. There are good examples of studies that use TAM model [18, 19], D&M Model [20, 21] and TOE Model [22, 23] to explain the antecedents of HA adoption. Unlike other studies on adoption of HA by hospitals, Lancry et al. [19] studies HA adoption by payers in the healthcare industry. Van Der Meijden et al. [20] use the D&M Model as a base to identify the determinants of the success factor.
- **Development of New Models:** Brooks et al. [24] develop a model to assess the maturity of the BI implementation in hospitals, which covers the aspects of the organization, people, and technology processes. Yusof et al. [25, 26] integrate D&M and IT organization fit models to create an HOT-Fit model that explains the antecedents of HA. Yu [21] proposes a multi-method (qualitative & quantitative) approach to evaluate healthcare IT.

Interestingly, based on years of practice, there have been two models developed and widely used by the industry namely "HIMSS Analytics EMR Adoption Model" (http://www.himssanalytics.org/provider-solutions) and "Healthcare Analytics Adoption Model (HAAM) [27]. Both the models are almost similar to each other and define the post-adoption maturity stages of HA in hospitals.

Ghosh and Scott [28], in their study, based on an in-depth study of cardiac surgery programs in a large hospital, find out many important antecedents of HA adoption such as (a) ensuring the quality of the input data collection; (b) building trust in the reliability of system outputs; (c) ensuring semantic interoperability through data standardization for aggregation and comparison across the distributed organization; (d) supporting effective decision-making and processes by providing integration of BI outputs into decision-making scenarios and processes; and (e) ensuring the metrics and measurements are put in place for hospital improvement.

The studies that use the (i) existing models, (ii) develop new ones, and (iii) explore the antecedents are useful to study the factors involved in HA adoption and build a theory. However, they cannot be used as a tool or an instrument readily by the hospitals to evaluate themselves on their level of readiness on those factors. Such instrument development needs a design science approach because there are activities of designing and building of an artifact involved in it and from our review no such research attempt has been carried out in the past to create such an instrument.

Secondly, the industry developed models referred earlier such as HAAM [27] is focused on "post adoption maturity review", whereas the instrument we are trying to develop in this research is focused on "pre-adoption HA readiness assessment".

Thirdly, Broad and general-purpose frameworks available for adoption-related issues are useful for evaluation, but due to the unique nature of healthcare IT, there is a need to narrow down to the context of HA. Also, while standard IS adoption or technology adoption models can be used to explore the antecedents of adoption, they can only serve as an input to an evaluation instrument. The design science can contribute here in advancing those inputs and the knowledge gained from past research through application of models into a valuable artifact. Our research precisely aims to achieve the said objective.

In the following section, we will on elaborate how we applied the design science methodology in developing the Healthcare-Analytics Pre-Adoption Readiness Assessment (HAPRA) Instrument.

3   DSRM Based Instrument Design

Our research (see Fig. 1) follows the classical six-step design science research methodology (DSRM) suggested by Peffers et al. [29] comprising, (i) problem identification and motivation, (ii) objectives setting, (iii) design and development, (iv) demonstration, (v) evaluation and, (vi) communication. The focus and scope of this paper are first three stages. We will detail these stages below:

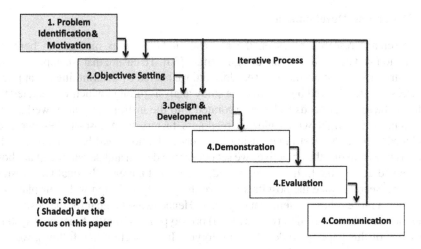

Fig. 1. DSRM framework used in our research (Source: Ken Peffers (2004)).

3.1 Problem Identification

According to Hevner et al. [30] one of the guiding principles of design science research is the "problem relevance", which means that the design science must work on developing technology-based solutions to the important and relevant business problems. The problem that we are trying to solve here is to provide clarity to the hospitals about their organizational readiness to adopt HA technology. This clarity is required because, hospitals before investing money, need to be confident that, the HA adoption would be successful and be able to create value for their business. Adopting a technology when the organization is not ready or unprepared will result in a failure of the initiative. Markus et al. [31] articulates a need for the IS to be "linked" to the real world of practical significance. Also, working on the said problem is of practical importance now especially, when the HA technologies will get diffused mainstream in health information systems in next few years, and many organizations are already on the cusp of HA adoption.

3.2 Objectives Setting

Our core objective was to develop an artifact (an instrument) to support an assessment of the readiness of hospitals to adopt HA. The major requirement was to integrate both the qualitative and quantitative parameters into our methodology and at the same time provide an easy to use interface hiding the technical complexity behind it. The second requirement was to ensure that, the post-assessment results are available in an easily understandable format, and it provides the information to the executives who make the decisions for the adoption of technology.

3.3   Design and Development

Design science research relies on the application of rigorous methods in both the construction and evaluation of the design artifact [30]. To ensure that we apply rigor in the construction of our artifact on HA adoption, we started by determining the application areas of HA followed by a multi-case study analysis through which we selected the readiness factors that needs to be incorporated into the instrument. Once, we had the basic foundations right with validated readiness factors from case-studies, we then developed a prototype instrument using low-cost technology and basic features. The idea was to ensure that the objectives we set out for the design and development are both feasible and achievable [29] and also to reduce risk and increase the quality of results from our research. Once the hospitals receive the prototype design well, our plan was to develop a more robust system that can scale. Hence, we set a goal for the design and development to be achieved in two stages: (i) prototype and (ii) fully functional system. The scope of this paper is to detail the prototype. In the section that follows, we will elaborate on the design and development stage of the process we adopted.

4   Design and Development of HAPRA Prototype

The design and development process (see Fig. 2) for HAPRA prototype involved the following four steps:

1. **Determination of HA Adoption Application Areas:** This lays the foundation for the HA application areas in hospitals and its adoption factors. The output from this step is used to design a case study research.
2. **Multi-case Study Analysis:** This empirically validates the factors impacting the readiness of hospitals to adopt HA using qualitative case study approach.
3. **Prototype Artifact Development Based on Case Study Analysis:** This helps determine the constructs/parameters to be used in the instrument based on in-depth case study analysis.
4. **Prototype Development of Instrument:** This helps in realization of the artifact incorporating the solution to the problem that we intend to address. The artifact takes the constructs that we developed in previous steps as inputs.

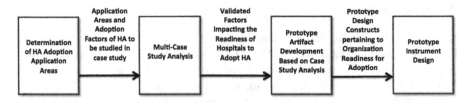

Fig. 2. The design and development process for HAPRA

We will look into each one of the above in detail.

4.1 Determination of HA Adoption Application Areas

HA technology works on data generated by systems in the hospitals such as EMRs, laboratory systems, diagnostic or monitoring instruments, insurance claims billing, pharmacy, human resources, supply-chain and real-time locating systems [7, 32]. The implementation of HA requires a good understanding of the various structured and unstructured data produced in the hospital, their organization and key business processes that they support. Since the topic of types of data in hospitals by itself is vast, we needed to have some reference point to start our design. Past research has developed a detailed HA adoption typology of applications (clinical, operational, administrative, strategic and financial) that generate the data for analysis and also identified the antecedents that impact the adoption of HA in a typical hospital [23]. We used the above as a foundation to design our semi-structured interviews for multi-case study, with an objective of validating the above-said application areas and organization specific adoption factors.

4.2 Multi-case Study Analysis

The past research suggests that currently HA adoption is at an early stage in the market [7]. This project is unique in investigating the HA adoption readiness factors, and hence we chose qualitative case study as a suitable approach [33]. We followed the following two key guidelines in our case study approach:

(i) Selection of case study samples based on their potential to illuminate the concept that we intend to study [34].
(ii) Ensuring that the data is collected from key informants and also triangulated with data from other credible resources to increase the validity of the same [35].

In keeping up with the guideline one and based on the past knowledge of the organizations, the location, accessibility, personal contacts and keenness of the respondents to support the research process, we selected the following three cases with different profiles to ensure diversity, coverage and holistic representation of the market:

A. A multi-specialty group hospital with six branches in India and uses predominantly external consultants as doctors (case 1),
B. An ophthalmology mission hospital with eighteen branches in India that has all its doctors/consultants as employees (case 2) and
C. One of the largest hospital chains in Asia-Pacific focused on corporate clients with sixty-four branches with a mix of employees and external consultants as doctors (case 3).

In keeping up with the guideline two, we collected the data primarily through semi-structured case study interviews of senior professionals (MD, CIO, Sr. Consultant levels) with many decades of experience in the industry. Our semi-structured interviews covered five broad themes *viz.* data types, data organization and access, applications that use the data, data analysis and antecedents of adoption of HA. To ensure the validity of data collected through interviews, we triangulated them with other sets of information like physical artifacts, presentations and also publically available data.

In two out three hospitals, we also viewed the demonstration of the hospital management software (HIS) by the IT team.

We carried out a multi-case analysis (using MAXQDA software), and coded the interview transcripts on the quotes given by case study participants. Based on the coding categorization, data triangulation, and multi-case analysis, we determined five organizational-readiness factors that impact the adoption of HA in hospitals. They are: Medical Technologies (Digital), IS & IT Infrastructure, User Adoption of IT Systems, Quality of Data Available for Analysis, and Management Alignment. Since these are the factors need to be evaluated to determine the organization's readiness to adopt HA, they formed the core construct of the artifact that we will discuss in next section.

4.3 Prototype Artifact Development Based on Case Study Analysis

The prototype artifact development involved the identification of the "best-known practices" followed in mature hospitals under the construct of HA readiness factors that we identified earlier, with appropriate literature support. The extent to which the organization follows these best practices was used as a basis to determine the readiness of the organization to adopt HA. We incorporated 50 such practices in the instrument (Note: due to space constraint we are not able to list all the 50 practices incorporated in the tool, but the information is available from authors on request). However, for an illustration, we show the portion of it in Fig. 3. We will now detail each of the constructs and the supporting case study analysis.

#	Best IT Practices Adopted in Mature Hospitals
	Medical Technologies (Digital)
1	The basic medical equipment (X Ray, ECG, Ultrasound etc.,) has capability to produce data in digital format [7].
3	The results of all the lab tests are captured and stored electronically [7], [36].
	IS & IT Infrastructure
6	The hospital has implemented ERP or Hospital Information System software [32]
7	The hospital has adopted EMR (Electronic Medical Record).[9]
	User Adoption of Technology
14	Hospital executives, administrative staff use systems for communication, data entry, retrieval, verification, reporting and analysis [14, 15], [17].
17	The visiting consultants also use the IT systems of the hospitals [14, 15], [17].
	Quality of Available Data
35	There are very minimum duplicate & invalid records in the systems.[41]
39	Systems are well integrated and it is easy to access the required data.[40]
	Management Alignment
42	Management views technology led transformation and IT-Business alignment as a critical part of their strategy [23].
43	Executives support the mandates for technology adoption in the hospital.[46]

Fig. 3. Partial list of best practices used in HAPRA.

Readiness Construct 1 - Medical Technology (Digital): The case study participants indicated that one of the basic requirements for HA is the availability of data in digital format. Past studies have described how hospitals use digital technologies and the extent of analytics possible on the data produced by the medical equipment [7, 36]. Our case study showed that mature hospitals implement real-time data acquisition technologies, digital monitors and medical equipment, instruments, sensors and image management systems. One of case hospital that was planning to adopt HA in all areas in the typology of applications had a good eco-system of digital clinical data availability, whereas, another case, which did not have the digital capability in their medical equipment, had adopted HA only in the operational processes.

We included five best practices in the instrument under this construct which covers the topics on the availability of medical equipment (such as XRAY, ECG, and Ultrasound) that produce data in digital format, the process of capturing data capture and storing and the integration of devices into the network.

Readiness Construct 2 - IS & IT Infrastructure: All the three cases that we analyzed had their HIS (Hospital Information Systems) in place to manage and operate the hospital. Every stage in their hospital's business process workflow from patient registration to discharge and all the hospital operational and administrative activities produce huge amounts of data that could be analyzed [7, 32]. However, only in two cases that we studied had EMR system in place. The case study participants also said that not many people in the industry have adopted EMR, although adoption of HIS is quite common, the primary reason being, HIS is needed to run the hospital as a business, but EMR adoption is driven more by the regulatory compliance. This observation also validates the fact as observed even in developed countries like the US where the EMR adoption rate is poor [9, 10]. Also, as per our findings across three cases, the implementation levels of EMR also varied in maturity. The case study participants indicated that, only when the hospital fully implements EMR, much of analysis on the clinical areas could be effectively carried out. The case study participants also expressed that, they need the basic IT systems with a robust connectivity across hospital branches for efficient the flow of information to the facilities.

We included eight best practices in the instrument that cover the topics on HIS and EMR, their integration, the basic IT infrastructure and the business processes (clinical, admin, operational) automated on HIS.

Readiness Factor 3 - User Adoption of IT Systems: All the case study participants viewed user adoption of existing underlying IT systems as a critical prerequisite for HA adoption. They believed that unless the users adopt basic HIS and EMR fully, and the managers effectively use the built-in analysis tools, implementing HA would not produce any business benefits. The user adoption of IT systems, a well-researched subject for long has established the same as critical to the success of any IT implementation, and there are many models such as TAM [14], D&M model [17] which researchers have developed to explain the user adoption of IT. Specifically, in the context of HA, the user adoption of systems has an impact on the achievement of organizational goals [37] and the behavior of users can have a bearing on the benefits derived from investments in analytics [38, 39]. The case study participants highlighted that this adoption behavior (or the lack of it) has many underlying reasons such as lack of time, lack of incentives, lack of accountability and demand-supply issues. Our case study analysis revealed that the hospital with doctors as their employees (case-2) has better adoption rate as compared to other ones (case-1 and case-3) where they employ many external consultants who do not have an incentive for using the system.

We included ten best practices in the instrument that cover the topics on the level adoption of IT by hospital executives, administrative staff, consultants, doctors, nurses, and paramedical staff for activities such as communication, data entry, retrieval, verification, and reporting.

Readiness Factor 4 - Quality of Available Data: The participants of the cases viewed the availability of quality data for analysis as a critical factor for HA success. Many dimensions of data quality management such as integration, accessibility, data transformation came up in the discussions. Researchers have highlighted data availability and data quality as the two biggest challenges faced by hospitals [40]. Poston et al. [41] in his research on EMR data-management details many issues related to data accuracies such as patient identity, erroneous medical records, medicine prescription errors, trend analysis problems and, reimbursement related issues, and also challenges related to data availability such as time lag and lack of readily available records. One of the case study participants highlighted the problem of multiple unmatched records for a single patient [42] causing confusion. McCoy et al. [43] highlight the implications of such duplicate records on patient safety. The participants said that availability of a well integrated HIS and EMR, and an automated real-time data acquisition were critical to ensuring data quality. Pipino et al. [44] lay down the guiding principles that can be used by organizations to develop data quality metrics. Taking it further Batini et al. [45] develop methodologies for data quality assessment and improvement. Case-1 participant said that fixing the data quality issue has been a daunting task by his hospital, and the most of the quality issues are also related to the skill level of the users, user adoption, the system related issues, and the extent of error-prone manual data entry practices.

We included seventeen best practices in the instrument that cover the topics on data validation, profiling, mapping, cleansing, transformation, conversion, purging, integration and change management.

Readiness Factor 5 - Management Alignment: All the participants that we interviewed echoed the importance of executive and management support [46] that helps to drive HA adoption. The management support is critical because the target users for HA technology are usually managers themselves. So, they need to believe in data-driven decisions, promote and encourage the user adoption, invest in hardware, software and services, drive & encourage analyst skills development [23]. One of the case study participants said that the management support for adoption of technology is critical when the complexity of hospital operations is high or when the size of the organization is significant. For the HA investment to create value to HCOs, a proper alignment of IT and Business is an essential prerequisite. Kearns and Lederar [47] develop a model focused on exploring the relationship between IT-business plan alignment and performance. The above is also echoed by SAM (Strategic Alignment Model) [48], which highlights the need for IT initiatives to be aligned with market demand. In the cases we studied, the participants reflected the similar view that management expects the IT investments and capabilities to be correctly aligned to market and patient (client) needs, and due process requirements be followed to ensure alignment [49].

We included ten best practices in the instrument that cover the topics on IT alignment to business strategies, management support, envisioning IS, setting expectations, and clarity on HA adoption goals.

4.4   Prototype Development of HAPRA Instrument

Based on the insight we gained through the study of typology and analysis of case studies, we finalized on the five key readiness constructs and their associated best practices (described in previous sections) to be assessed in an organization for HA adoption. We developed a pilot instrument (see Fig. 4) using Visual Basic (VBA) modules in MS Excel. The GUI Input and Output of the tool had four screens: The Home Screen, the interface for eliciting the response on maturity, the interface for eliciting the response on factor priority and screen for results of the evaluation. We further detail of each one of the above:

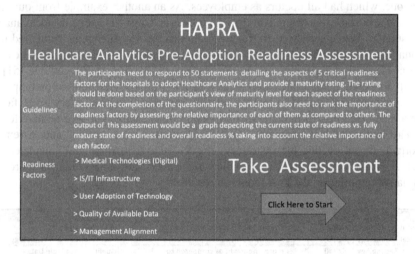

Fig. 4. HAPRA instrument: home screen.

(1) Home Screen: The home screen has the description of the tool with an arrow to click and start the assessment process. The click of the arrow takes the user to the next screen to enter responses for maturity.

(2) Interface for Eliciting Response for Maturity Level Scoring: On the instrument, the participants are prompted to the mark the level of maturity in their organization for the attribute described in each of the statements (see Fig. 5). The instrument uses a scale of 1 to 10 for a response, where 1 indicates the least ready state and 10 the highest. The approach is similar to the one carried out for CMM certification using "Software Process Maturity Questionnaire" [50] where the participants are asked to respond to a statement defining the process maturity. We take an average score of all the statements to describe the overall readiness level for a particular factor.

#	Best IT Practices Adopted in Mature Hospitals	Maturity Level (Select From Drop-Down)
	(Please Indicate the level of Maturity in your Hospital in the next Column (1 = Least Mature to 10 = Most Mature)	
	Medical Technolohgies (Digital)	
1	The basic medical equipment (X Ray, ECG, Ultrasound etc.,) has capability to produce data in digital format.	2
2	PACS system is in place.	4
3	The results of all the lab tests are captured and stored electronically.	5
4	The hospital has the capability to capture, store and access the data in real-time from medical equipment in digital format.	6
5	All the equipment are integrated on network and the data from these equipment are available on demand to consultants, doctors, nurses and others who need it.	3

Fig. 5. HAPRA instrument: eliciting response (maturity score).

(3) Interface for Eliciting Response on Relative Importance of Factors: Not all the readiness factors are equally important for a hospital, and this can also change between hospitals. As an example from our case study, in the hospital that had many visiting consultants on contract, the user adoption of EMR was a major challenge as compared to the one, which had all doctors as employees. As an another example from our case study, in the hospital that catered more to corporates and high-value clients, the management support for technology investment was not as big a challenge as compared to a hospital that was primarily a mission that runs on donations and hence tends to be a lot more conservative in investments. In our instrument, we use AHP technique [51] to quantify the relative importance of readiness factors from the viewpoint of participants. The participant is prompted to select a relative importance level of every given factor from a menu (see Fig. 6) in comparison to every other factor. The five relative levels are: least important, less important, equally important, more important, and extremely important. Based on this the instrument creates an AHP matrix and calculates the weightage of factors. Finally, based on the weighted average of the readiness score and the relative importance, the final report on readiness score is derived.

Readiness Factor Relative Importance		
Medical Technology (Digital)	is equally Important as compared to	IS/IT Infrastructure
Medical Technology (Digital)	is less important as compared to	User Adoption of Technology
Medical Technology (Digital)	is more Important as compared to	Quality of Available Data
Medical Technology (Digital)	is extremely important as compared to	Management Alignment
IS/IT Infrastructure	is more Important as compared to	User Adoption of Technology
IS/IT Infrastructure	is extremely important as compared to	Quality of Available Data
IS/IT Infrastructure	is more Important as compared to	Management Alignment
User Adoption of Technology	is equally Important as compared to	Quality of Available Data
User Adoption of Technology	is extremely important as compared to	Management Alignment
Quality of Available Data	is more Important as compared to	Management Alignment

Fig. 6. HAPRA instrument: eliciting response (factor relative importance).

(4) Reports Screen: We used the macros to automate the user interaction and also embedded the logic of the readiness level calculation and report generation. The Fig. 7 above shows the output report from the pilot study that we carried out in a hospital to test the instrument. The results are given both in numerical form and as well graphical from using radar graphs. The results have two parts: (i) the individual scores of each readiness factor i.e. "as-is state" and the gap between the "as-is state" and "to-be state" and (ii) the overall computed % of readiness. The radar graph gives a visually appealing picture of same, where the area of the smaller pentagon and its points represents the current readiness state as within the larger one, which represents the ideal state.

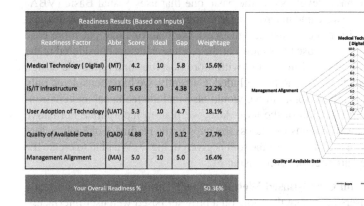

Readiness Results (Based on Inputs)					
Readiness Factor	Abbr	Score	Ideal	Gap	Weightage
Medical Technology (Digital)	(MT)	4.2	10	5.8	15.6%
IS/IT Infrastructure	(ISIT)	5.63	10	4.38	22.2%
User Adoption of Technology	(UAT)	5.3	10	4.7	18.1%
Quality of Available Data	(QAD)	4.88	10	5.12	27.7%
Management Alignment	(MA)	5.0	10	5.0	16.4%
Your Overall Readiness %					50.36%

Fig. 7. HAPRA screen showing results from a pilot assessment carried out.

4.5 Normative Guidance to Improve Readiness and Maturity

A hospital aspiring to increase their "HA adoption readiness" needs to focus on the improvement of the underlying processes related to the readiness factors. As a part of evaluation, the practitioner compares his current processes related to a given HA readiness factor with the known best practices followed in mature hospitals. Hence, the inclusion of "known best practices" in the instrument (based on literature support) by itself is guidance for the hospitals to understand their area of improvement. The executives should focus on the areas where the readiness score is low. However, the readiness improvement is more than an emphasis on isolated areas of improvement, as the factors are also inter-dependent. As an example, unless there is sufficient management alignment, the investment of IS/IT infrastructure and medical technologies to enhance the digital capability would not be possible. Secondly, since not hospitals are of same profile and as a result, the relative importance of the readiness factors could change between hospitals. So, the executives planning the improvement measures should assign appropriate weight and priority for various factors accordingly.

The prototype version of the instrument provides an indicative guidance to executives, but the design science lens could be used to inform practitioners, the HA capabilities or maturity beyond the readiness measurements that we covered in this research. Maturity assessment involves understanding the current state, envisaging the target state, and determining the gaps and appropriate initiatives to fill the gaps. Using the same technique and approach that we used in this research, we can measure a more exhaustive set of technical factors such as features, deployment models, the level of adoption (descriptive, prescriptive, predictive, cognitive); organizational factors such as culture, partnerships; and environmental aspects such as regulation and compliance.

4.6   Planned Enhancements to the Tool

The prototype that we have developed is the basic one that uses Visual Basic (VBA) modules in MS Excel software and macro programming. We plan to scale up as the next phase of our project with more robust design. Also, we plan to carry out more case studies (15 to 18 cases) to increase the validity of the readiness factors considered in the design and also evaluate the tool iteratively with more hospitals and refine the design with additional best practices and factors included. Currently, we have considered only the organizational readiness factors, but we would also include technical and environmental factors in the full version of the tool. Also, we plan to incorporate normative guidance with specific action items to address the gaps in the readiness of each factor.

The envisaged future architecture of the tool is given in Fig. 8. We plan to create the tool with a 3-tier based architecture comprising of:

1. **Presentation Tier on Cloud-Based Web Interface:** This would be a cloud-ready application with users accessing the same on a browser based web user interface.
2. **Logic Tier with AHP & DEA:** This would be an application that computes readiness score, compares with the industry average and best practices, and also includes AHP & DEA. In HAPRA, the readiness factors are qualitative. In reality, even if hospitals are qualitatively ready for adoption, they may not still adopt HA because of other quantitative factors like cost of technology, even if the technology can provide long-term benefits. Especially when the organization has short-term financial goals such as reduction of cash flow or capital expenses, the above behavior is expected. In short, readiness for HA may be a necessary condition, but not a sufficient one for adoption. On the contrary, even if the organization is not yet fully ready, if they get an attractive commercial value proposition, they may still invest. To accommodate this pattern, we plan to use DEA technique to measure the efficiency of the input (investment) vs. output (returns/benefits). There are many examples of AHP-DEA integration from the past, but we plan to the technique suggested by Ramanathan [52].
3. **Data Tier:** This would be a database (Knowledge base) containing the data of multiple hospitals and can be used for comparison the hospital participating in the assessment with statistical metrics of industry. It also gives hospitals a view on their maturity as compared to their peers in the industry.

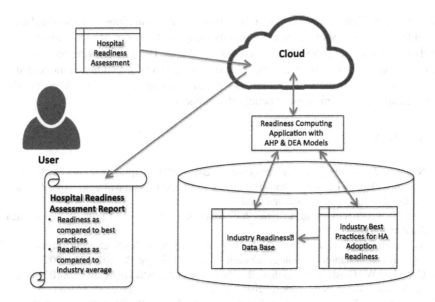

Fig. 8. The conceived architecture of the full version of HAPRA

5   Implications

Managerial Implications: Our research has important implications for hospitals. First, it provides useful information for the executives of the HCOs to assess the typical organizational conditions under which analytics is adopted in a hospital. Second, the exercise of understanding the current processes followed in the hospitals benchmarked against the best-practices can give valuable insights to the executives to drive business process improvements. Third, a well-informed decision to adopt HA timed well after fixing all readiness issues can significantly increase the probability of success of HA implementation. Fourth, our research also helps HCOs drive focus and prioritize on areas that need to be improved.

Research Implications: Our research also has many implications for the academics. Though our first part of our journey is to measure the readiness of HA adoption, we can extend the same concept into many other related areas such as (i) post HA implementation maturity analysis (iii) HA solution selection decision support or a combination of them. There is also an excellent scope for "Action-Design" research involving practitioners, and this has far-reaching implications for industry and academics collaboration.

6   Conclusions

We discussed our approach to integrating the case study based qualitative study with DSRM in our research, which is unique in many aspects. First, the problem is motivated based on real-life issues and hence has a greater significance. Second, we root our constructs considered in the design both on theoretical foundations and also the data are drawn from the viewpoint of industry and its analysis. Thus, our design is informed by the theory. Third, the proposed application of AHP & DEA integration techniques in the context of HA adoption is also novel and unique. HA adoption is in a nascent stage in the industry, and we believe that this research along with other related possible extended studies will immensely benefit the industry.

References

1. National Health Expenditure Projections 2014–2024. https://www.cms.gov/Research-Statistics-Data-and-Systems/Statistics-Trends-and-Reports/NationalHealthExpendData/NationalHealthAccountsProjected.html
2. Prewitt, E.: Effective data analytics for a data-rich industry. The Promise of Healthcare Analytics (2012)
3. Raghupathi, W., Tan, J.: Information systems and healthcare XXX: charting a strategic path for health information technology. Commun. Assoc. Inf. Syst. **23**, 501–522 (2008)
4. Cortada, J.W., Gordon, D., Lenihan, B.: The Value of Analytics in Healthcare. IBM Institute for Business Value, New York (2010)
5. Davenport, T.H., Harris, J.G.: Competing on Analytics: The New Science of Winning. Harvard Business School Press, Boston (2007)
6. Andreu-Perez, J., Poon, C.C.Y., Merrifield, R.D., Wong, S.T.C., Yang, G.Z.: Big data for health. IEEE J. Biomed. Heal. Inform. **19**, 1193–1208 (2015)
7. Ward, M.J., Marsolo, K.A., Froehle, C.M.: Applications of business analytics in healthcare. Bus. Horiz. **57**, 571–582 (2014)
8. Frost and Sullivan: Drowning in Big Data? Reducing Information Technology Complexities and Costs for Healthcare Organizations (2011)
9. Adler-Milstein, J., Jha, A.K.: Health information exchange among U.S. hospitals: who's in, who's out, and why? Healthcare **2**, 26–32 (2014)
10. Buntin, M.B., Jain, S.H., Blumenthal, D.: Health information technology: laying the infrastructure for national health reform (2010)
11. Sherer, S.A.: Advocating for action design research on IT value creation in healthcare. J. Assoc. Inf. Syst. **15**, 860–878 (2014)
12. Angst, C.M., Agarwal, R.: Adoption of electronic health records in the presence of privacy concerns: the elaboration likelihood model and individual persuasion. MIS Q. **33**, 339–370 (2009)
13. Bonney, W.: Applicability of business intelligence in electronic health record. Procedia - Soc. Behav. Sci. **73**, 257–262 (2013)
14. Venkatesh, V., Davis, F.D.: A theoretical extension of the technology acceptance model: four longitudinal field studies. Manag. Sci. **46**, 186–204 (2000)
15. Venkatesh, V., Morris, M.G., Davis, G.B., Davis, F.D.: User acceptance of information technology: toward a unified view. MIS Q. **27**, 425–478 (2003)
16. Tornatzky, L.G., Fleischer, M., Chakrabarti, A.K.: The Processes of Technological Innovation. Lexington Books, Lexington (1990)
17. DeLone, W.H., McLean, E.R.: The DeLone and McLean model of information systems success: a ten-year update. J. Manag. Inf. Syst. **19**, 9–30 (2003)
18. Bhattacherjee, A., Hikmet, N.: Reconceptualizing organizational support and its effect on information technology usage: evidence from the health care sector. J. Comput. Inf. Syst. **48**, 69–76 (2008)

19. Lancry, P.J., Oconnor, R., Stempel, D., Raz, M.: Using health outcomes data to inform decision-making: healthcare payer perspective. Pharmacoeconomics **19**(Suppl 2), 39–47 (2001)
20. Van Der Meijden, M.J., Tange, H.J., Troost, J., Hasman, A.: Determinants of success of inpatient clinical information systems: a literature review. J. Am. Med. Inform. Assoc. **10**, 235–243 (2003)
21. Yu, P.: A multi-method approach to evaluate health information systems. Stud. Health Technol. Inf. **160**, 1231–1235 (2010)
22. Malladi, S., Arbor, A.: Adoption of business intelligence and analytics in organizations – an empirical study of antecedents. pp. 1–11 (2013)
23. Venkatraman, S., Sundarraj, R.P., Seethamraju, R.: Healthcare analytics adoption-decision model: a case study. In: Proceedings of PACIS 2015 (2015)
24. Brooks, P., El-Gayar, O., Sarnikar, S.: A framework for developing a domain specific business intelligence maturity model: application to healthcare. Int. J. Inf. Manag. **35**, 337–345 (2015)
25. Yusof, M.M., Kuljis, J., Papazafeiropoulou, A., Stergioulas, L.K.: An evaluation framework for health information systems: human, organization and technology-fit factors (HOT-fit). Int. J. Med. Inform. **77**, 386–398 (2008)
26. Yusof, M.M., Papazafeiropoulou, A., Paul, R.J., Stergioulas, L.K.: Investigating evaluation frameworks for health information systems. Int. J. Med. Inform. **77**, 377–385 (2008)
27. Sanders, D., Burton, D., Protti, D.: The healthcare analytics adoption model: a framework and roadmap (2013). https://www.healthcatalyst.com/white-paper/healthcare-analytics-adoption-model
28. Ghosh, B., Scott, J.E.: Antecedents and catalysts for developing a healthcare analytic capability. Commun. Assoc. Inf. Syst. **29**, 1 (2011)
29. Peffers, K., Tuunanen, T., Rothenberger, M.A., Chatterjee, S.: A design science research methodology for information systems research. J. Manag. Inf. Syst. **24**, 45–77 (2008)
30. Hevner, A.R., March, S.T., Park, J., Ram, S.: Design science in information systems research. MIS Q. **28**, 75–105 (2004)
31. Markus, M.L., Majchrzak, A., Les, G.: A design theory for systems that support emergent knowledge processes. MIS Q. **26**, 179–212 (2002)
32. Zhang, N.J., Seblega, B., Wan, T., Unruh, L., Agiro, A., Miao, L.: Health information technology adoption in U.S. acute care hospitals. J. Med. Syst. **37**, 1–9 (2013)
33. Yin, R.K.: Case Study Research. 4th edn. (2009)
34. Eisenhardt, K.M., Graebner, M.E.: Theory building from cases: opportunities and challenges. Acad. Manag. J. **50**, 25–32 (2007)
35. Creswell, J.W.: Qualitative Inquiry and Research Design - Choosing Among Five Approaches (2007)
36. Shneiderman, B., Plaisant, C., Hesse, B.W.: Improving healthcare with interactive visualization. Comput. IEEE Comput. Soc. **46**, 58–66 (2013)
37. Jourdan, Z., Rainer, R.K., Marshall, T.E.: Business intelligence: an analysis of the literature. Inf. Syst. Manag. **25**, 121–131 (2008)
38. Chasalow, L.C.: A model of organizational competencies for business intelligence success. ProQuest dissertations and thesis, pp. 191–276 (2009)
39. Shanks, G., Sharma, R., Seddon, P., Reynolds, P.: The impact of strategy and maturity on business analytics and firm performance : a review and research agenda. In: Proceedings of ACIS 2010, p. 51 (2010)
40. Lau, F.: Toward a conceptual knowledge management framework in health. Perspect. Health Inf. Manag. **1**, 8 (2004)

41. Poston, R.S., Reynolds, R.B., Gillenson, M.L.: Technology solutions for improving accuracy and availability of healthcare records. Inf. Syst. Manag. **24**, 59–71 (2006)
42. Bell, G.B., Sethi, A.: Matching records in a national medical patient index. Commun. ACM **44**, 83–88 (2001)
43. McCoy, A.B., Wright, A., Kahn, M.G., Shapiro, J.S., Bernstam, E.V., Sittig, D.F.: Matching identifiers in electronic health records: implications for duplicate records and patient safety. BMJ Qual. Saf. **22**, 219–224 (2013)
44. Pipino, L.L., Lee, Y.W., Wang, R.Y.: Data quality assessment. Commun. ACM **45**, 211 (2002)
45. Batini, C., Cappiello, C., Francalanci, C., Maurino, A.: Methodologies for data quality assessment and improvement. ACM Comput. Surv. **41**, 1–52 (2009)
46. Jarvenpaa, S.L., Ives, B.: Executive involvement and participation in the management of information technology. MIS Q. **15**, 205–227 (1991)
47. Kearns, G.S., Lederer, A.L.: The effect of strategic alignment on the use of IS-based resources for competitive advantage. J. Strateg. Inf. Syst. **9**, 265–293 (2000)
48. Henderson, J.C., Venkatraman, H.: Strategic alignment: leveraging information systems and transforming organizations. IBM Syst. J. **32**, 472–484 (1999)
49. Bush, M., Lederer, A.L., Li, X., Palmisano, J., Rao, S.: The alignment of information systems with organizational objectives and strategies in health care. Int. J. Med. Inform. **78**, 446–456 (2009)
50. Zubrow, D., Hayes, W., Siegel, J., Goldesson, S.: Maturity Questionnaire - CMM - SEI (1994)
51. Saaty, T.L.: The Analytic Hierarchy Process. McGraw-Hill Inc., New York (1980)
52. Ramanathan, R.: Data envelopment analysis for weight derivation and aggregation in the analytic hierarchy process. Comput. Oper. Res. **33**, 1289–1307 (2006)

Short Papers

The Structure of DSR Knowledge as Reflected by DESRIST – A Citation Analysis (2009–2015)

Jacky Akoka[1,2], Isabelle Comyn-Wattiau[1,3], and Nicolas Prat[3(✉)]

[1] CEDRIC-CNAM, Paris, France
{akoka,wattiau}@cnam.fr
[2] TEM-Institut Mines Telecom, Evry, France
[3] ESSEC Business School, Cergy-Pontoise, France
prat@essec.edu

Abstract. The design science research (DSR) paradigm is now established and reco gnized within the information systems (IS) community. The members of the DSR community have a common language and shared perceptions. However, it remains to define what constitutes the fundamental issues, theories, applications, and the main findings in this area. In other words, how may the knowledge of the field be characterized? The aim of this paper is to determine and analyze the DSR body of knowledge, based on publications in the DESRIST conference. To this end, we perform a citation and co-citation analysis of the papers published in this conference between 2009 and 2015. The co-citation analysis leads to the identification of several clusters representing what we believe to be a good overview of the structure of the DSR body of knowledge. We contend that our findings will help researchers to identify DSR areas likely to lead to future research.

Keywords: Design science research · Citation analysis · Body of knowledge · DESRIST

1 Introduction

In a mature field, the sharing of language, concepts, and theories is well established. In the case of DESRIST, the field, i.e., DSR, is relatively recent and in development. However, DSR remains a relatively new field, which only gained wide recognition after Hevner et al's MISQ publication. In addition, there is a lack of a real agreement on its basic concepts. Finally, the rate at which thinking about the field has developed is relatively slow, given the fact that one of the first contributions related to the sciences of the artificial has been published in 1969 [1].

Our first aim is to mitigate apparent contradictions which seem to characterize the field, especially in differentiating between Design Science (DS), Design Research (DR), and Design Science Research (DSR). Following [2], DS is the knowledge form of constructs, techniques, and methods. It is a research paradigm allowing researchers to build artifacts, in our case IS/IT artifacts. On the other hand, *"DSR is the research that creates this type of knowledge using design abstraction"*. It is a research using design as a research method. Finally, DR can be defined as a research about design.

© Springer International Publishing Switzerland 2016
J. Parsons et al. (Eds.): DESRIST 2016, LNCS 9661, pp. 177–185, 2016.
DOI: 10.1007/978-3-319-39294-3_12

Other confusions may stem from the concept of artifact, the way design science relates to theory, and the existence of adequate evaluation [3]. Our second aim is to choose a framework which can be the basis for the interpretation of our co-citation analysis. Hevner et al. [4] propose a framework combining three design science research cycles. These three cycles will help us to interpret the clusters obtained using the co-citation analysis. Finally, our main aim is to identify the body of knowledge of DESRIST publications given the diversity of subjects covered.

This paper is organized as follows. Section 2 presents a brief state literature review and concludes with our research questions. Section 3 describes our research method. The citation analysis is outlined in Sect. 4. The co-citation analysis is performed in Sect. 5, with an interpretation of the clusters revealed by this analysis. Section 6 concludes the paper and points to future research.

2   Literature Review

An overview of the common body of knowledge of ISDSR can be found in [2, 5–7] or books [8, 9]. Indulska and Recker [10] analyzed papers published at IS conferences (ACIS, AMCIS, ECIS, ICIS, and PACIS) from 2005 to 2007. Offermann et al. [11] performed a systematic review on ISDSR literature. They identified ISDSR contributions in the DESRIST conference, but not in top IS journals. Vaishnavi and Kuechler [2] provide an ordered list of ISDSR literature. Fischer [12] identified 50 ISDSR articles published in the AIS basket of six journals from 2007 to 2010. He found that ISDSR was developing a common body of knowledge. The assertion related to the existence of a body of knowledge is based on a citation analysis of 221 sources that have been cited by at least two papers. Among them, 148 sources were cited by exactly two papers, while 48 sources were cited by three papers. These figures may be considered too small in order to establish a complete body of knowledge. Besides, the time range is relatively narrow, since the author considered publications between 2007 and 2010. In this work, we propose to focus on papers published in the DESRIST conference. Based on these papers, we aim to answer the following research questions: RQ1: What are the most cited DSR publications and authors? RQ2: What is the current structure of the DSR body of knowledge? To answer these questions, we perform a citation analysis (RQ1) and a co-citation analysis (RQ2). Before the analyses, we describe our research method.

3   Research Method

In this work, we chose to perform the citation and co-citation analysis on DESRIST papers: DESRIST was our source of citing papers. We initially considered starting from the first edition of DESRIST (2006). However, given some practical constraints we considered the 2009 to 2015 time period only. For each edition of DESRIST in this period, we selected all papers, except product and prototype papers. We obtained a total of 234 citing papers, distributed as follows: DESRIST 2009: 32, DESRIST 2010: 45, DESRIST 2011: 34, DESRIST 2012: 31, DESRIST 2013: 33, DESRIST 2014: 26,

DESRIST 2015: 33. After the selection of the 234 citing papers, we downloaded the bibliometric information of the papers from Scopus. For a practical reason, the sample was reduced to 233 papers. We had to perform deduplication on cited references using Citespace [13] to map bibliometric information from Scopus format into Web of Science (ISI) format and then MySQL. We then performed data cleaning and deduplication within MySQL, sorting references by author and year to identify duplicates. In the MySQL database, we had 6,573 valid cited references. The number of unique references was 5,460. After deduplication, this number was reduced to 4,615. After cleaning the MySQL database, we exported it back into Web of Science format. We did a preliminary citation analysis with Citespace, and decided to keep only the most cited references (at least four citations) and their citing papers. Finally, we came up with ninety-nine references including journal papers, conference papers, books, etc. In the co-citation analysis, we performed clustering with Gephi, based on the algorithm for community detection by Blondel et al. [14].

4 Citation Analysis

In this section, we analyze the citations according to different criteria.

Types of resources cited. The basket of 99 papers contains mainly journal and conference papers. Twenty-one papers were published in MIS Quarterly. Eleven papers belong to DESRIST proceedings. Seven are EJIS papers and five are ISR papers. The remaining papers are scattered among several journals or conferences.

Age of cited references. The basket of ninety-nine papers spans from 1969 to 2013 only, since the DESRIST 2014 and 2015 publications cannot already have been cited sufficiently to appear in the final basket. Fifty-eight papers were published between 2001 and 2010. Thus researchers tend to reference the same recent papers, increasing considerably the size of the DESRIST common body of knowledge.

Frequency of authors. Even if some authors appear several times as first authors of several papers, the set of ninety-nine papers contains sixty-five different first authors.

Most cited papers. The table below illustrates the ranking of the most cited papers (papers cited at least fifteen times) (see Table 1).

Comparison with other studies. In order to better characterize the basket that can be considered as DESRIST body of knowledge, we performed a comparison with two other baskets of papers. First we analyzed the basket of 113 papers selected in [15]. This basket results from the selection of all DSR papers published in the AIS basket of eight journals between April 2004 and March 2014. In this basket we also extracted the most cited papers. If we consider the ten most cited papers, nine out of ten are also in the basket of 99 most cited papers in DESRIST proceedings. Four common papers are in the top 6 of both baskets: [1, 4, 16, 17]. That means that DESRIST references mainly the same papers as DSR papers published in top IS journals. This analysis confirms that DESRIST focuses on DSR seminal papers. Second we compared the basket of 99 papers to the basket of 25 papers selected by Fisher [12]. Fischer had identified 50 DSR papers in top IS journals in the four-year period 2007-2010. Collecting all the papers cited in

Table 1. Most cited papers with numbers of citations

Hevner, 2004, Misq, V28, P75-105	151	Markus , 2002, Mis, V26, P179-212	24
March S, 1995, Dss, V15, P251-266	81	Vaishnavi V, 2008, Design Science Research Methods And Patterns	23
Peffers K, 2007, Jmis, V24, P45-77	66		
Walls J, 1992, Isr, V3, P36-59	64	Hevner A, 2010, Design Research in IS: Theory and Practice, V, P	22
Gregor S, 2007, Jais, V8, P312-335	61		
Simon H, 1969, V, P	59	Hevner, 2007, Scand. J. IS, V19, P87-92	21
Gregor, 2006, Misq, V30, P611-462	40		
Gregor, 2013, Misq, V37, P337-355	31	Goldkuhl G, 2004, Jitta, V6, P59-72	19
Sein M, 2011, Misq, V35, P37-56	27	Van Aken, 2004, J. Mgt Studies, V41, P219-246	18
Winter, 2008, Ejis, V17, P470-475	27		
Iivari 2007, Scand. J. IS, V19, P39-64	24	Venable, 2012, Desrist, V, P423-438	17
Kuechler 2008, Ejis V17, P489-504	24	Nunamaker, 1991, Jmis, V7, P89-106	17
		Walls J, 2004, Jitta, V6, P43-58	16

these 50 DSR papers, he came with a set of 25 papers cited by four or more papers among the 50. Five common papers are in the top 6 of both baskets: [1, 4, 16–18]. Finally, we conclude that the body of knowledge of DESRIST proceedings is aligned with the main top-journal DSR baskets.

5 Co-citation Analysis

The previous analysis shows that DESRIST gathers not only DSR researches but also many papers on Design Science and Design Research. The body of knowledge over-laps strongly with that of other DSR studies. In order to have a better understanding of DESRIST publications, we conducted a co-citation analysis of the previous basket of 99 papers using Citespace. The resulting graph, composed of 99 nodes and only 97 edges, is weakly connected. However, it contains only two connected components. More specifically, except one node (node 19 representing Becker's 2009 paper), the whole graph is connected. Becker's paper was cited several times but never co-cited. It focuses on maturity models and does not reference the seminal papers of DSR.

Based on the co-citation graph, we performed different clustering algorithms leading to insightful interpretations. The first interpretation may start with three clusters (domains[1] A and C, domains B and D, domain E). Domain E only contains Becker's paper. The other two clusters allowed us to identify two major domains of research. The first one focuses mainly on early theory (domains B and D). It seems to be the core of DSR and contains the theoretical foundations of DSR. Using Hevner's framework, it represents the knowledge base, and therefore the Rigor Cycle. The second domain focuses mainly on the application aspect of DSR. It can be considered as Hevner's Design Cycle (domains A and C). Domain D includes papers on ontology building, business process reengineering, design patterns language, and some considerations on

---

[1] Domains are characterized by letters and listed in column 5C of Table 2.

Table 2. Basket of ninety-nine papers

#	Paper_label	5C	10C	#	Paper_label	5C	10C
1	Aken J, 2004, J Management Studies, V41, P219-	A	4	51	Jarvinen P, 2007, Quality And Quantity, V41, P3	B	2
2	Alavi M, 2001, Misq, V25, P107-136	C	8	52	Klein H, 1999, Misq, V23, P67-94	B	3
3	Alexander C, 1977, A Pattern Language: Towns,	D	0	53	Kuechler W, 2008, Ejis, V17, P489-504	A	7
4	Alexander C, 1979, The Timeless Way Of Buildin	D	0	54	Kuechler W, 2008, Journal Of Design Research, V	B	1
5	Alturki A, 2011, Desrist, V, P107-123	B	2	55	Kuechler W, 2012, Jais, V13, P395-423	A	7
6	Arazy O, 2010, Jais, V11, P455-490	A	7	56	Lee A, 1989, Misq, V13, P33-50	A	4
7	Au Y, 2001, Cais, V7, P1-15	B	3	57	Lee A, 2003, Isr, V14, P221-243	B	2
8	Baldwin C, 2000, Design Rules, V1.,	B	3	58	Lee J, 2008, Misq, V32, P757-778	C	8
9	Baskerville R, 1996, Jit, V11, P235-246	B	3	59	March S, 1995, Dss, V15, P251-266	A	6
10	Baskerville R, 1998, Ejis, V7, P90-107	B	3	60	March S, 2008, Misq, V32, P725-730	B	6
11	Baskerville R, 2004, Misq, V28, P329-335	B	3	61	Markus Ml, 2002, Mis, V26, P179-212	C	8
12	Baskerville R, 2007, Desrist, V, P18-38	D	0	62	Moore G, 1991, Isr, V2, P192-222	A	7
13	Baskerville R, 2008, Ejis, V17, P441-443	B	2	63	Nunamaker J, 1991, Jmis, V7, P89-106	B	1
14	Baskerville R, 2009, Desrist, V, P.1-11	B	2	64	Offermann P, 2010, Desrist, V, P77-92	B	1
15	Baskerville R, 2010, Bise, V5, P271-282	A	7	65	Orlikowski W, 2001, Isr, V12, P121-134	B	1
16	Baskerville R, 2011, Ejis, V20, P11-15	A	4	66	Osterle H, 2011, Ejis, V20, P7-10	A	4
17	Baskerville R, 2011, Ejis, V20, P251-254	C	8	67	Pawson R, 1997, Realistic Evaluation, V, P	C	8
18	Becker J, 2007, Reference Modeling - Efficient Is	A	5	68	Peffers K, 2006, Desrist, V, P83-106	A	5
19	Becker J, 2009, Bise, V1, P213-222	E	9	69	Peffers K, 2007, Jmis, V24, P45-77	A	6
20	Benbasat I, 1987, Misq, V11, P369-386	A	4	70	Peffers K, 2012, Desrist, V, P398-410	A	7
21	Benbasat I, 1996, Isr, V7, P389-399	A	4	71	Popper K, 1959, The Logic Of Scientific Discover	D	0
22	Benbasat I, 1999, Misq, V23, P3-16	B	1	72	Pries-heje J, 2008, Ecis, V, P255-266	B	2
23	Benbasat I, 2003, Misq, V27, P183-194	A	4	73	Pries-heje J, 2008, Misq, V32, P731-755	C	8
24	Brinkkemper S, 1996, Information And Software	A	5	74	Purao S, 2002, Design Research In The Technolog	B	3
25	Bunge M, 1967, Scientific Research Ii: The Search	D	0	75	Rittel H, 1973, Policy Sci., V4, P155-169	B	1
26	Bunge M, 1977, Treatise On Basic Philosophy.	D	0	76	Rogers E, 1995, Diffusion Of Innovations, V, P	C	8
27	Carlsson S, 2007, Scandinavian Journal Of Is, V19	B	3	77	Rosemann M, 2008, Misq, V32, P1-22	A	4
28	Checkland P, 1990, Soft Systems Methodology I	B	2	78	Rossi M, 2003, Presentation At Iris, V26, P9-12	B	1
29	Chen P, 1976, Acm Tods, V1, P9-36	A	4	79	Sein M, 2011, Misq, V35, P37-56	B	3
30	Clark Jr, 2007, Misq, V31, P579-615	A	5	80	Simon H, 1969, The Sciences Of The Artificial, V,	A	6
31	Cole R, 2005, Icis, V, P325-336	B	3	81	Takeda H, 1990, Ai Magazine, V11, P37-48	B	1
32	Creswell J, 2002, Research Design: Qualitative, V	A	5	82	Vaishnavi V, 2004, Design Research In Informatio	B	1
33	Cross N, 2001, Design Issues, V17, P49-55	D	0	83	Vaishnavi V, 2008, Design Science Research Meth	B	2
34	Davenport T, 1993, Process Innovation: Reengine	D	0	84	Van Aken J, 2004, Journal Of Management Studie	D	0
35	Davis Fd, 1989, Misq, V13, P318-340	A	5	85	Van Aken J, 2005, British Journal Of Manag., V16	D	0
36	Davison R, 2004, Isj, V14, P65-86	B	2	86	Venable J, 2006, Desrist, V, P1-18	B	2
37	Delone W, 2003, Jmis, V19, P9-30	A	5	87	Venable J, 2006, Irma Conference, V, P. 21-24	B	2
38	Eekels J, 1991, Design Studies, V12, P197-203	B	1	88	Venable J, 2010, Desrist, V, P109-123	B	2
39	Gamma E, 1995, Design Patterns: Elements Of R	D	0	89	Venable J, 2012, Desrist, V, P423-438	A	7
40	Goldkuhl G, 2004, Jitta, V6, P59-72	A	7	90	Venkatesh V, 2003, Misq, V27, P425-478	A	5
41	Goldkuhl G, 2010, Desrist, V, P45-60	A	1	91	Vom Brocke J, 2009, Ecis, V, P2206-2217	A	5
42	Gregor S, 2006, Misq, V30, P611-462	A	6	92	Walls J, 1992, Isr, V3, P36-59	A	6
43	Gregor S, 2007, Jais, V8, P312-335	A	6	93	Walls J, 2004, Jitta, V6, P43-58	B	2
44	Gregor S, 2013, Misq, V37, P337-355	A	7	94	Wand Y, 1990, Ieee Transactions On Software Eng	D	0
45	Hammer M, 1993, Reengineering The Corporatio	D	0	95	Wand Y, 1995, Dss, V15, P285-304	D	0
46	Hevner A, 2004, Misq, V28, P75-105	A	6	96	Webster J, 2002, Misq, V26, Pxiii-xxiii	A	5
47	Hevner A, 2007, Scandinavian Journal Of Is, V19	A	7	97	Wieringa R, 2009, Desrist, V, P1-12	C	8
48	Hevner A, 2010, Design Research In Information	A	4	98	Winter R, 2008, Ejis, V17, P470-475	A	6
49	Hevner A, 2010, Design Research In Information	B	1	99	Yin R, 1994, Case Study Research: Design And M	A	4
50	Iivari J, 2007, Scandinavian Journal Of Is, V19, P	B	6				

design science. This is not a homogeneous cluster. If we perform a clustering based on one more cluster, this cluster is discarded from the rigor cycle and constitutes one cluster. As a consequence, the cluster representing the rigor cycle (domain B alone) is reinforced and becomes more homogeneous. If we ask for one more cluster, domains A and C are separated. A close analysis of domain A shows a preeminence of the Relevance Cycle. Domain C mainly characterizes the Design Cycle. Domain B fits with the Rigor Cycle. Finally the clustering into five components is globally aligned with the three cycles of Hevner [4], illustrating how papers concentrate mainly on one cycle. We performed several other steps of clustering, zooming into the major clusters showing the most influential contributions and the way they are connected. We superimposed the 5 clusters (called domains) and the 10 clusters[2] thus showing the way they are connected. An interpretation of these 10 clusters is provided below.

Cluster 6 (*DS in IS*) is the central one in the graph. If we consider the meta-graph in Fig. 1, it has the highest degree (4). This is probably the most coherent cluster dealing with Design Science (Winter 2008, Hevner 2004) and DS in ISR (Hevner 2004, Peffers 2007, Iivari 2007, March 2008, Gregor 2007). It contains the most cited papers. The global average number of citations per paper is about 13. In cluster 6, this average number is about 56. The degree of cluster 1 (*DR-DS*) in the meta-graph is 3. This cluster is heavily oriented towards Design Research (Kuechler 2008, Vaishnavi 2004, Rossi 2003, Hevner 2010) and design process (Takeda 1990, Goldkuhl 2010). Scientific bases are mentioned (Rittel 1973, Eekels 1991). Finally artifacts in DS are cited (Offermann 2010). Cluster 2 (*DSR*) is clearly a DSR cluster including evaluation aspects (Alturki 2011, Venable 2006, Vaishnavi 2008, Pries-Heje 2008, Venable 2010). Let us mention the existence of papers related to Action Research (Jarvinen, 2007) and to soft systems approach to DS (Baskerville 2008). We could also call it DESRIST cluster since it contains a majority of DESRIST papers. Cluster 0 is not homogeneous. It is composed of articles related to design science (Baskerville 2007, Van Aken 2004/2005) as well as papers on ontologies (Wand 1990, Bunge 1977). In addition contributions on business process reengineering (Davenport 1993, Hammer 1993) as well as design patterns (Gamma 1995, Alexander 1977) are cited.

Cluster 4 (*ISR*) covers mainly ISR (Rosemann 2008, Benbasat 1996/2008, Osterle 2011) and design oriented ISR (Baskerville 2011). However some contributions on case study research are present (Benbasat 1987, Yin 1994, Lee 1989). Cluster 7 (*DSR positioning and evaluation*) is not homogeneous but connects two clusters (DS in IS and ISR). It is composed of papers related to DSR evaluation (Peffers 2012, Venable 2012, DSR positioning (Kuechler 2012, Gregor 2013, Hevner 2007) and Design Theory (Baskerville 2010, Kuechler 2008, Goldkuhl 2004). Cluster 5 (*IS models*) encompasses different articles on IS success model, user acceptance of IT, UTAUT model and situational methods (Venkatesh 2004, Davis 1989, Delone 2003, Brinkkemper 1996). It is worth mentioning some contributions on literature review (Webster 2002, Vom Brocke 2009) and on research design (Peffers 2006, Creswell 2002). Cluster 3 (*Action Research*) is dominated by Action Research contributions (Cole 2005, Baskerville 1996, Baskerville 2004, Sein 2011, Davison 2004).

---

[2] Clusters are numbered from 0 to 9 and defined in column 10C of Table 2.

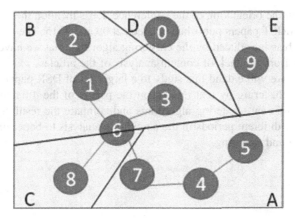

Fig. 1. The five domains and ten clusters

A connected paper related to interpretive field study research is mentioned (Klein 1999). Finally Cluster 8 (*Design theory for problem solving*) is mainly concerned by problem solving issues (Wieringa 2009, Markus 2002, Alavi 2001, Baskerville 2011). Let us mention contribution by Pries-Heje (2008) dealing with Design Theory and strongly connected to the contributions of the authors mentioned above.

6 Conclusions and Future Research

In this paper, we have performed a citation analysis to better understand the DSR body of knowledge, as reflected by the DESRSIT conference. To perform the citation analysis, we have considered the last seven editions of DESRIST, including all papers from these editions except products and prototypes. Our goal was threefold: Determine the most cited publications and authors (RQ1), better understand the current structure of the DSR body of knowledge (RQ2). To answer RQ1, we performed citation analysis. We found similarities between the most frequent citations revealed by this study and those revealed by other studies. To answer RQ2, we performed clustering on the co-citation network. Thanks to this clustering, we gained a clearer picture of the organization of the DSR body of knowledge. The set of clusters can be regarded as convergence points for communities of researchers. Most of the clusters found in the analysis deal with theories or methodologies of DSR (as opposed to applications of DSR to specific domains like e.g. system analysis or business processes). Interestingly, the clustering did not reveal a marked separation between the artefact view and the design-theory view of DSR: the opposition between these two views, which has been underlined in several publications, thus appears more theoretic than real (We note that similarly to the present study, the co-citation analysis performed on the sample of papers of Prat et al. [19] found that "artefact view" and "design-theory view" papers were not clearly separated in different clusters).

This paper confirms that DESRIST, as well as DSR mainly produces method papers and not enough applications. This may impact future DESRIST conference program chairs in the orientation of the conference. Let's mention the limitation of our research on DESRIST papers published between 2009 and 2015. The second limitation is related to the bias introduced by the clustering algorithm that we have used. A third limitation stems from the lack of content analysis of the articles.

In the future, we will extend this study to a larger set of DSR papers. We will also complement the clustering by text mining on the papers of the different clusters. We will also apply different clustering algorithms and compare the resulting clusters. We will also consider different periods in the co-citation analysis to better understand how DSR is evolving and maturing.

References

1. Simon, H.A.: The Sciences of the Artificial. MIT Press, Cambridge (1969)
2. Vaishnavi, V., Kuechler, B. (eds.) Design Science Research in Information Systems. http://desrist.org/desrist/content/design-science-research-in-information-systems.pdf. (Accessed on Nov 2015)
3. Niederman, F., March, S.T.: Design science and the accumulation of knowledge in the information systems discipline. ACM Trans. MIS 3(1), 1–15 (2012)
4. Hevner, A.R., March, S.T., Park, J., Ram, S.: Design science in information systems research. MIS Q. 28(1), 75–105 (2004)
5. Venable, J.: The role of theory and theorising in design science research. In: Chatterjee, S., Hevner, A. (eds.) Proceedings of the First International Conference on Design Science in Information Systems and Technology (DESRIST 2006), pp. 1–18, Claremont (2006)
6. Kuechler, W., Vaishnavi, V.K., Kuechler Sr., W.L.: Design [science] research in IS – a work in progress. In: Proceedings of the Second International Conference on Design Science Research in Information Systems and Technology (DESRIST 2007), pp. 1–17 (2007)
7. Fischer, C., Winter, R., Wortmann, F.: Design theory. Bus. Inf. Syst. Eng. 2(6), 387–390 (2010)
8. Vaishnavi, V.K., Kuechler, W.: Design Science Research Methods and Patterns: Innovating Information and Communication Technology. Auerbach Publications, NY (2007)
9. Hevner, A.R., Chatterjee, S.: Design Research in Information Systems: Theory and Practice. Springer, Dordrecht (2010)
10. Indulska, M., Recker, J.: Design science in IS research: a literature analysis. In: Hart, D.N., Gregor, S.D. (eds.) Information Systems Foundations: The Role of Design Science Workshop. The Australian National University E Press, Canberra (2010)
11. Offermann, P., Blom, S., Schönherr, M., Bub, U.: Artifact types in information systems design science – a literature review. In: Winter, R., Zhao, J., Aier, S. (eds.) DESRIST 2010. LNCS, vol. 6105, pp. 77–92. Springer, Heidelberg (2010)
12. Fischer, C.: The information systems design science research body of knowledge – a citation analysis in recent IS top journal publications. In: Proceedings of PACIS 2011 (2011)
13. Chen, C.: CiteSpace II: detecting and visualizing emerging trends and transient patterns in scientific literature. J. Am. Soc. Inform. Sci. Technol. 57(3), 359–377 (2006)
14. Blondel, V., Guillaume, J., Lambiotte, R., Mech, E.: Fast unfolding of communities in large networks. J. Stat. Mech: Theor. Exp. 2008, P10008 (2008)

15. Schöler, M., Mauermann, M., Majschak, J.-P.: Application of hollow sphere structures and composites in processing machines. In: Öechsner, A., Augustin, C. (eds.) Multifunctional Metallic Hollow Sphere Structures. Eng.Mat., vol. 1, pp. 213–222. Springer, Heidelberg (2009)
16. Walls, J.G., Widmeyer, G.R., El Sawy, O.A.: Building an information system design theory for vigilant EIS. Inf. Syst. Res. 3(1), 36–59 (1992)
17. March, S.T., Smith, G.F.: Design and natural science research on information technology. Decis. Support Syst. 15(4), 251–266 (1995)
18. Gregor, S., Jones, D.: The anatomy of a design theory. J. Assoc. Inf. Syst. 8(5), 312–335 (2007)
19. Prat, N., Comyn-Wattiau, I., Akoka, J.: A taxonomy of evaluation methods for information systems artifacts. J. MIS 32(2), 229–267 (2015)

Information System Design Theory:
A Lifecycle Perspective

Ahmad Alturki[(✉)]

Information Systems Department, King Saud University, Riyadh, Saudi Arabia
alturkiahmad@hotmail.com

Abstract. For Design Science Research (DSR) to gain wide credence as a research paradigm in Information Systems (IS), DSR must contribute to theory. "Theory cannot be improved until we improve the theorizing process, and we cannot improve the theorizing process until we describe it more explicitly, operate it more self-consciously, and decouple it from validation more deliberately" [2 p. 516]. With the aim of improved design science theorizing, we propose Information System Design Theory (ISDT) should be viewed and analyzed through the concept of ISDT lifecycle. The nature of this lifecycle distinguishes the ISDT from other types of theories in IS discipline. Each ISDT has one lifecycle which has several waves (versions) - the relation here is one to many. A wave of DSR is a special instance of independent DSR project which may produces new ISDT or refined existed ISDT. This paper attempts to contribute to theorizing in DSR. The concept of ISDT lifecycle will contribute and help researchers to identify and crystallize the position of their theorizing contributions in DSR. The lifecycle concept provide with traceability capability which allows researchers to anticipate future theorizing contributions. The ISDT lifecycle can utilized in teaching DSR especially for novice DSR researchers.

Keywords: Design Theory · Information System Design Theory · Design Science Research · Design research

1 Introduction

There has been growing interest in Design Science Research (DSR) in Information System (IS). DSR has become an accepted methodology for research in IS [3, 4] and its importance is well established [3, 5–9]. DSR can be seen as a third major form of science, artificial science, in addition to the natural and human sciences [10].

To gain wide credence as a research paradigm in IS, DSR must contribute to design theory (defined in the next section) which is part of DSR efforts. With the aim of facilitating design theory, researchers, e.g. Lee et al. [11], Kuechler and Vaishnavi [12] and Fischer and Gregor [13], call for increased attention to theorising - the process of creating theories in DSR – and have suggested valuable concepts intended to aid in DSR theorising.

Though theorizing, or the abstraction process, has been the subject of healthy discussion in DSR, theoretical development in DSR needs more investigation [4, 14]. Furthermore, most attention to this area has focused on: (1) the structure of design

© Springer International Publishing Switzerland 2016
J. Parsons et al. (Eds.): DESRIST 2016, LNCS 9661, pp. 186–194, 2016.
DOI: 10.1007/978-3-319-39294-3_13

theory such as [6, 15–17]; and (2) theorizing process for DSR – where the emphasis is on how a specific designed output can be abstracted/generalized in the form of Information System Design Theory (ISDT) and how this design theory (abstracted design) can be situated and implemented in many yet similar contexts such as [11, 12, 18, 19].

The aim of this manuscript is to introduce a design theory lifecycle, and its waves, concept. This lifecycle relatively distinguishes the design theory from other types of theories in IS discipline. This lifecycle concept gives clear relationships between different ISDTs focused on specific problem/need in one context; i.e. investigating ISDTs through the lens of this concept provides researchers with complete history. Therefore, the design theory lifecycle concept will contribute to DSR conduction in terms of inspiring researchers to identify problems/needs and/or opportunities and crystallize the position of their design theory (contributions) in DSR in general. Through this concept, DSR researchers can also anticipate future theorizing contributions.

The remainder of the paper is organized as follows. Firstly, the literature is shortly[1] reported based on extensively content analysis of the literature. Subsequently, the concept of ISDT lifecycle is explained. The conclusion summarizes the paper's contributions and identifies areas for future work.

2 Literature Review

A detailed comprehensive literature review was conducted on DSR in IS discipline; ISDT and its theorizing process was one of the main aspect of this literature review. There are other important areas of DSR but out of our scope such as DSR outputs [20], DSR methodologies [8, 21, 22], DSR abstraction layer and patterns [23, 24], and DSR contributions [25] and [1].

2.1 Information System Design Theory, and Its Structures and Frameworks

Development of good theories is very important to any discipline; researchers aim to build theories as an ultimate goal [26]. "[A] particular kind of model that is intended to account for some subset of phenomena in the real world. … It is an artifact built by humans to achieve some purpose. It is a conceptual thing rather than a concrete thing. Nonetheless, it has a concrete manifestation as a neuronal pattern in some person's brain" [26 p. 4]. Theories can be defined as "abstract entities that aim to describe, explain and enhance understanding of the world and, in some cases, to provide predictions of what will happen in the future and to give a basis for intervention and action" [27 p. 7]. Gregor [27] identifies four goals of theories: Analysis and description, Explanation, Prediction, Prescription "recipe". Based on these goals, Gregor [27 p. 13] identifies five types of theories: analysis, explanation, prediction, explanation and prediction, and design and action (or known ISDT), for more details see Table 2 in [27].

---

[1] Due to space limitation, the literature review is not presented in this paper.

ISDT has been defined in different ways, as we summarized below:

- Walls et al. [17] define ISDT as a "prescriptive theory which integrates normative and descriptive theories into design paths intended to produce more effective information systems" [17 p. 36]. It is "a *prescriptive* theory based on theoretical underpinnings which says how a design process can be carried out in a way which is both effective and feasible" [17 p. 37].
- ISDT provides a complete set of general principles and guidelines for developing a system in a particular situation [28].
- "Design theories consist of knowledge of a *practical* character; i.e., for practical purposes" [29 p. 61].
- Aken [30] defines management theory as a form of design science: it is "*prescription-driven* research and to be used largely in an instrumental way to design solutions for management problems" [30 p. 221].
- "The distinguishing attribute of theories for design and action is that they focus on 'how to do something'. They give explicit *prescriptions* on how to design and develop an artifact, whether it is a technological product or a managerial intervention" [6 p. 313]. ISDT is defined as "something in an abstract world of man-made things, which also includes other abstract ideas such as algorithms and models. A design theory [ISDT] instantiated would have a physical existence in the real world" [6 p. 320]; it addresses "how to do something".

There are very extensive discussion of different approaches to the structure of ISDT and ISDT development process. Walls et al. [17], Markus, et al. [28], Goldkuhl [29], Gregor and Jones [6], Kuechler and Vaishnavi [35], Goldkuhl and Lind [19], Baskerville and Pries-Heje [15], Arazy et al. [18], Fischer and Gregor [13], Lee et al.'s [11], and Kuechler and Vaishnavi [12] represent main contribution under this subject[2].

3 Information System Design Theory Lifecycle

It can be concluded from the literature review that there is much research, such as [9, 11, 17–19, 24, 33, 37], emphases on the process of how ISDT is developed and theorized during one single DSR project/research. However there is not much discussion about ISDT in terms of how different ISDTs, resulted from different DSR, relate to each other. Additionally, the ISDT has special characteristics which differentiate it from other types of theories. One of these characteristics is that ISDT in nature evolves in several iterations in one and across different DSR efforts. Put it differently, every ISDT goes through various advancements[3] through different DSR efforts. We label this phenomena *ISDT lifecycle*.

The rationale behind *ISDT lifecycle* concept and its waves is that resulted design from DSR is strongly influenced by the following:

---

[2] Due to space limitation, these efforts are not discussed in this paper.

[3] These advancements could have any form of contributions; this is out the scope of the current paper.

- There is no optimum design solution in any DSR [7]; there may be design options for one situation (same requirements and context).
- Technologies are perishable and have been evolving [20]; advances in technology may inspire better designs/solutions, or even generate new needs/problems which create new opportunities for researchers to investigate.
- Needs, problems and opportunities keep changing for different reasons [7, 8, 21, 37].

ISDT should reflect these three issues; the results (i.e. ISDT as one of the main outputs) of DSR are continuously changed. Based on this, we propose that one ISDT should be viewed and analyzed through the concept of *ISDT lifecycle*. Each ISDT has one *lifecycle* and each *lifecycle* has several *waves* (versions) - the association here is *one-to-many*. A wave of *ISDT lifecycle* means a special instance of independent DSR project which may produces new ISDT or refined existed ISDT (i.e. new *wave*).

Figure 1 below depicts the concept *ISDT lifecycle* and its *waves*; the figure shows that one *ISDT lifecycle* is advanced and improved through many *waves* of DSR projects. Any ISDT, in its original/first *wave* (ISDT wave#1), is developed with an innovation. The ISDT development in the initial *wave* has many inputs[4]; problems or opportunities, kernel theories (also may be DREPT), and may be some parts from other ISDT. The main output of the first successful *wave* is an innovative artifact presented in ISDT form; usually with some limitations, constraints or issues.

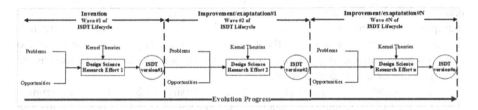

Fig. 1. Information System Design Theory (ISDT) lifecycle and its waves

Once there are emergent problems/needs to be resolved, opportunities (as a result of new advancements of technology) for enhancement, or better kernel theories that suggest changes, another (subsequent) *improvement wave* of *ISDT lifecycle* can start. In this subsequent *wave*, there are also many and similar inputs: problems or opportunities, kernel theories (also may be DREPT), and parts from other ISDT including the ISDT from previous *wave* of *ISDT lifecycle*. Thus, various subsequent new *improvement waves* may continue if there is an impetus for them. Each ISDT resulting from any *wave* can be *adopted* in practice by practitioners who *instantiate* the developed ISDT in their context, or used by other researchers in other DSR opportunities (different *ISDT lifecycle*) or in any social science research.

We also introduce what we so-call *sweet wave* to distinguish between waves of *ISDT lifecycle*. The *sweet wave* is the best wave of *ISDT lifecycle* in which DSR effort

---

[4] Regardless of which of DSR frameworks is followed by DSR researchers.

has the best of all required capabilities and resources such as design and creativity skills, technology, hardware, or best kernel theories in domain knowledge. Availability of these capabilities and resources is not enough, yet their *harmonization* is very important to be attained. The *harmonization* means that there is a *decent fit* between the ISDT in of internal design (i.e. all ISDT's components and their relations) and external environment which affects and effected by a design emerged from ISDT. For instance, we might find a developed and published ISDT based on a kernel theory, however there was better kernel theory which provides advancements to the ISDT, and could lead to superior harmonization which then helps to get the best impact of the ISDT. Social networks show real examples of the harmonization idea; indeed they are not new innovation yet the current version them attain harmonization (there is fit between the internal logic and its kernel theories, mobile devices, telecommunication, and people and society). This harmonization of social networks may explain one of the success factors of social networks' widely usage by people and adoption in organization.

3.1 The Waves Resulting from ISDT Lifecycle vs. DSR Contribution

Järvinen [25] proposes a four-fold classification of DSR outputs: (1) a totally new artefact; (2) an artifact whose value is equal to that of the best earlier one; (3) an artifact whose value is superior to that of the best earlier one; and (4) a failed artifact construction. Gregor and Hevner [1] have proposed a DSR Knowledge Contribution Framework (a 2 × 2 matrix) to depict DSR contributions (Fig. 2). This framework has four quadrants: invention, improvement, exaptation, and routine design. The X (high to low) axis represents the maturity of the domain for a particular problem. The Y (high to low) axis represents the maturity of currently available artifacts that can be used as the starting point for a new design/solution.

Using Gregor and Hevner's [1] 2 × 2 matrix, firstly we believe that the original (first) wave of ISDT is under the quadrant of *invention*. Any advancement to the first wave is considered as *improvement*. Any wave resulted from ISDT lifecycle, including original wave, may be *exaptated* (adopted or adapted) into a problem in a different field. We believe the innovation quadrant has one wave which then may have several waves under the improvement and exaptation quadrants.

Finally, each wave resulted[5] from ISDT lifecycle can be adopted in the practice by practitioners who instantiate the developed ISDT in the same context defined by the ISDT producer, this is considered as a *routine design*. Figure 3 below shows how the waves of ISDT lifecycle are integrated with the four quadrants of Gregor and Hevner's [1] 2 × 2 matrix.

---

[5] We assumed the resulting ISDT is scientifically evaluated which definitely affects interest in its adoption in practice.

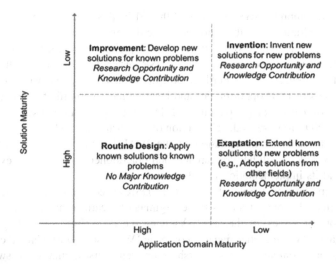

Fig. 2. DSR Knowledge Contribution Framework (Gregor and Hevner [1]).

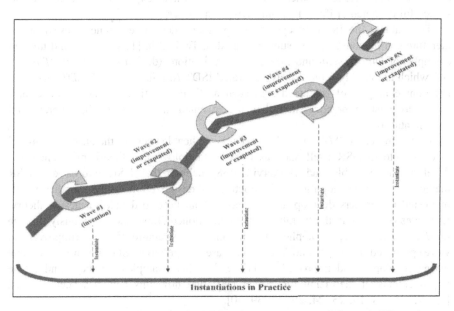

Fig. 3. The integration between ISDT lifecycles and Hevner and Gregor's [1] matrix

3.2 The Implications and Evaluation of the ISDT Lifecycle

The ISDT lifecycle concept, and its waves, provide with *traceability* capability which permits DSR researchers and practitioners to keep track of all ISDT innovations, advancements, motivations, changes, constraints, and limitations; i.e. the *history* of the ISDT. The *traceability* benefits DSR researchers to attain a good contribution by providing a comprehensive overview of the ISDT; this overview includes (1) ISDT motives and inspirations, (2) the rationale of the design, (3) the reasons why the ISDT has many waves, and (4) the sweet wave which explains why the ISDT has significant impact on targeted context/practice. Thus, DSR researchers can justify their contributions and differences easily. Furthermore, the *traceability* could work as a tool to offer researchers of DSR opportunities and inspire them to contribute (new version) to ISDT. Based on *traceability* capability of ISDT lifecycle, it can be used for *expecting future*. Since ISDT represents the abstraction of real instantiations/implementations and an artifact represents an instantiation of the ISDT [6, 11, 12, 23], viewing ISDT through lifecycle lens will help researchers and practitioners to expect the evolution of the ISDT and its implementation in the practice.

Another implication is related to *teaching* DSR especially for novice researchers. The ISDT lifecycle concept allows these beginners to learn from the history, original and development waves, of the ISDT. Viewing the ISDT from lifecycle perspective helps to create very comprehensive and complete DSR case studies which therefore can be used as a main content for DSR workshops or even courses. Finally, the sweet wave, explained above, could point to and justify why at different time some similar artifacts have dissimilar effects. In other words, the sweet waves expose the rationale behind successful designed artifacts that built based on ISDTs.

To evaluate the ISDT lifecycle concept, many design researches (cases) in the literature can demonstrate and support this idea. Table 2 in [1] shows around thirteen examples of *improvement* and *exaptation* contributions (design *waves* of *ISDT lifecycle*) which are based on previously innovated ISDT (original *wave* of *ISDT lifecycle*). Different examples of routine design such as ERP or rational database are clearly shown to exist in practice after they are invented and improved in different and incremental *waves*.

Furthermore, the *ISDT lifecycle* concept is applicable even for the efforts conducted to contribute to DSR itself such as DSR methodology and theorizing frameworks development. Venable and Baskerville [38] believe that DSR efforts, e.g. DSR methodology or developing ISDT structure, is design effort itself; in other words interested researchers develop design theory about how to develop a design theory. Examples of efforts in the literature review mentioned above show obviously that the *ISDT lifecycle* concept is applied. For instance, the structure of ISDT (improvement wave) proposed by Gregor and Jones [6] is based on previous ISDT invention (original wave) developed and improved by [17, 32]. Other examples can be found in the improvements of theorizing process in DSR and how this area has been evolved [11, 12, 15, 18, 19, 23, 24, 29, 37, 39, 40].

4 Conclusion

This paper attempts to contribute to the DSR theorizing area by proposing the *lifecycle* concept for ISDT- an abstract knowledge of the development of a specific IS. The motivation for this concept is the special characteristics of ISDT; these characteristics are: (1) no optimum design solution in any DSR; (2) technologies are perishable; and (3) needs, problems and opportunities keep changing. The concept of ISDT lifecycle, and its waves, assists DSR researchers with *traceability* and *teaching* capabilities. The lifecycle of ISDT originally starts with innovation wave and then many improvement waves could emerge based on needs, problems, and opportunities. Each wave of the resulting from ISDT innovation or improvements could be adopted in different contexts and used in practice.

For future work, the ISDT lifecycle concept needs further validation by using the illustrative scenario method [22]. Doing this will show more importance of the *ISDT lifecycle* concept and encourage DSR researchers to consider the ISDT lifecycle when they develop their design theories. Furthermore, we will investigate of grounding the *ISDT lifecycle* by using promising theories.

References

1. Gregor, S., Hevner, A.R.: Positioning and presenting design science research for maximum impact. Manag. Inf. Syst. Q. **37**(2), 337–355 (2013)
2. Weick, K.E.: Theory construction as disciplined imagination. Acad. Manag. Rev. **14**(4), 516–531 (1989)
3. Iivari, J.: A paradigmatic analysis of information systems as a design science. Scand. J. Inf. Syst. **19**(2), 39–64 (2007)
4. Kuechler, B., Vaishnavi, V.: The emergence of design research in information systems in North America. J. Des. Res. **7**(1), 1–16 (2008)
5. Gregor, S.: Design theory in information systems. Aust. J. Inf. Syst. **10**, 14–22 (2002)
6. Gregor, S., Jones, D.: The anatomy of a design theory. J. Assoc. Inf. Syst. **8**(5), 312–335 (2007)
7. Hevner, A.R., et al.: Design science in information systems research. MIS Q. **28**(1), 75–106 (2004)
8. Peffers, K., et al.: A design science research methodology for information systems research. J. Manag. Inf. Syst. **24**(3), 45–77 (2007)
9. Vaishnavi, V., Kuechler, W.: Design research in information systems, 20 February 2004 [cited 10 January 2010]. http://www.isworld.org/Researchdesign/drisISworld.htm
10. Gregor, S.: Building theory in the sciences of the artificial. In: DESRIST 2009, pp. 1–10. ACM, Malvern, PA, USA
11. Lee, J.S., Pries-Heje, J., Baskerville, R.: Theorizing in design science research. In: Jain, H., Sinha, A.P., Vitharana, P. (eds.) DESRIST 2011. LNCS, vol. 6629, pp. 1–16. Springer, Heidelberg (2011)
12. Kuechler, W., Vaishnavi, V.: A framework for theory development in design science research: multiple perspectives. J. Assoc. Inf. Syst. **13**(6), 30 (2012)
13. Fischer, C., Gregor, S.: Forms of reasoning in the design science research process. In: Jain, H., Sinha, A.P., Vitharana, P. (eds.) DESRIST 2011. LNCS, vol. 6629, pp. 17–31. Springer, Heidelberg (2011)
14. Venable, J.R.: Identifying and addressing stakeholder interests in design science research: an analysis using critical systems heuristics. In: Dhillon, G., Stahl, B.C., Baskerville, R. (eds.) CreativeSME 2009. IFIP AICT, vol. 301, pp. 93–112. Springer, Heidelberg (2009)
15. Baskerville, R., Pries-Heje, J.: Explanatory design theory. Bus. Inf. Syst. Eng. **2**(5), 271–282 (2010)
16. Venable, J.: The role of theory and theorising in Design Science research. In Proceedings of DESRIST 2006, Claremont, CA

17. Walls, J.G., Widmeyer, G.R., El Sawy, O.A.: Building an information system design theory for vigilant EIS. Inf. Syst. Res. **3**(1), 36–59 (1992)
18. Arazy, O., Kumar, N., Shapira, B.: A theory-driven design framework for social recommender systems. J. Assoc. Inf. Syst. **11**(9), 455–490 (2010)
19. Goldkuhl, G., Lind, M.: A multi-grounded design research process. In: Winter, R., Zhao, J., Aier, S. (eds.) DESRIST 2010. LNCS, vol. 6105, pp. 45–60. Springer, Heidelberg (2010)
20. March, S.T., Smith, G.F.: Design and natural science research on information technology. Decis. Support Syst. **15**(4), 251–266 (1995)
21. Alturki, A., Gable, G.G., Bandara, W.: A design science research roadmap. In: Jain, H., Sinha, A.P., Vitharana, P. (eds.) DESRIST 2011. LNCS, vol. 6629, pp. 107–123. Springer, Heidelberg (2011)
22. Peffers, K., Rothenberger, M., Tuunanen, T., Vaezi, R.: Design science research evaluation. In: Peffers, K., Rothenberger, M., Kuechler, B. (eds.) DESRIST 2012. LNCS, vol. 7286, pp. 398–410. Springer, Heidelberg (2012)
23. Alturki, A., Gable, G.G.: Theorizing in design science research: an abstraction layers framework. In: PACIS 2014 Proceedings, p. Paper 126 (2014)
24. Iivari, J.: Distinguishing and contrasting two strategies for design science research. Eur. J. Inf. Syst. **24**(1), 107–115 (2015)
25. Järvinen, P.: On reviewing of results in design research in the 15th European Conference on Information Systems, Switzerland (2007)
26. Weber, R.: Evaluating and developing theories in the information systems discipline. J. Assoc. Inf. Syst. **13**(1), 2 (2012)
27. Gregor, S.: The nature of theory in information systems. MIS Q. **30**(3), 611 (2006)
28. Markus, M.L., Majchrzak, A., Les, G.: A design theory for systems that support emergent knowledge processes. MIS Q. **26**(3), 179–212 (2002)
29. Goldkuhl, G.: Design theories in information systems-a need for multi-grounding. J. Inf. Technol. Theory Appl. **6**(2), 59–72 (2004)
30. Aken, J.E.: Management research based on the paradigm of the design sciences: the quest for field-tested and grounded technological rules. J. Manag. Stud. **41**(2), 219–246 (2004)
31. Gregor, S., Hevner, A.: Introduction to the special issue on design science. IseB **9**(1), 1–9 (2010)
32. Dubin, R., Theory building (Rev. ed.). New Symptoms of depression in adolescents with epi (1978)
33. Simon, H.A.: The Sciences of the Artificial, 3rd edn. The MIT Press, Cambridge (1996)
34. Takeda, H., et al.: Modeling design process. AI Mag. **11**(4), 37 (1990)
35. Kuechler, B., Vaishnavi, V.: On theory development in design science research: anatomy of a research project. Eur. J. Inf. Syst. **17**(5), 489–504 (2008)
36. Merton, R.K.: Social Theory and Social Structure. Simon and Schuster, New York (1968)
37. Venable, J.: A framework for design science research activities. In: Information Resource Management Association Conference (CD), Washington, DC, USA. Idea Group Publishing, Hershey, Pennsylvania, USA
38. Venable, J., Baskerville, R.: Eating our own cooking: toward a more rigorous design science of research methods. Electron. J. Bus. Res. Methods **10**(2), 141–153 (2012)
39. Gregor, S., Mueller, O., Seidel, S.: Reflection, abstraction and theorizing in design and development research (2013)
40. Purao, S., et al.: The sciences of design: observations on an emerging field. Harvard Business School Finance Working Paper (2008)

Prototypes

A Prototype System for Collecting and Analyzing Credible Online Medical Content

Ahmed Abbasi[1,2(✉)], Kevin Zhao[2], and Brendan Abraham[2]

[1] Information Technology Area, McIntire School of Commerce, University of Virginia,
Charlottesville, VA, USA
abbasi@virginia.edu
[2] Center for Business Analytics, McIntire School of Commerce, University of Virginia,
Charlottesville, VA, USA
{rz2db,bea3ch}@virginia.edu

Abstract. Regulators, analysts, policy-makers, and advocacy groups are increasingly interested in utilizing the abundance of available online Health 2.0 content to support key decision-making tasks. However, existing systems are ill-suited to deal with the plethora of medical spam and variety of relevant online channels. We present a prototype system for collecting, analyzing, aggregating, and presenting key topics and sentiments encompassed in online medical content. By incorporating modules for examining credibility, relevance, and context, the system is able to present users with information that is markedly better with respect to credibility, coverage, precision, and timeliness.

Keywords: Health 2.0 · Online sentiment · Credibility assessment · Design science

1 Introduction

The increased presence and utilization of health portals and infomediaries, social media, and health-related e-tailers has ushered the era of Health 2.0, with consumers and/or patients all turning to the Web to purchase health-related products and services, attain information, share experiences, seek advice, and express concerns [1]. Various stakeholders are interested in leveraging the wealth of user-generated content encompassed in such online data sources. Health regulatory agencies are interested in more accurate and timelier warning indicators [2]. Private sector health firms wish to gather insights that can protect brand reputation and manage risk [3]. Consumer advocacy groups seek indicators that can inform and influence policy. Consequently there is great interest in IT artifacts that can collect, analyze, aggregate, and present timely insights from large collections of online health content. For the back-end collection and analysis, most prior work has developed traditional website-oriented topical crawling systems, or forum or blog-specific focused crawlers [7]. However, existing methods for collecting and analyzing such content have a couple of major shortcomings [4–6].

Limited credibility assessment of online health content: Content credibility concerns remain paramount [4]. In 2011, Google settled a U.S. government investigation for $500

J. Parsons et al. (Eds.): DESRIST 2016, LNCS 9661, pp. 197–201, 2016.
DOI: 10.1007/978-3-319-39294-3_14

million after it was discovered that their search engine ad results for online pharmacy-related searches for several years had been including fraudulent pharmacy websites [4]. However, the problem is far more extensive. Some estimate that over 20 % of the entire Web is comprised of spam, with the proportion of questionable content even greater in the context of health-related content [5]. Our own prior experiments found that at any given time, between 65 and 85 of the top 100 search results for online pharmacies were not credible [4], with similarly high levels of web spam for health information and health institution websites.

Lack of inclusion of various online health information sources: Health information is present in various online sources, including health portals, infomediaries, discussion forums, patient-centric social networking sites, medical blogs, and general-purpose social media such as Twitter and Facebook. Systems capable of effectively capturing information from an array of relevant online channels must consider nuanced inter-linkage patterns [7, 9]. Furthermore, they must also factor the sentiment polarity of content, as opposed to merely considering topical relevance. For instance, social media postings expressing positive or negative opinions pertaining to a health topic are highly likely to link to others also containing opinions on the topic [8]. Prior topical crawling systems or social media-specific focused crawlers fail to incorporate multi-channel context, and its implications for content and linkage, in their design [7].

In order to address these deficiencies, we develop a prototype system for collecting, analyzing, aggregating, and presenting large volumes of online medical content in a timely manner. The contribution of our work is two-fold. First, we add to the growing body of design science research exploring credibility assessment artifacts in online and offline settings [10, 11]. Additionally, by accounting for many characteristics of Big Data in our design, including volume, velocity, variety, and veracity, our system also contributes to the nascent design science work on IT artifacts for Big Data analytics [12]. Second, we present a novel prototype system (instantiation) in the Health 2.0 domain which incorporates new algorithms (methods) for credibility assessment and efficient real-time omni-channel collection and analysis of online medical content.

2   Design of the Artifact

Based on our extensive interviews with potential users at health and regulatory agencies and industry analysts, assessment of existing systems, and review of the academic literature, we determined the following three critical user requirements for the system.

(1) *Credibility assessment module* – Given the extensiveness of online medical spam, identifying and filtering non-credible content is of paramount importance to users seeking to leverage online medical content as a decision-making aid. Accordingly, the system's credibility assessment module incorporates a link analysis algorithm for determining whether a candidate URL is credible by analyzing its page and site-level hyperlink graphs. Only credible URLs are given further consideration.

(2) *Relevance assessment module* – In light of the abundance of user-generated content encompassing varying opinions and emotions in online Health 2.0 channels, users are increasingly interested in the sentiments pertaining to key topics. For instance,

post-marketing drug surveillance entails examination of negative reaction-related discussion about a particular drug. Hence, the system's relevance assessment module includes topic and sentiment classification, and both topical and sentiment relevance are factored into the collection and analysis process.

(3) *Context assessment module* – Users interviewed noted a lack of diversity in the existing online channels analyzed – with most relying on the CAPHIS 100 websites, a few prominent health-related web forums, and select social networking sites. Effectively capturing multi-channel medical content necessitates the use of "tunneling" methods capable of burrowing through layers of unrelated contents' hyperlinks to get from one cluster of relevant content to another. The context assessment module incorporates a labeled graph comprised of topic, sentiment, and source labels. For instance, a given URL node in the graph may be labeled as social media (source) having positive sentiment about a relevant topic. The module learns key contextual patterns from a training set comprising hundreds of relevant and irrelevant pages manually labeled by domain experts.

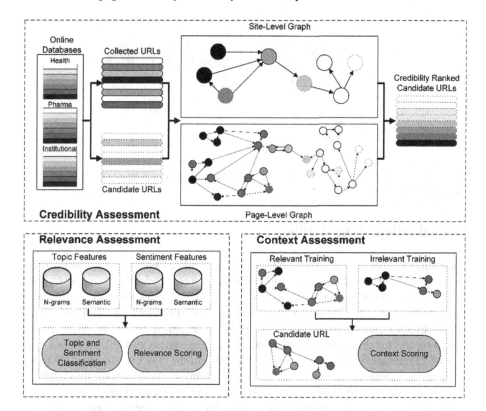

Fig. 1. Overview of system's collection and analysis components

Figure 1 presents an overview of the system's collection and analysis components. During the collection phase, URLs deemed credible are examined by the relevance assessment module. Those deemed relevant are added to the collection queue in descending rank order based on their relevance scores. Those considered irrelevant are assessed using the context module to determine their "tunneling potential" and possible addition to the collection queue. As later discussed, the three modules collectively facilitate more accurate and timely collection of relevant online medical content.

Figure 2 shows screenshots of the system's user interface, where the aggregated results are presented to analysts. The system is extensible such that the front-end can support various use cases related to topics and sentiments present in credible online medical content. The dashboards in Fig. 2 relate to post-marketing drug surveillance. The chart on the right shows aggregated sentiment and mention time series for various pharmaceutical drugs related to adverse drug events. Users can click on various spikes to attain details regarding underlying content, key discussion items, etc. The chart on the left side shows a user dashboard which depicts users' drug-related post frequencies on social media, the influence measured based on content repost rates, sentiment trends over time, and individual drug-related posts with accompanying sentiment labels.

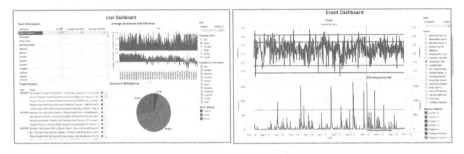

Fig. 2. Screenshots of system's interface depicting aggregated results related to medical topics and sentiments

3   Evaluation of the Artifact

Consistent with design science guidelines, we rigorously evaluated the system using a multi-method approach. First, a series of experiments were conducted on a large test bed encompassing over 40 million pages from websites, forums, blogs, and social networking sites. For the post-marketing drug surveillance use case, the system significantly outperformed several existing topical spiders and focused crawlers in terms of precision, recall, f-measure, and timeliness of the collection. In fact, the system was able to collect over 80 % of all relevant credible content in the first 20 % of the crawl, relative to 40 % recall for the top benchmark methods – underscoring its ability to effectively sift through large volumes of low-veracity, high-velocity content across various online channels. Additional results demonstrated the utility of each module in the collection component of the system: the credibility, relevance, and context assessment modules each significantly contributed to the system's overall performance. Second, we received positive qualitative feedback through preliminary user studies involving ten analysts in public and private sector organizations examining health-related topics and sentiments using the system.

We are also considering conducting a larger user study to analyze the system's effectiveness in supporting decision tasks involving the use of online medical content.

4   Significance of the Artifact to Research and Practice

Our contributions to research include the credibility assessment and context assessment methods, as well as the prototype system which signifies an instantiation of how credibility, context, and relevance can be effectively incorporated in an IT artifact. Our work contributes to the growing body of knowledge on credibility artifacts [10, 11]. By incorporating design guidelines related to Big Data's 4Vs, we also contribute to the emerging literature on Big Data IT artifacts [12]. The practical contributions of our work extend to various practitioner groups, including health and regulatory agencies, pharmaceutical companies, and consumer advocacy groups interested in leveraging such credibility-centric artifacts to inform critical real-time decisions and actions.

Acknowledgements. We would like to thank the U.S. National Science Foundation for their support through grants IIS-1236970, IIS-1236983, IIS-1552860, and IIS-1553109.

References

1. Eysenbach, G.: Medicine 2.0: social networking, collaboration, participation, apomediation, and openness. J. Med. Internet Res. **10**(3), e22 (2008)
2. Adjeroh, D., Beal, R., Abbasi, A., Zheng, W., Abate, M., Ross, A.: Signal fusion for social media analysis of adverse drug events. IEEE Intell. Syst. **29**(2), 74–80 (2014)
3. Abbasi, A., Adjeroh, D.: Social media analytics for smart health. IEEE Intell. Syst. **29**(2), 60–64 (2014)
4. Abbasi, A., Zahedi, F.M., Kaza, S.: Detecting fake medical web sites using recursive trust labeling. ACM Trans. Inf. Syst. **30**(4), 22 (2012)
5. Fu, T., Abbasi, A., Zeng, D., Chen, H.: Sentimental spidering: leveraging opinion information in focused crawlers. ACM Trans. Inf. Syst. **30**(4), 24 (2012)
6. Abbasi, A., Fu, T., Zeng D., Adjeroh, D.: Crawling credible online medical sentiments for social intelligence. In: The ASE/IEEE International Conference on Social Computing, Washington D.C., 8–14 September 2013
7. Fu, T., Abbasi, A., Chen, H.: A focused crawler for dark web forums. J. Am. Soc. Inform. Sci. Technol. **61**(6), 1213–1231 (2010)
8. Tremayne, M., Zheng, N., Lee, J., Jeong, J.: Issue publics on the web: applying network theory to the war blogosphere. J. Comput.-Med. Commun. **12**(1), 290–310 (2006)
9. Fu, T., Abbasi, A., Chen, H.: A hybrid approach to web forum interactional coherence analysis. J. Am. Soc. Inform. Sci. Technol. **59**(8), 1195–1209 (2008)
10. Jensen, M.L., Lowry, P.B., Burgoon, J.K., Nunamaker, J.F.: Technology dominance in complex decision making: the case of aided credibility assessment. J. Manag. Inf. Syst. **27**(1), 175–202 (2010)
11. Jensen, M.L., Averbeck, J.M., Zhang, Z., Wright, K.B.: Credibility of anonymous online product reviews: a language expectancy perspective. J. Manag. Inf. Syst. **30**(1), 293–323 (2013)
12. Abbasi, A., Sarker, S., Chiang, R.H.L.: Big data research in information systems: toward an inclusive research agenda. J. Assoc. Inf. Syst. **17**(2), 3 (2016)

Lost in Antarctica: Designing an Information Literacy Game to Support Motivation and Learning Success

Linda Eckardt[✉] and Susanne Robra-Bissantz

Chair Information Management, Technische Universität Braunschweig,
Braunschweig, Germany
{linda.eckardt,s.robra-bissantz}@tu-braunschweig.de

Abstract. The acquirement of information literacy skills is associated with a number of challenges (e.g. less motivation because often no grades are given). This paper presents a new method for developing information literacy – the gameducation application "Lost in Antarctica". Gameducation describes the integration of game design elements into education and, within that concept, learners have to act as realistic characters in a realistic environment. It uses the beneficial effects of games to positively influence the student's motivation and learning success.

Keywords: GamEducation · Gamification · Education · Information literacy game · Learning success · Motivation

1 Introduction

Information Literacy (IL) describes the ability of a person "to recognize when information is needed and […] to locate, evaluate, and use effectively the needed information" [1]. This skill is increasingly recognized as a key competence in order to be successful at school or work in today's information and knowledge society [2].

Teaching IL to students is associated with a number of challenges. Disagreements about how to learn IL (e.g. self-study, in-class lecture) or the lack of positive assessment for learning these skills are such examples [3–5]. Consequently, maintaining motivation is difficult and learning success is frequently not achieved.

This paper demonstrates a new approach for IL instruction – the GamEducation application "Lost in Antarctica". The research follows the design science process proposed by Peffers et al. [6].

GamEducation is a combination of the words gamification and education. It describes the integration of game design elements within the context of education. Students act as realistic characters in a realistic story [7]. A strong connection between game story and activities during the game play promotes the context for learning [8]. Firstly, the integration of game design elements can encourage the participation and interaction of students, so that an effective and active acquirement of IL skills takes place [9]. Furthermore, motivation, fun and engagement of students can be increased, and thus the learning success can be positively influenced [9].

© Springer International Publishing Switzerland 2016
J. Parsons et al. (Eds.): DESRIST 2016, LNCS 9661, pp. 202–206, 2016.
DOI: 10.1007/978-3-319-39294-3_15

2   Design of the Information Literacy Game

2.1   Differences to Other Information Literacy Games

Game design elements are already being used in different ways to learn IL [9]. Previous applications focus on several aspects of IL (e.g. plagiarism, search strategies) but the instruction of an extensive knowledge is non-existent [10–12]. While most applications encourage competition, collaboration is rarely considered. Indeed, collaboration is integrated among students but mainly outside of the accompanying websites during in-class lectures [13]. Solving tasks together during the process of game play is rare. The applications are too often characterized by repetitive task types (e.g. multiple choice tasks) [12, 14]. Therefore, there is little variety in activities for the students.

This is why "Lost in Antarctica" instructs a fundamentally extensive knowledge about IL. In addition, the background story is strongly connected with the tasks completed during game play, and both collaboration and competition among the students should be supported in the same dimensions.

2.2   Game Design of "Lost in Antarctica"

According to Zichermann and Cunningham, most educational games fail because the learners do not enjoy themselves while playing and learning [15]. During the design of corresponding applications, the focus is on the learning outcome instead of a combination of learning outcome and a gaming experience that is fun [15]. Fullerton emphasizes the importance of the process of testing and an iterative design process. Moreover, the need for an interdisciplinary team with different skills for a game design that is completely thought through is recommended [16]. Therefore, the development of the "Lost in Antarctica" game concept was carried out in several iterative steps in a project course with the target group, students of mechanical engineering. In addition, a graphic designer, a programmer and librarians worked on the project.

"Lost in Antarctica" is a browser game designed as a 'point and click' adventure. In the game, the students act as scientists traveling in teams to a research expedition to the South Pole, but due to a snow storm they have crash-landed. Consequently, in addition to their research they must repair the defective aircraft.

Figure 1 shows six screenshots of the gameducation application. In the beginning of the game students can create their own avatar (screen 1 and 2). The selected career further influences the course of the game and serves as basis to randomly put together the teams. The career choice is based on the area of concentration in the mechanical engineering degree program.

The students are able to move freely within a research station and choose between twelve different levels. The levels are hidden behind doors and represent topics of IL (screen 3). Each level has an identical structure. The students have to follow a checklist (screen 4) and appropriate new knowledge or solve tasks alternately. The knowledge transfer is done based on videos, presentations or stories to scroll down. The associated task types vary. Drag and drop (screen 5), cloze texts, multiple choice questions, tasks where students have to connect lines (screen 6), crossword puzzles, memory games, free

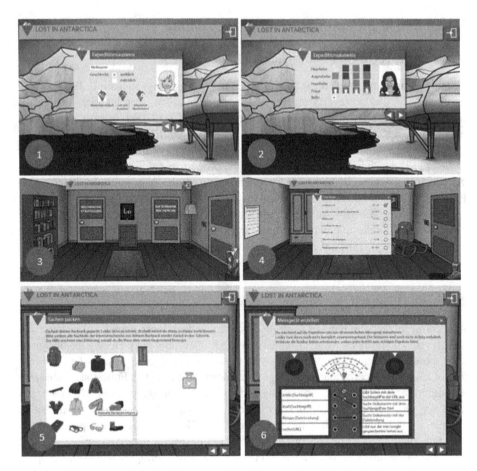

Fig. 1. Screenshots of the information literacy game "Lost in Antarctica"

text tasks and tasks that students have to solve as team, are examples of such tasks. In every level students can gain up to 300 points, but they need only 100 points to progress within the game context. Additional points can be exchanged in mini games (e.g. penguin shooter). The students receive an airplane component for a successful level completion. These components represent the game progress.

3   Significance of "Lost in Antarctica" for Research and Practice

3.1   Significance for Research

The integration of game design elements for gaining IL skills is not totally new but the game design of "Lost in Antarctica" offers new insights into the effects of gameducation through this compilation of game design elements. Answers to the following questions should be found, among others:

- Is the leaner's motivation positively influenced by identification with the game story and the avatar?
- Does a balance between collaboration and competition promote the motivation and the student's learning success?
- Does the strong connection between task types and game story influence the motivation?
- Does gameducation positively influence the learning success?

3.2 Significance to Practice

The game "Lost in Antarctica" offers a new method to students for learning IL skills. Librarians can use the game in order to expand their portfolio for IL instruction, and faculty staff can use it in the field of education in order to better prepare students for scientific writing.

4 Evaluation of "Lost in Antarctica" and Future Research

In order to enhance the gaming experience and ensure that the students have fun while learning with the "Lost in Antarctica" IL game, playtests are initially planned. The playtests are based on Fullerton's ideas and may be followed up with some improvements [16].

The IL game is then introduced within a course. An evaluation is carried out in order to indicate whether motivation and learning success are positively influenced by using the game. Learning success is not an easy aspect to measure and consists of different components (e.g. motivation) [17]. For this reason, different methods for gathering information are used. One possibility for collecting information about motivation and learning success is through game play-based interaction [18]. For example, this objective assessment can record how often a student repeats a task and how many points were received. Another possibility is to use a subjective method for assessment. Obtaining information through dialog-based interaction is an example of such a method [18]. Students have to answer questions that are usually presented as questionnaires or interviews, thereby enabling the collection of information about learner beliefs and thoughts.

References

1. American Library Association: Presidential committee on information literacy: final report. Chicago (1989)
2. Markey, K., Leeder, C., Rieh, S.Y.: Designing Online Information Literacy Games Students Want to Play. Rowman & Littlefield, Maryland (2014)
3. Saunders, L.: Faculty perspectives on information literacy as a student learning outcome. J. Acad. Librarianship **38**(4), 226–236 (2012)
4. McGuinness, C.: What faculty think: exploring the barriers to information literacy development in undergraduate education. J. Acad. Librarianship **32**(6), 573–582 (2006)

5. Markey, K., Swanson, F., Jenkins, A., Jennings, B.J., Jean, B., Rosenberg, V., Yao, X., Frost, R.L.: The effectiveness of a web-based board game for teaching undergraduate students information literacy concepts and skills. D-Lib Mag. **14**(9/10), 1082–9873 (2008)

6. Peffers, K., Tuunanen, T., Rothenberger, M.A., Chatterjee, S.: A design science research methodology for information systems research. J. Manag. Inf. Syst. **24**(3), 45–77 (2007)

7. Eckardt, L., Huttner, J.P., Robra-Bissantz, S.: GamEducation in einer virtuellen 3D-Umgebung mit Googles virtual-reality-brille cardboard. In: GI-Jahrestagung 2015, pp. 1295–1306 (2015)

8. Broussard, M.J.: Digital games in academic libraries: a review of games and suggested best practices. Ref. Serv. Rev. **40**(1), 75–89 (2012)

9. Branston, C.: From game studies to bibliographic gaming: libraries tap into the video game culture. Bull. Am. Soc. Inf. Sci. Technol. **32**(4), 24–26 (2006)

10. Sittler, R.L., Sherman, C., Kepperl, D.P., Schaeffer, C.E., Hackley, D.C., Grosik, L.A.: A planet in peril: plagiaris: using digital games to teach information literacy skills. In: McDevitt, T.R. (ed.) Let the Games Begin! Engaging Students with Field-Tested Interactive Information Literacy Instruction, pp. 134–137. Neal-Schuman Publishers, New York (2011)

11. Baker, B., Shanley, C., Wilkinson, L.: Nightmare on vine street: librarians, zombies, and information literacy. In: McDevitt, T.R. (ed.) Let the Games Begin! Engaging Students with Field-Tested Interactive Information Literacy Instruction, pp. 30–31. Neal-Schuman Publishers, New York (2011)

12. Rice, S.: Education on a shoestring: creating an online information literacy game. In: Harris, A., Rice, S. (eds.) Gaming in Academic Libraries: Collections, Marketing and Information Literacy, pp. 175–188. Association of College and Research Libraries, Chicago (2008)

13. Knautz, K., Soubusta, S.: Aufbruch nach Zyren: Game-based Learning in der Hochschullehre. Universitätsbibliothek Hildesheim, Hildesheim (2013)

14. Broussard, M.J.: Secret agents in the library: integrating virtual and physical games in a small academic library. Coll. Undergraduate Libr. **17**(1), 20–30 (2010)

15. Zichermann, G., Cunningham, C.: Gamification by Design: Implementing Game Mechanics in Web and Mobile Apps. O'Reilly, Köln (2011)

16. Fullerton, T.: Game Design Workshop: A Playcentric Approach to Creating Innovative Games. Taylor & Francis, Boca Raton (2014)

17. Mager, R.F., Küper, B., Schweim, L., Speichert, H.: Motivation und Lernerfolg: Wie Lehrer ihren Unterricht verbessern können. Beltz, Weinheim (1972)

18. Ghergulescu, I., Muntean, C.H.: measurement and analysis of leaner's motivation in game-based e-learning. In: Ifenthaler, D., Eseryel, D., Ge, X. (eds.) Assessment in Game-Based Learning. Springer, New York (2012)

Interactive Dynamic Learning Environment (IDLE)

Belinda Gibbons[✉], Karlheinz Kautz, Mario Fernando, and Trevor Spedding

Faculty of Business, University of Wollongong, Wollongong, Australia
{bgibbons,kautz,mariof,spedding}@uow.edu.au

Abstract. The global business community requires graduates with skills and capabilities to cope with real-world interdisciplinary problems. Two key issues frequently noted are the silo disciplinary focus and the lack of exposure to responsible decision-making (RDM). IDLE (Interactive Dynamic Learning Environment) is a web-based computer simulated enterprise delivered through a systems approach broadening students' understanding of the interrelationship between corporations, society and the environment. Engagement in IDLE develops students' understanding and application of corporate social responsibility (CSR) and sustainability through the identification of business interdependencies. In IDLE, integrating systems dynamics with agile dynamic system development methods enabled the intricate multifaceted relationships of organisational decision-making that includes CSR and sustainability interrelationships to be explored. The resulting unique design ensures real organisation decision-making dynamics, while not being so complex that the interrelationships were overlooked during student engagement.

Keywords: Responsible decision-making · Systems dynamics methodology · Dynamics systems development methodology · Simulation · Business higher education

1 Introduction

Academic and practitioner literature express serious concerns about the current approach to business higher education in developing an understanding of organisation interdependencies and responsible decision-making attributes. Understanding and being able to consider these interrelationships in decision-making is significant in order to cultivate holistic thinking business graduates. Unfortunately many current teaching approaches to business higher education are strictly discipline-based and fail to develop and organise knowledge in a way that is useful to practicing managers [1]. IDLE provides a technologically-rich simulated learning environment where students experience the intricacies and interactions of business decisions, the environment and society within an organisational framework.

IDLE is experienced by over 1500 business higher education students annually and has been adopted by a number of tertiary and secondary education programs. Designed around the manufacturing industry, multidisciplinary teams of business students compete across a performance matrix which includes profit, environmental impact, sustainability, social innovation and quality of service. Students describe the simulated

© Springer International Publishing Switzerland 2016
J. Parsons et al. (Eds.): DESRIST 2016, LNCS 9661, pp. 207–211, 2016.
DOI: 10.1007/978-3-319-39294-3_16

learning environment in a positive way; "I think the best thing about the simulation is that it reflects the nature of the 21st century business world. The interactive dynamic learning environment reflects the complexity of modern business from which I now have a better understanding of company operations. I can apply theory to practice through the simulation" (Student Reflection 2011).

2 Design

2.1 Goals

The goal of IDLE is to develop responsible decision-making skills in future leaders by anchoring corporate social responsibility and sustainability decision-making in the strategy and activities that arise during the running of a web-based computer simulated enterprise (IDLE) within facilitated laboratory curricula. Integrating knowledge across disciplines, this innovative approach aims to broaden students' understanding of the interrelationship between corporations, society and the environment with multidisciplinary teams running an online simulated manufacturing enterprise for a period of several weeks. The students work at their own pace during a laboratory session, discussing ideas amongst one another, trying a range of decision-making options, evaluating consequences, seeking mentor assistance when required and enjoying learner-learner collaboration. Inbuilt videos and comprehensive scenarios designed around an evolution of timed events, from the present to four years into the future allows business students engaging in the simulation to achieve a more realistic feel for the organisation they are managing. These information and communication technological resources ensure the student's learning environment is practice-based and hands-on.

2.2 Scenarios

The dynamic relationships built into the design of IDLE allow the interdependencies that exist in responsible decision-making to be experienced by those engaging in the simulation. The scenarios deliver the model in a way that provides a realistic feel for the simulated manufacturing organisation they are managing.

To achieve the outcomes, the scenarios chosen during the design stage had to allow for the uncertainties that underlie the different decision-making areas to be experienced while considering various options and possibilities.

The scenarios were designed and developed around the topic area of the United Nations Global Compact [2] principles of human rights, labour standards, environment and anti-corruption. Designing and developing the scenarios around the UN Global Compact [2] principles allowed the simulation to demonstrate complex societal forces at work within an organisation. An example of this is under the environment topic area. Figure 1 visually represents the e-Waste management decision areas in IDLE. Students are required to evaluate the cost of implementing a waste management strategy for their business versus possible penalties and non-efficiencies for noncompliance and adverse publicity.

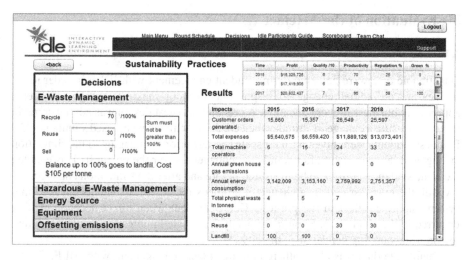

Fig. 1. e-Waste management decision screen

2.3 Users

IDLE is predominately engaged by business higher education students at UOW Australia, Singapore and Malaysia. It has been piloted for use at the University of Western Australia and Monash University, Melbourne. IDLE has also been engaged by high school students, post-graduate students and industry personnel during verification and validation.

2.4 Design Process

Designing and constructing IDLE required a fusion between simplicity and elaboration. The key objective was to develop a simulation based on a simplified abstraction of a system that retained the key elements of organisation dynamics without unduly complicating the learning environment. In order to identify and portray these dynamics, Systems Dynamics methodology [3] was integrated with an agile Dynamic Systems Development method [4]. Integrating the methods enabled:

- The exploration of the intricate multifaceted relationships of organisational decision-making that includes CSR and sustainability interrelationships;
- The creation of dynamic models that represent the behaviour of the interrelationships overtime;
- Verification and validation of the dynamic models by students and industry representatives;
- The creation of a web-based user interface to allow scenario interaction during decision-making to be accessed by a large number of students; and
- The evaluation of a web-based computer simulation in business higher education.

3   Evaluation of the Artefact

3.1   Lab Study

Quantifiable data were gathered during student engagement with IDLE in order to try to measure attitudinal change to responsible decision-making through a systems approach to business higher education. A pre- and post-test design was administered in order to measure a change in attitude when engaging with the web-based simulation [5]. Business students were given a Likert scale pre-test prior to engaging in the simulation and again five weeks later after simulation engagement for the post-test. This enabled the same student's attitude to be measured before and after the simulation engagement. Overall, the post-test reveals a change of attitudes for business students engaged in a systems approach than in the pre-test. This is evident when direct decision-making occurred in the simulation. Exploratory analysis revealed interesting results for future research surrounding gender and ethnicity.

Qualitative data was also gathered during student engagement with IDLE. Observations revealed learning through systems simulation to be engaging, thought provoking, challenging, stimulating and enjoyable. To support the quantitative and observation findings, qualitative business student reflections after the web-based simulation engagement were also collected and analysed. Key themes were collated into three overarching concepts which together characterised the positive evaluation: First a unique learning experience, second an interdisciplinary learning environment and finally a collaborative engagement. Experience, environment and engagement combined to an overarching theme that resulted from providing a systems approach to learning.

4   Significance to Research

The study findings have theoretical implications for simulation design and development. These include:

- Simulation design – Multiple Identification Theory (MIT) [6] conclude that simulations can foster attitudinal change by adopting affective, cognitive and behavioural identification design dimensions. This research supports MIT simulation principles but also reveals the importance of the experience, the learning environment and direct simulation engagement when designing a simulation for attitudinal change.
- Simulation development – Integrating Systems Dynamic methodology with an agile Dynamic Systems Development method revealed the interdependencies between system dynamics (SD) [3] and agile software development activities [4]. The construction of IDLE required the understanding of nonlinear behaviours that occur between a business, the environment and society. System dynamics provided a method for framing and understanding these complex dynamic interrelationships. IDLE development also required a user-interface for application in the classroom. Agile software development processes allowed the dynamic models to evolve through early delivery and continuous improvement into a software product for use

in business higher education. This study supports further research integrating SD into the software development cycle.

5   Significance to Practice

Applying a systems approach to responsible decision making in undergraduate business education has many potential implications to practice. These include:

- Enhancing curriculum design — the availability of a unique web-based systems simulation model provides an experiential learning experience that can be integrated into existing or new curriculum. This engaging learning approach can be used to improve curriculum design in undergraduate business education.
- Systems approach application — the dynamic model that underlies the calculations and interdependencies in IDLE can be used as the basis for understanding complex responsible decision-making interrelationships in other sectors such as service, mining, transportation, agriculture and government. The implications of this are significant in ensuring responsible decision making is applied on a global scale.

6   Link to Implementation

Please refer to associated video 'Products & Prototypes Submission IDLE', https://youtu.be/pNNDZcln6Ug.

References

1. ABDC (Australian Business Deans' Council): The Future of Management Education, Australian Government, Department of Industry, NSW, Australia (2014)
2. UNGC (United Nations Global Compact): Architects of a Better World, Accenture CEO Study on Sustainability (2013). http://www.accenture.com/SiteCollectionDocuments/PDF/Accenture-UN-Global-Compact-Acn-CEO-Study-Sustainability-2013.PDF. Accessed 20 Oct 2013
3. Maani, K.E., Cavana, R.Y.: Systems Thinking, System Dynamics: Managing Change and Complexity, 2nd edn. Pearson Education New Zealand, North Shore, New Zealand (2007)
4. DSDM 2014, DSDM Consortium: Driving Strategy Delivery More (2014). http://www.dsdm.org/. Accessed 30 April 2011
5. Kumar, R.: Research Methodology: A Step-By-Step Guide for Beginners. Addison Wesley Longman Australia, Melbourne (1997)
6. Williams, A., Williams, R.: Multiple identification theory: attitude and behavior change in a simulated international conflict. Simul. Gaming 42(6), 733–744 (2007)

TheoryOn: Designing a Construct-Based Search Engine to Reduce Information Overload for Behavioral Science Research

Jingjing Li[1(✉)], Kai R. Larsen[2], and Ahmed Abbasi[1]

[1] McIntire School of Commerce, University of Virginia, Charlottesville, VA 22904, USA
{Jingjing.Li,Abbasi}@comm.virginia.edu
[2] Leeds School of Business, University of Colorado at Boulder, Boulder, CO 80309, USA
Kai.Larsen@colorado.edu

Abstract. The accumulated literature base in the behavioral sciences represents a great source of knowledge on human behaviors, and yet the same literature has grown beyond human comprehension. We address this information overload problem by proposing a novel IT artifact – TheoryOn. Based on the design science paradigm, we identify five design requirements. We first adapt the ontology learning layer cake framework to develop a four-step process – hypothesis extraction, construct extraction, construct relationship extraction and theory extraction – to automatically extract integral "parts" of behavioral theories. We then design four functionalities allowing researchers to quickly access synonymous constructs, construct relationships and theoretically related constructs (e.g. antecedents and consequents), as well as integrate related theories. To illustrate the applicability and usefulness, we use a dataset of all the relevant behavioral studies from three top journals in Information Systems and Psychology and conduct an A/B test between the prototype TheoryOn system and the EBSCOhost full-text search engine.

Keywords: Ontology learning from text · Theories · Constructs · Theoretical models · Behavioral science research

1 Introduction

The IS field and every other behavioral discipline continually search for and reify concepts designed to improve disciplinary understanding of key phenomena. As a field, IS has been extraordinarily successful with many models or theories that enjoy tens of thousands of extensions and citations. However, it is also widely accepted that the rich academic literature on human behavior has become expansive to the point of incognizance, bringing with it information overload in theory development and testing [1]. Academics are unable to track and use behavioral knowledge, even within a relatively narrow domain such as information systems adoption.

Existing IT artifacts, such as Google Scholar and EBSCOhost, are ineffective in addressing this information overload problem. One reason is that they operate at the article level and do not extract theory-relevant meta-data inside articles. As a result, they

© Springer International Publishing Switzerland 2016
J. Parsons et al. (Eds.): DESRIST 2016, LNCS 9661, pp. 212–216, 2016.
DOI: 10.1007/978-3-319-39294-3_17

cannot distinguish between *ease of use*, the behavioral construct, and *ease of use*, the loosely used phrase; a search for the construct "ease of use" at Google Scholar will result in 410,000 articles (as of 3/5/2016). Furthermore, the focus on relationships in much of contemporary behavioral research reveals the second weakness of these types of search engines: it is not possible to specify a search for any paper positing a relationship between construct X and construct Y or find antecedents and consequents for a construct X. Finally, existing search engines are based on exact keyword matching, thereby rendering them incapable of returning a construct that refers to the same latent variable but uses different words from a search query, e.g. returning the construct *performance expectancy* for the query *perceived usefulness*.

Following in the same vein as recent text mining-based design artifacts [2, 3], this article proposes an IT artifact to alleviate the information overload problem in parts of the behavioral sciences. Following the design science paradigm [4, 5], we design and develop an academic support IT artifact – TheoryOn – to extract constructs, construct relationships, and theories from a set of published papers. With the extracted theory parts, TheoryOn allows researchers to directly search for synonymous constructs, construct relationships and statistically related constructs (antecedents or consequents), and finally, integrate related theories through synonymous constructs.

2   Design of the Artifact

A review of information overload research identified five categories of causes for information overload, two of which we believe are particularly relevant to the current state of IS theory research: information characteristics, and task and process parameters [6]. Particularly, information characteristics entail increases in the number, diversity and ambiguity of constructs, construct relationships, theories, and articles in behavioral research. Task and process parameters manifest in the complex process to identify relevant literature, related constructs, and their relationships when conducting behavioral science research.

In light of these two causes, and following Hevner et al.'s (2004) design principles, we interviewed several IS behavioral researchers and identified five design requirements:

1. It should distinguish the theory "parts"—which, as defined in Weber (2012), consist of constructs and their relationships in behavioral theories—from other initially irrelevant texts in papers.
2. It should identify synonymous constructs. We define a construct, C', to be synonymous with another construct, C, if some construct measurement items for C' could also be used to measure the latent variable referred to or connoted by C. This allows researchers to build a comprehensive collection of related literature.
3. It should enable construct-pair search (e.g., return only articles containing those two constructs). This functionality is important to understand the research context, related literature, and variables for a construct relationship of interest.
4. It should allow searching of statistically related constructs. We define a construct, C', to be statistically related to another construct, C, if they both appear in the same

hypothesized theoretical model, e.g., antecedents and consequents of a construct of interest. This functionality is useful when researchers need to identify control, moderating and mediating variables related to a construct of interest as well as find its role in a larger theoretical network.

5. It should facilitate theory integration. Theory integration is achieved by clustering synonymous constructs shared by different theories. Such integration is useful for nomological network construction [7, 8] and meta-analysis.

We then implement the prototype according to the presented requirements (see Fig. 1). We also provide links to a more detailed video demonstration of the system.

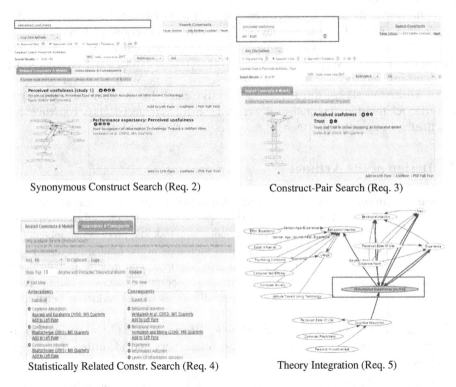

Synonymous Construct Search (Req. 2)   Construct-Pair Search (Req. 3)

Statistically Related Constr. Search (Req. 4)   Theory Integration (Req. 5)

Fig. 1. Screenshots of TheoryOn's four major functionalities (Color figure online)

Requirement 1. We restrict our focus to behavioral positivist research, which generally is variance-focused and quantitative in nature. However, the IT artifact should in the future be extendable to positivist case studies, interpretive studies, or process studies as well as other approaches.

We first identified two embedding patterns of behavioral theories in behavioral positivist research articles. First, an article testing a quantitative positivist behavioral theory usually presents its theory through hypotheses. Second, a hypothesis usually includes a statement describing the relationships between constructs and variables, thereby representing a link connecting two or more nodes in the theoretical model.

We then adapted the ontology learning layer cake framework [9] to identify suitable extraction methods, i.e. the natural language processing techniques, and machine learning models. We further designed a four-step process to extract integral "parts" of behavioral theories (extraction methods denoted in parentheses): hypothesis extraction (rule-based learning), construct extraction (conditional random fields), construct relationship extraction (tree-kernel support vector machine) and theory extraction (latent semantic analysis and network visualization).

Requirement 2. Once the theory parts have been successfully extracted, TheoryOn allows searches of articles containing a construct exact matching or synonymous with a search query. Users can also save the related constructs and articles in a sorting hierarchy. For more details, watch the video "TheoryOn: Synonymous Construct Search".

Requirement 3. TheoryOn allows construct-pair search on the extracted construct relationships. The constructs and their relationships are shown in the extracted theoretical models in the left part of the search results. For more details, watch the video "TheoryOn: Construct-Pair Search".

Requirement 4. A user should see not only the theoretical models related to the search query (highlighted in yellow) but also the list and network visualization of antecedents and consequents by exploring the "Antecedents & Consequents" tab. For more details, watch the video "TheoryOn: Theoretically Related Construct Search".

Requirement 5. All the related theories can be saved in the sorting hierarchy and visualized on the canvas. A user can then integrate theories by clustering synonymous constructs or customize the theoretical networks by editing, deleting or adding any nodes and links. For more details, watch the video "TheoryOn: Theory Integration".

3   Evaluation of the Artifact

To demonstrate and evaluate TheoryOn, we used articles that contained at least one construct from MIS Quarterly (MISQ), Information Systems Research (ISR) and Journal of Applied Psychology (JAP) in the period of 1990 to 2009. Regarding requirement 1, we adopted the standard information extraction metrics – Precision, Recall and F-measure to compare our automatic methods with human-annotated datasets. The F-measures for all the steps range from 74 % to 92 %, suggesting promising results. Regarding requirement 2 to 5, we designed four closely related tasks and will conduct an A/B test between TheoryOn and a state-of-the-art search engine – EBSCOhost – using an experiment user pool encompassing behavioral researchers. In addition to comparing the precision, recall and F-measures between these two systems, we plan to use several fitness-utility metrics following [10].

4   Significance of Research and Practice

TheoryOn alleviates information overload facing behavioral research by addressing two key causes: information characteristics, and task and process parameters. Particularly, TheoryOn addresses the information characteristics by effectively retrieving theory parts from large sets of articles so that researchers can quickly access the theory-relevant parts of articles without having to read all the paper contents. For task and process parameters, TheoryOn provides four major functionalities to standardize and streamline the four routine tasks facing behavioral researchers.

With quicker access to a more comprehensive set of behavioral constructs and relationships, TheoryOn users can conduct a more thorough literature review to guide their research process, potentially leading to higher research quality and rigor. With the ability to "glue" related theories through synonymous constructs, TheoryOn can help researchers to discover research gaps consisting of several untested theoretical relationships across studies, domains or even disciplines, thus encouraging innovation and promoting research progress.

Our work also has practical significance. By providing our ontology learning toolkit and domain-specific design guidelines, TheoryOn can significantly address gaps pervasive in existing academic search engines such as Google Scholar and EBSCOhost to improve their design for behavioral research area.

References

1. Weber, R.: Evaluating and developing theories in the information systems discipline. J. Assoc. Inf. Syst. **13**(1), 1–30 (2012)
2. Abbasi, A., Chen, H.: CyberGate: a design framework and system for text analysis of computer mediated communication. MIS Q. **32**(4), 811–837 (2008)
3. Lau, R.Y., Liao, S.S., Wong, K.F., Chiu, D.K.: Web 2.0 environmental scanning and adaptive decision support for business mergers and acquisitions. MIS Q. **36**(4), 1239–1268 (2008)
4. Hevner, A., March, S., Park, J., Ram, S.: Design science research in information systems. Manag. Inf. Syst. Q. **28**(1), 75–105 (2004)
5. Gregor, S., Hevner, A.: Positioning and presenting design science research for maximum impact. Manag. Inf. Syst. Q. **37**(2), 337–355 (2013)
6. Eppler, M.J., Mengis, J.: The concept of information overload: a review of literature from organization science, accounting, marketing, MIS, and related disciplines. Inf. Soc. **20**(5), 325–344 (2004)
7. Cronbach, L.J., Meehl, P.E.: Construct validity in psychological tests. Psychol. Bull. **52**(4), 281–302 (1955)
8. Lee, Y., Kenneth, A.K., Larsen, K.: The technology acceptance model: past, present, and future. Commun. AIS **12**(1), 50 (2003)
9. Buitelaar, P., Philipp, C., Bernardo, M.: Ontology Learning from Text: Methods, Evaluation and Applications, vol. 123. IOS Press, Amsterdam (2005)
10. Gill, T., Hevner, A.: A fitness-utility model for design science research. ACM Trans. Manag. Inf. Syst. **4**(2), 5 (2013)

Designing a Competence Management System 'Knome' for a Knowledge-Intensive Project Organization

Erkka Niemi[⊠] and Sami Laine

Aalto University, Espoo, Finland
{erkka.niemi,sami.k.laine}@aalto.fi

Abstract. Knome is a Competence Management System (CMS) developed during a 33-month long Action Design Research (ADR) program in a knowledge-intensive project organization. It can be used to match customer demand with the present and future competences and interests of the employees. The artifact contains data on every employee of the case organization and most of the information is transparently open to all employees. The ADR program will result in scientific contribution with the generalized design principles of a CMS.

Keywords: Competence management system · Action design research · Design principles · Knowledge management · Enterprise system

1 Introduction

The importance of knowledge-intensive organizations increases constantly. They form an essential part of the service sector, which is already the sector that is the biggest employer in the world economy. For service organizations, it is essential to match customer demand with the competences of the employees and to improve competence management with the help of enterprise systems (ES). There exists a lot of research on ES and knowledge management but only a limited amount of research on Competence Management Systems (CMSs). Particularly, there is a need to study how to design, implement, and deploy such technology in a real business environment. The authors published a literature review and presented the initial contributions of an Action Design Research (ADR) program in another paper [5].

This paper extends existing CMS research by describing the ES artifact, 'Knome,' designed in a 33-month long ADR program [8]. During the program we utilized CMS design principles [4] and complemented them with the hedgehog concept [1].

2 Design of the Artifact

The case organization Siili Solutions PLC (Siili) conducted an R&D initiative to improve competence management between October 2013 and June 2016. Siili employs over 400 persons, its annual sales revenue amounts to over €40 M (+ 42 % in 2015) and it operates in Finland, Germany, and Poland. During the CMS development program, there have been three major organizational changes and four major releases of the CMS. The service

© Springer International Publishing Switzerland 2016
J. Parsons et al. (Eds.): DESRIST 2016, LNCS 9661, pp. 217–222, 2016.
DOI: 10.1007/978-3-319-39294-3_18

vision for Siili's CMS is founded on the hedgehog concept [1] —the company should focus on the intersection of what it can be best at in the world (competence), how its economics work best (customer demand), and what most interests its employees (passion).

Siili has many ES supporting its main business capabilities: customer relationship management, resource management and invoicing, document and content management, communications, master data management, and data warehouse and business intelligence. However, in 2013, there was still no formal framework or process for competence management. The ES development program was initiated to systematize competence management and to support service-offering design. The resulting enterprise-wide CMS would be made accessible to all employees.

The main data entities in Knome are employees, competence-based tribes (15–20 employees each), customers, projects, and partners. These master data entities are enriched with many categorizations and linked with competence data, following typology: competence-in-stock, competence-in-use, and competence-in-the-making [4].

There are three main features of Knome: (1) edit: profile data (2) search: person, competence (3) report: competences, tribes. Authentication is done with Active Directory for internal users and with LinkedIn for external users. KnoMe is integrated with a resource management system and data warehouse.

The design followed lean development principles (DevOps, CI, TDD) and was managed in the Trello Kanban board with Flowdock collaboration, Gitlab version control, and testing in Jenkins. The software development utilized CoachDB and ElasticSearch for the database layer, Node.js and REST for the application layer, and Angular.js for the user interface. The development infrastructure was implemented using Amazon's cloud (AWS) with an automated Chef environment. Knome is fully responsive and scales automatically for all common devices, including web and mobile.

Realization of the Service Vision

Competence data is stored as profiles of every individual employee, recruit, and many partners (see Fig. 1). The profile includes, for example, personal details, certificates, training, and, most importantly, methodology and technological skills.

Customer demand data covers all historical and ongoing customer and internal projects (see Fig. 2). The data includes a description of each customer as well as ongoing and implemented projects. The projects are linked with each participating employee including his/her role in the project as well as the required technological skills.

Passion data is implemented on profiles by providing each employee with the possibility to rate each unique skill on two scales: *skill level* and *interest to use it* (see Fig. 3). These ratings are used to generate many reports and visualizations, such as skill clouds on both tribe and company levels (see Fig. 3).

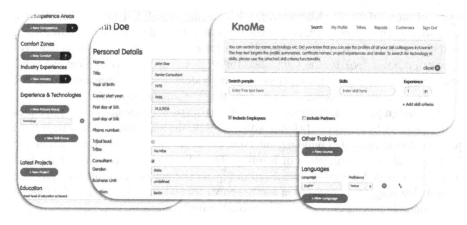

Fig. 1. Competence: Profile content screenshots.

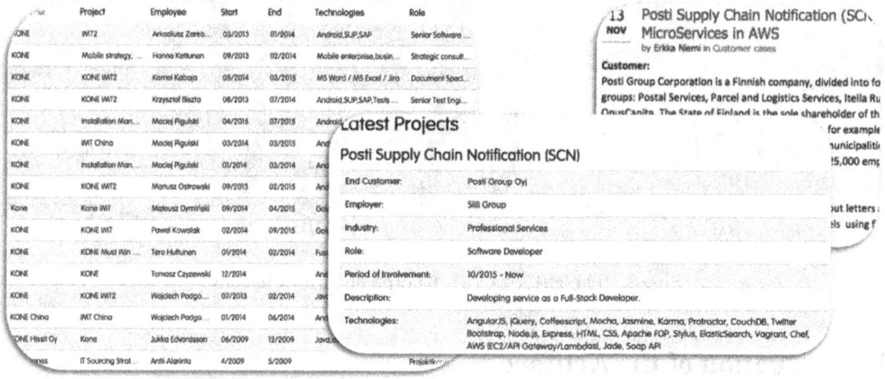

Fig. 2. Demand: ongoing and historical customer and internal projects.

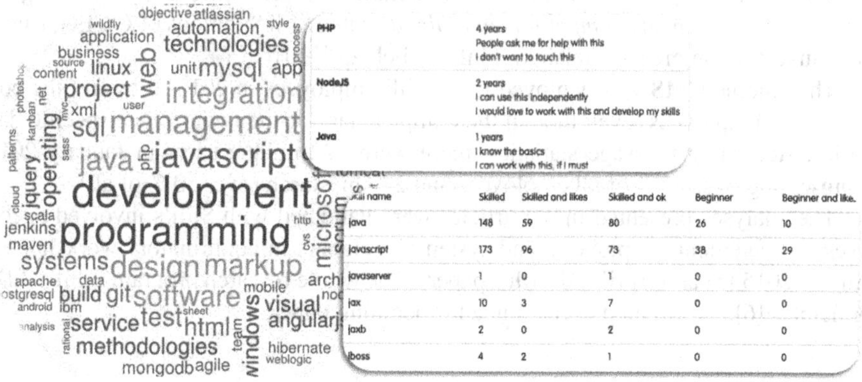

Fig. 3. Passion: skills clouds derived from skill ratings on employee profiles.

Usage of the artifact. The Knome artifact is accessible for all Siili employees, recruits, and partners. There they can manage their own competence data and to find information on their colleagues. There are many use cases for Knome: sales and business management can use it to look for the right talent for projects; service development and tribal leads can plan and manage competences on individual tribe and company levels; HR administration and development can manage the recruitment process.

The design process follows the ADR method [6] and implemented design principles introduced by Lindgren et al. [4]. According to ADR, design consists of four stages: (1) problem formulation, (2) building, intervention, evaluation (BIE), (3) reflection and learning, and (4) formalization of learning. The BIE stage—here including the four major releases of Knome—is visualized in Fig. 4. The authors described the problem formulation stage in more detail in another paper [5] and the BIE and formalization of the learning in this paper, as well as in two other forthcoming papers.

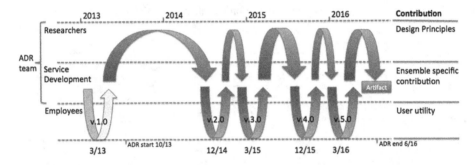

Fig. 4. The BIE of CMS Knome at Siili Solutions.

3   Evaluation of the Artifact

'The competence management system we have implemented increases the utilization of our experts and improves our forecasting capabilities. According to my knowledge, it is the best system among competitors in Finland' stated Siili Solutions PLC CEO, Kuula, at an investor conference, Helsinki, Finland, Feb 25th, 2016.

The Knome CMS was deployed to all Siili employees in 2013. It covers the core data of all employees, even though the completeness of the competence-specific data varies. According to usage statistics, there were 122 unique users in January 2016, representing over 30 % of all employees and 239 in March (over 50 % of all).

The analyses presented in our articles were validated with Siili's involved executives, management, employees, and system developers in confirmatory workshops in August 2015 [5] and April 2016 (this paper). The whole research program fulfills ADR principles [6], as will be presented in a forthcoming paper.

4 Significance to Research and Practice

Scientific significance. Hevner [2] argues that design science research differs from routine system design by clearly identifying the scientific contribution. Kasanen et al. [3] introduced the concept of market-based validation for constructive research. Our research fulfills the criteria of a 'weak market test,' because one company has applied this design and found it useful in a real business environment. Sein et al. [6] argue that ADR research should result in publishing design principles (DP). Lindgren et al. [4] introduced CMS DPs in 2004, but apart from their own research the principles have not been rigorously tested in another scientific research and real business environment. In this research we have utilized the DPs of Lindgren et al. [4] and propose improvements to them by adding the customer demand point of view.

Practical significance. This is practice-inspired research resulting in a theory-ingrained artifact [6]. The case organization needed a CMS and has deployed the Knome artifact to all its employees, investing over €2 M in the program with four major releases and three organizational changes. During the program the case organization has grown from €18 M to €42 M in annual revenue and the stock market value has increased by 243 %, which could at least partly be the result of this program. The contributions published in this and other papers can be useful to other knowledge-intensive organizations willing to implement a CMS.

5 Conclusions

This research provides new knowledge regarding CMS design principles by implementing an ES artifact in a real business environment during 33 months, from 2013 to 2016. The resulting data governance organization, as well our proposal for improved design principles, will be published in other publications. In the future, it would be interesting to study the wider adaption of the designed artifact and improved principles in other knowledge-intensive organizations.

Acknowledgments. We would like to thank all the employees in Siili Solutions for giving their time and sharing their ideas and experiences with us. This study was funded by the Academy of Finland (grant number 259454).

Material. Knome can be accessed from https://knome.siilicloud.com/ and Siili Solutions PLC's website from http://www.siili.com. Please note that external users (partners and recruits) can only edit their own personal profiles, but employees can see the rest of the features and reports.

References

1. Collins, C.: Level 5 leadership: The triumph of humility and fierce resolve. Harvard Bus. Rev. **83**(7/8), 136–146 (2001)
2. Hevner, A.R., March, S.T., Park, J., Ram, S.: Design science in systems research. MIS Q. **28**(1), 75–105 (2004)

3. Kasanen, E., Lukka, K., Siitonen, A.: The constructive approach in management accounting research. J. Manag. Acc. Res. **5**, 243 (1993)

4. Lindgren, R., Henfridsson, O., Schultze, U.: Design principles for competence management systems: a synthesis of an action research study. MIS Q. **28**(3), 435–472 (2004)

5. Niemi, E., Laine, S.: Competence management as a dynamic capability: a strategic enterprise system for a knowledge-intensive project organization. In: Hawaii International Conference on System Sciences (HICSS-49), USA (2016)

6. Sein, M., Henfridsson, O., Purao, S., Rossi, M., Lindgren, R.: Action design research. MIS Q. **35**(2), 37–56 (2011)

Communication Platform for Disaster Response

Mihoko Sakurai[✉]

University of Agder, Kristiansand, Norway
mihoko.sakurai@uia.no

Abstract. The present research proposes an information platform for enhanced communication and information sharing in municipalities struck by disasters. Once a disaster happens, collecting and sharing information with and among citizens is the most important tasks for municipalities. However, empirical research of the Great East Japan Earthquake in 2011 revealed a marked lack of tools supporting municipal communication and data sharing activities at the initial stage. A smartphone and tablet based application was subsequently developed and evaluated in the field as a means of first response in future disasters. The application is based on the notion of frugality, which proved to be very useful in the field drill. Frugality is shown to be a requirement of the system as well as an evaluation indicator.

Keywords: Disaster management · Communication · Frugal information system

1 Introduction

The largest earthquake on record struck Japan on March 11, 2011. The movement of tectonic plates along the Pacific Rim created a rupture zone 500 km long. Measuring 9.0 on the Richter scale, the earthquake produced a tsunami of 40 m hitting the coastline and devastating cities and towns. The earthquake was named the Great East Japan Earthquake. The Fire and Disaster management Agency reported 19,335 deaths, 6,219 injuries and 2,600 missing as of September 2015. It also reported 124,690 houses totally lost and more than 1,000,000 partially destroyed. This earthquake was unique in that it caused severe damage to a very wide area, above all due to a massive tsunami beyond any prior assumptions.

All business operations including public organizations were suspended and remained so for some time in areas directly affected by the earthquake and tsunami. In some areas power supply and connectivity were completely lost at the most critical life saving phase immediately after the earthquake. In those areas people were instantly faced with a situation they had never experienced and which had never been anticipated in any disaster management plan.

Constrained by a severely degraded information and communication technology (ICT) environment, local authorities in the most damaged areas had to conduct five critical life-saving missions following the disaster, namely (1) confirming the whereabouts and safety of residents, (2) establishing and operating evacuation centers, (3) transporting and managing relief goods, (4) supporting evacuees and recording their

© Springer International Publishing Switzerland 2016
J. Parsons et al. (Eds.): DESRIST 2016, LNCS 9661, pp. 223–227, 2016.
DOI: 10.1007/978-3-319-39294-3_19

status, and (5) issuing disaster victim certificates. To conduct these operations smoothly, information sharing among relief staff is important. Due to ICT failure and lack of supportive tools, however, information sharing among municipal offices was mostly done with pencil and paper, which made it quite difficult to share information readily.

The most intricate job that information department personnel had to undertake immediately following the earthquake was to prepare a list of evacuees and confirm the names of survivors. In some towns, more than hundreds of people evacuated to gymnasiums of elementary schools and community centers. Relatives of evacuees simultaneously ran to these places to find their families or friends. A message board with evacuee names was set up at each evacuation center, which helped to find dislocated people. Collecting evacuee names and writing them down on the message board was a labor-intensive task that turned out to be a severe burden on information department personnel.

2   Design of the Artifact

The present study has the purpose of designing a communication platform that can be used for information sharing between local authorities, i.e., staff at municipal governments, and citizens. In earlier research this author has shown that in a disaster situation simple tools have an increased likelihood of readiness and ease of use than other more complex devices [1]. Whereas other studies insist on the importance of exploiting existing infrastructure when designing a communication platform [2], the approach suggested here minimizes the adoption barrier for the user and lowers implementation cost [3].

In addition to these findings, design principles of the artifact employ the notion of a frugal information system [4]. The frugal information system is defined as an information system that is developed and deployed with minimum resources to meet the preeminent goal of the client. The notion is useful especially after a disaster because it forces people to manage with very limited resources. The frugal information system has four information requirements, i.e., universality, ubiquity, uniqueness and unison [5]. Universality is the drive to overcome the friction of information systems' incompatibilities. Ubiquity means information access unconstrained by time and space. Uniqueness requests to know precisely the characteristics and location of a person or entity. Unison refers to information consistency.

Looking toward the future, the smartphone is likely to be the tool to meet frugal design requirements better than any other device. First, it can be kept operational easily with a manually cranked charger. Second, it can be connected either via a cellular network or, if the cellular network is down, via WiFi. Third, a smartphone carries a unique phone number and SIM card. By associating the information of individuals collected with the number of a personal smartphone, the compatibility of the individual data is maintained. It is also be easy to link information of the same individual collected in different locations. In addition to this, a smartphone is a readily available tool with which people are already familiar.

Based on design the features described above, the author and a Japanese systems developer created a prototype information sharing system, which is predominantly a smartphone and tablet based application. Expected users are both municipal officials and citizens. The application can be used in evacuation centers and disaster management headquarters within municipal government. The application enables five key operations; (1) interactive information sharing on specific situations between disaster management headquarters and evacuation centers, (2) identification and registration of people at evacuation centers, (3) recording individual arrivals and departures, (4) assessing required relief resources (water, food and so on) at each evacuation center and, (5) creating an evacuee and resource list. These key operations were derived from empirical research on the Great East Japan Earthquake which the author conducted eight months after the earthquake. Smartphones were used mainly by evacuees (citizens) and tablets were used by city officials. This was based on the assumption that a tablet device has a more suitable interface for browsing the database.

3   Evaluation of the Artifact

A drill which used the prototype system in the field was conducted in November 2014 in Tome City, which occupies about 536 square km of land and holds a population of around 80,000. This city was not included in the empirical research on the earthquake but is one of the municipalities damaged by the Great East Japan Earthquake. During the earthquake, Tome accepted over 800 evacuees from a neighboring town, Minami-sanriku. They had never assumed to have evacuees from outside the city. This caused all-round confusion. It was difficult to figure out the whereabouts of people, what was happening in the field, what was needed, who needed it and what resources they already had or did not have. As a result, the city was quite eager to develop a solution for sharing such information in any future disaster situation.

The initial test was planned with the operation of evacuation centers, which would test the use of smartphones and tablets for supporting disaster relief. In this drill, we set up two temporary evacuation centers. Each center was located 10 to 14 km away from headquarters, a drive of about 20 min. Since important conditions for system development are said to be a small team and simple technology [6], the number of participants was kept small with two officials from headquarters and five officials and five citizens at each evacuation center.

A dummy unison database was prepared in advance and available to be accessed through a tablet application. Once the drill started, the tablet application provided officials with access to information on the stages of the disaster as posted by headquarters and other staff (key operation 1). Five evacuees in each evacuation center registered their location to the smartphone application (key operations 2 and 3). At the same time, they were able to send their demands for relief goods such as water, food, medicine through the application (key operation 4). The system created an evacuee database automatically and officials were able to reference the evacuee list and needs for relief goods through their tablet application (key operation 5).

The drill was accomplished smoothly because people were already familiar with the devices and easily got to understand how to use it in these operations. Nevertheless, the result of the drill was mixed. The use of smartphones and tablets for accessing the database was effective. In other words, *universal* devices enable *unison* of evacuee information. In this regard we could verify that the use of smartphones is certainly a possibility, although the scalability of the system should be questioned because of the limited number of smartphones tested. While accessing the database was realized, using *universal* devices to share posted information on disaster status caused information overflow. This is an issue for future research. In addition, the identification of evacuees by using the phone number of their SIM ID was not realized because of a privacy issue. *Uniqueness* was not accomplished in this sense. To compensate, a dummy database was created in advance and once the fire drill started, evacuees logged in the application and updated their status (location) by themselves. We should also note that we did not conduct any connectivity measures (*ubiquity*) in this drill. Rather we simply assumed continuous network connectivity. Although it was dummy information, we confirmed the importance of both preparing a unison database which every relief staff could access and providing information uniqueness on the database. This allowed smooth information sharing among different sites at the same time.

4   Significance to Research and Practice

Massive disasters like the Great East Japan Earthquake will likely become more common, as the number of natural disasters in the world is increasing.[1] There were three times as many natural disasters between 2000 and 2009 as there were between 1980 and 1989.[2] Thus, a communication platform which enables smooth information sharing between stakeholders during an emergency situation will be demanded both in Japan and around the world. Not only local authorities but also the notional governments tend to build large, complex and robust systems to support disaster management operations. While noting its limitations, we conclude that a frugal solution that employs devices that citizen use in their daily lives are worth incorporating in the lists of options which may save countless lives under severe conditions.

Let us briefly look at the significance of this paper to research and practice. First, the field drill focused mainly on the response stage which in emergency management literature is defined in terms of mitigation, preparedness, response, and recovery [7–9]. However, we found little discussion of information systems at those stages. Given the drill we could evaluate five key operations and see how the proto-type application might work out for each of them. The result of the field drill convinces us that each operation is essential in responding to a situation. However, the drill also pointed to some issues to be solved in the future. Information over-flow, scalability of the system and evacuee identification by unique number will be future issues which we expect to affect design requirements. In addition, the drill made clear the importance of both keeping the citizen database up-to-date in its daily basis operations and connecting it to emergency operations.

---

[1] Last accessed Mar. 3rd 2016, at http://www.emdat.be/disaster_trends/index.html.
[2] Last accessed Mar. 3rd 2016, at http://www.accuweather.com/en/weather-blogs/climatechange/steady-increase-in-climate-rel/19974069.

Second, the aim of designing an information system based on the notion of frugal IS has been accomplished in the present research. In this sense, we can say that we took both the bootstrap and adaptability approach [2]. While design requirements were generated from experience in the field, the application employs four information requirements advocated in the literature. The drill tells us that those requirements are useful as indicators in evaluating the system itself. This finding contributes to research in this area by proposing how to evaluate the artifact from the view of requirements, rather than functional perspective.

There are several directions for future research. This research is based on a single type of disaster, i.e., an earthquake and tsunami that occurred in Japan. For further generalizations of findings, a comparison with other types of disasters and cases is necessary. To make the application useful in practice, we also need to consider how to create and maintain the database and how to connect it to an ordinary residential record system. Because of privacy issues, the registration of evacuees would perhaps be the most difficult part of this challenge.

References

1. Sakurai, M., Watson, R.T.: Securing communication channels in severe disaster situations – lessons from a Japanese earthquake. In: Palen, L., Büscher, M., Comes, T., Hughes, A. (eds.) Information Systems for Crisis Response and Management, Kristiansand, Norway (2015)
2. Hanseth, O., Lyytinen, K.: Design theory for dynamic complexity in information infrastructures: the case of building internet. J. Inf. Technol. 25(1), 1–19 (2010)
3. Aanestad, M., Jensen, T.B.: Building nation-wide information infrastructures in healthcare through modular implementation strategies. J. Strat. Inf. Syst. 20(2), 161–176 (2011)
4. Watson, R.T., Kunene, K.N., Islam, M.S.: Frugal information systems (IS). Inf. Technol. Dev. 19(2), 176–187 (2013)
5. Junglas, I.A., Watson, R.T.: The U-constructs: four information drives. Commun. Assoc. Inf. Syst. 17, 2–43 (2006)
6. Grisot, M., Hanseth, O., Thorseng, A.A.: Innovation of, in, on infrastructures: articulating the role of architecture in information infrastructure evolution. J. Assoc. Inf. Syst. 15(4), 197–219 (2014)
7. McLoughlin, D.: A framework for integrated emergency management. Public Adm. Rev. 45(Special), 165–172 (1985)
8. Settle, A.K.: Financing disaster mitigation, preparedness, response, and recovery. Public Adm. Rev. 45(Special), 101–106 (1985)
9. Shoaf, K.I., Rottman, S.J.: The role of public health in disaster preparedness, mitigation, response, and recovery. Prehospital Disaster Med. 15(04), 18–20 (2000)

Design of a Real-Time Data Market
Based on the 21 Bitcoin Computer

Dominic Wörner[✉]

Department of Management Technology and Economics,
ETH Zurich, Zurich, Switzerland
dwoerner@ethz.ch

Abstract. An ever increasing number of physical and virtual sensors are digitizing the world around us. Today, most of this data is trapped in application-specific environments, and even if accessible in principle, discovery remains a problem. An open and transparent data market brings incentives for sensor owners to offer measurement data and provides means for discovery. We envision a decentralized data market based on peer-to-peer data exchange and payments. The presented prototype is an iteration of this idea based on the 21 Bitcoin computer, a computer with an embedded Bitcoin mining chip, as well as tools and services to simplify machine-to-machine payments based on Bitcoin.

1 Introduction

Data are the fuel of the digital economy. With the emergence of the Internet of Things (IOT) and the spread of connected devices the Internet gets additional senses to perceive the physical world. Currently most Internet of Things applications are vertically integrated and data are collected and used solely for their designated purpose. In order to free data, incentives have to be provided. An open data market with a simple interface opens the possibility for data providers, e.g. sensors, to offer their measurement data to other people, applications, and devices in exchange for money. Digital peer-to-peer payment systems like Bitcoin promise to deliver global, frictionless value transfer via the Internet without having to rely on intermediaries. So far, this promise has not been met, at least for micro- and nanopayments which would be needed for machine-to-machine payments on a data market. Nevertheless, we embrace Bitcoin as a lower level protocol on which additional layers will eventually allow for IOT-scale payments [1,2]. The here presented prototype is an iteration on an earlier instantiaton of the concept [3,4]. We chose the 21 Bitcoin Computer [5] as a basis. It allows to easily create Bitcoin-payable API endpoints and provides a virtual overlay network between 21 Bitcoin Computers to facilitate peer-to-peer data delivery. Moreover, this kind of infrastructure may become deployed widespread in all kinds of connected devices, first and foremost smartphones [6].

© Springer International Publishing Switzerland 2016
J. Parsons et al. (Eds.): DESRIST 2016, LNCS 9661, pp. 228–232, 2016.
DOI: 10.1007/978-3-319-39294-3_20

2   Design of the Artifact

2.1   Design Principles

The main goal is to establish an open data market with particular scope on real-time sensor data which is one of the main value propositions of the Internet of Things. Interactions between data providers and data requesters should be as immediate as possible to prevent data leakage and rent-seeking behavior of a central platform provider. This means in particular that data delivery should be peer-to-peer instead of mediation via a platform provider. An important function of a data market is the discovery between requesters and providers. This is provided by an open, queryable registry.

2.2   System Overview

The system is based on the 21 Bitcoin Computer which provides two important features that simplify the implementation significantly. First, a library is provided that allows to integrate Bitcoin-payable HTTP REST endpoints. Payments can either be made on- or off-chain. Off-chain payments are handled by 21 internally and therefore allow instant micropayments below Bitcoin's dust limit (currently 576 satoshi[1]) and without fees. Hence, we sacrifice direct peer-to-peer payments, at least for the moment, in exchange for the possibility to handle individual payments as tiny as 1 satoshi. Second, each 21 Bitcoin Computer is already part of a virtual network enabled by software defined networking. Thus, peer-to-peer communications, e.g. for data delivery, between requesters and providers are directly possible.

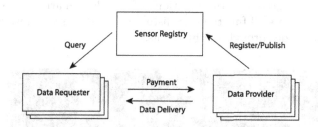

Fig. 1. General architecture of the data market artifact.

A graphical representation of the system is shown in Fig. 1. In the following we will briefly describe the individual components.

---

[1] Satoshi is the smallest fraction of a bitcoin. 1 satoshi corresponds to 10^{-8} bitcoin.

Sensor Registry. The sensor registry provides the means of discovery for data providers and data requesters. Notably, discovery between requesters and providers could be implemented on top of a distributed hash table like Blockstack [7]. However, we chose a centralized registry based on a MongoDB for practical reasons. Data providers are able to publish their offerings on the data market by creating an entry in the sensor registry. This is currently done with the command line interface, which will be presented in Sect. 2.2. Entries in the sensor registry have the following form[2]

```
{
    "name": "Air Quality Zurich Downtown"
    "endpoint" : "http://10.147.17.77:3002/measurement",
    "datatype" : "int",
    "type"     : "co2",
    "unit"     : "ppm",
    "price"    : 10,
    "location" : "47.37246913,8.54426892"
    "description": "Zurich air quality measurements"

}
```

and can be queried using the datamarket command line interface. Entries also have a time-to-live (TTL) after which they expire. TTL can be extended by payment. This provides a revenue stream for the data market provider and should lead to a higher fraction of available data providers.

Data Provider. A data provider is represented by a simple HTTP webserver with a payable API endpoint that returns a measurement value and a timestamp as JSON. Since the 21 Bitcoin Computer is essentially a Raspberry Pi physical sensors can be attached easily. Moreover it can act as bridge to external sensor data. An example would be an endpoint which is fed by a MQTT consumer.

Datamarket Command Line Interface. The datamarket command line interface provides access to the functions of the data market. Figure 2 shows the help screen where all functions are listed. In the next section we will present a step-by-step guide through the functions.

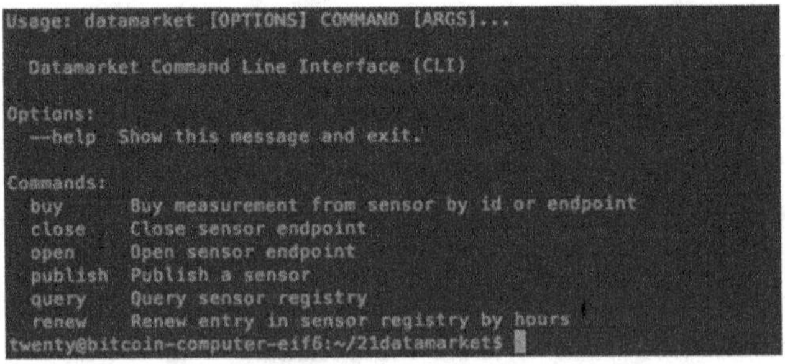

```
Usage: datamarket [OPTIONS] COMMAND [ARGS]...

    Datamarket Command Line Interface (CLI)

Options:
    --help  Show this message and exit.

Commands:
    buy      Buy measurement from sensor by id or endpoint
    close    Close sensor endpoint
    open     Open sensor endpoint
    publish  Publish a sensor
    query    Query sensor registry
    renew    Renew entry in sensor registry by hours
twenty@bitcoin-computer-eif6:~/21datamarket$
```

Fig. 2. Help screen of the datamarket command line interface provides an overview of its functions.

---

[2] Additional fields such as accuracy or measurement interval might be available.

3   Evaluation of the Artifact

In the following, we will use the datamarket artifact to offer real-time data of air quality measurements in Zurich. We assume a 21 Bitcoin Computer with a CO_2 sensor, which acts as a proxy for air quality, attached and the datamarket cli installed. The sensor.py represents the actual webserver that will serve the measurement data upon payment. Thus, sensor.py has to be configured to access and serve the measurement data. Furthermore the configuration file config.json which provides essentially the sensor registry entry as presented in Sect. 2.2 has to be adapted. After that we are ready to publish the sensor on the data market with

```
datamarket publish --hours 72
```

The hours option defines how long the entry will stay valid. To start up the webserver and serve measurement data to potential data requesters we type

```
datamarket open
```

Now a potential requester can query the datamarket to find this offering by using

```
datamarket query '{"type": "co2", "location:"Zurich"}'
```

which will return matching sensors. The current measurement value can then be bought directly from a sensor node either using the returned id or the endpoint url. Here we use the id.

```
datamarket buy '56698e32961b6b64b473e71c'
```

If funds are sufficient the current measurement value is returned along with a timestamp.

4   Significance of the Artifact

4.1   Significance to Research

Significance to research is twofold. On the one hand, progress towards data markets enables new data sources for research in general. Eventually, the vast amount of data generated by individually owned connected sensing devices like smartphones, wearables and other connected consumer products could become available to form a planetary nervous system [8]. On the other hand, to our knowledge this is the first usage of directly-payable API endpoints in Information Systems and Design Science research. This novel paradigm, essentially possible due to the proliferation of digital currencies like Bitcoin, provides a new design space where value can flow as easily as information.

4.2   Significance to Practice

A recent report by consulting firm McKinsey [9] estimated a potential economic impact of the Internet of Things of as much as \$11.1 trillion per year in 2015.

At least 40 % of this sum can only be unlocked by interoperability. Since most of the value is tied to data that connected devices produce, an open data market is contributing to the interoperability by providing immediate financial incentives to share data.

5   Demonstration of the Artifact

Code of the artifact together with instructions are available on GitHub[3]. Readers with access to a 21 Bitcoin computer are able to use the data market by installing the datamarket command line interface. The datamarket system is open source under the MIT license.

Acknowledgements. This work was supported by the Bosch Internet of Things Lab and the Swiss National Science Foundation.

References

1. Poon, J., Dryja, T.: The bitcoin lightning network. Accessed 18 Feb 2016
2. Decker, C., Wattenhofer, R.: A fast and scalable payment network with bitcoin duplex micropayment channels. In: Pelc, A., Schwarzmann, A.A. (eds.) SSS 2015. LNCS, vol. 9212, pp. 3–18. Springer, Heidelberg (2015)
3. Noyen, K., Volland, D., Woorner, D., Fleisch, E., When money learns to y: Towards sensing as a service applications using bitcoin. CoRR, abs/1409.5841 (2014)
4. Woorner, D., von Bomhard, T.: When your sensor earns money: Ex-changing data for cash with bitcoin. In: Proceedings of the 2014 ACM International Joint Conference on Pervasive and Ubiquitous Computing: Adjunct Publication, Ubi-Comp 2014 Adjunct, pp. 295–298, New York, USA. ACM (2014)
5. Srinivasan, B.S.: The 21 bitcoin computer (2015). https://medium.com/@21/the-21-bitcoin-computer-1d28d652b57b#.jxrbo1j7m. Accessed 25 Feb 2016
6. Srinivasan, B.S.: A bitcoin miner in every device and in every hand (2015). https://medium.com/21/a-bitcoin-miner-in-every-device-and-in-every-hand-e315b4 0f2821#.e3zt672gh. Accessed 22 Feb 2016
7. Ali, M., Nelson, J., Shea, R., Freedman, M.J.: Blockstack: design and implementa-tionof a global naming system with blockchains. Accessed 25 Feb 2016
8. Giannotti, F., Pedreschi, D., Pentland, A., Lukowicz, P., Kossmann, D., Crowley, J., Dirk Helbing, A.: Planetary nervous system for social mining, collective awareness. Eur. Phys. J. Spec. Top. **214**(1), 49–75 (2012)
9. Manyika, J., Chui, M., Bisson, P., Woetzel, J., Dobbs, R., Bughin, J., Aharon, D.: Unlocking the potential of the internet of things. McKinsey Global Institute (2015)

---

[3] https://github.com/domwoe/21datamarket.

Designing Information as a By-Product

Sruthi Yaramreddy, Kyle Knight, Nitin Ram Kona, Nitin Jain, Adriana Salgado,
and Roman Lukyanenko[✉]

Florida International University, Miami, FL, USA
{syara002,kknig021,nkona001,njain006,asalg009,rlukyane}@fiu.edu

Abstract. Much of IS design theory makes an assumption that if data is required by data consumers, it needs to be captured by the information systems (IS) explicitly and directly. With the pervasiveness of direct representation in IS development and research, academia has offered little support for cases where not all data elements required by data consumers are collected and stored directly. With the explosive proliferation of business analytics, it is becoming increasingly effective to mine existing data sources for unanticipated and novel insights. We developed and implemented GroceryBer - an online prototype for the crowdsourcing grocery delivery service in which we intentionally designed information as a by-product of the grocery delivery process.

Keywords: Crowdsourcing · Business analytics · Conceptual modeling · Hybrid intelligence · Machine learning

1 Introduction

In a provocative *New Yorker* article, George Packer [1] claims that the true reasons driving Jeff Bezos in launching the Internet giant Amazon.com were not books. Rather, Bezos, saw books - a product ripe for Internet sales - as a kind of trampoline that could propel his company into more lucrative markets of everyday products such as lawnmowers, computers, diapers, shoes, printers. To get there, long before Facebook and Google, "Bezos had realized that the greatest value of an online company lay in the consumer data it collected" [1].

Among other things, the Amazon's story is interesting from the point of view of the design of information systems (IS). It points to the fact that when an organization needs data, there are a variety of strategies for acquiring it, including capturing it indirectly. Thus, in the case of Amazon, the explicit purpose of the project may very well be secondary to its more implicit, but no less important objective of tracking book-buying patterns of customers to better understand their broader needs.

Yet, much of IS design theory makes an assumption that if data is required by data consumers, it needs to be captured by the IS explicitly and directly [2]. For example, this assumption is quite prominent in conceptual modeling – a phase of information systems development that captures and represents user requirements that are then used to design databases, programming code, and often, user interfaces [2, 3]. In particular, to the extent possible, conceptual models need to include "all the statements which

© Springer International Publishing Switzerland 2016
J. Parsons et al. (Eds.): DESRIST 2016, LNCS 9661, pp. 233–237, 2016.
DOI: 10.1007/978-3-319-39294-3_21

would be ... relevant about the domain" [4]. Once represented in a conceptual model, these statements (e.g., concepts, attributes, relationships describing entities of interest) are typically modeled as database elements (e.g., attributes, relations) and components of the user interface design (e.g., textboxes requiring certain values; dropdown lists; radio buttons). We summarize this general design principle as: if data is specified in a conceptual model, it needs to be collected and stored. Here we term this approach to IS development as the *principle of direct information collection.*

With the pervasiveness of direct information collection in IS research, academia has offered little guidance for cases where not all data elements required by data consumers are collected and stored directly. This results in an increasing gap between IS theory and growing computational capabilities. With the explosive proliferation of data mining, business analytics, artificial intelligence, natural language processing, computer vision, it is becoming increasingly common to mine existing data sources for unanticipated and novel insights. The promise of business analytics is in the ability to extend a data set beyond its immediate purpose [5]. This new philosophy stands in opposition to the traditional focus of IS that upholds the principle of direct information collection. Thus, the question can be raised whether projects should be designed with an explicit aim to collect information as a by-product of the focal project's activity or *information as a by-product principle.*

We developed and implemented GroceryBer - an online prototype for the crowd-sourcing grocery delivery service modeled after such popular crowd platforms as Uber, Lyft and Airbnb [6]. However, in building this project, we intentionally implemented the information as a by-product design principle. Below, we elaborate on the project and the design choices we made.

2   Design of the Artifact

While the principle of direct information capture dominates traditional thinking about IS design, with the explosive growth of data production, organizations have access to plethora of data sets created by third parties. For example, a market researcher hoping to better understand customer demand can subscribe to a variety of datasets (e.g., data.gov, https://datahub.io). Despite increased pervasiveness, there are several common limitations of publicly available sources, including:

- Non-restricted nature, availability to everyone, including competitors;
- Generic orientation, frequently not suitable for specific business needs;
- Anonymized content to comply with privacy and ethics restrictions.

These limitations motivated us to design an information system that would collect data that would remain proprietary (not accessible to competitors, or third-parties), be narrowly focused on the products in a specific geographic location (e.g., food items in South Florida), and having data to be consumed within the application itself thereby satisfying the legal and ethical restrictions. Despite the wealth of third-party datasets, we could not identify the source that would contain real-time grocery demand in a highly narrow local area. This led us to the development of GroceryBer.

GroceryBer is an on-demand community-driven grocery delivery service that provides rapid delivery of thousands of grocery items. The process begins when a customer selects preferred grocery store and grocery items available from the store using a mobile app (see Fig. 1). The app requires real-time access to grocery stores' inventory – thus cooperation with grocery stores is a key to its commercial success. GroceryBer sends the request to trained delivery helpers (who are similar to Uber drivers and are members of the same local community) as well as the grocery store – to notify it of the pending order. The delivery helpers pick up items in a local grocery store that has the items ready for pickup. The items are then delivered to the customer.

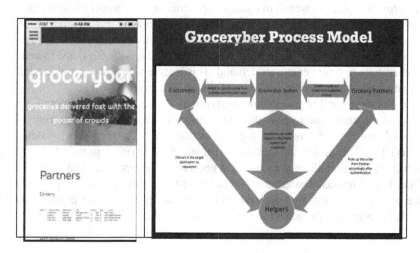

Fig. 1. Prototype of the GroceryBer app and the process model

Through a user-friendly app and a local network of reliable helpers, GroceryBer connects members to fresh groceries and everyday essentials. Saving time, fuel and headspace, next-hour, same day grocery delivery is quickly becoming an everyday necessity for people looking for an extra few hours.

While GroceryBer stands to generate revenue, its main design objective is to generate unique, proprietary real-time data and leverage these data in cross-selling and product improvement. Unlike existing grocery delivery services (e.g., favordelivery.com), the key to GroceryBer is in real-time integration between the app and the grocery partners' inventories. As customer chooses grocery items, the app processes the data for any real-time cross-selling opportunities and makes recommendation on addition items to purchase. The recommendations are driven by the analytics that performs market basket analysis (i.e., association rule mining). Importantly, the recommendation agent is trained on unique local data including previous orders by similar customers as well as the customer him/herself. This differs from traditional applications of market basket analysis [5] where transactions are mined without tying them to individual customers and individual customer characteristics (e.g., food allergies, dietary restrictions). Finally, the helpers can also make real-time recommendations of the items to purchase by suggesting items to be included in the order (in which case the customer receives a notification and can either accept or reject the recommendations). This augments the machine intelligence engine with creativity and insight of humans from the same local area (i.e., likely from people of similar cultural and ethnic background). This results in a *hybrid intelligence* solution (combined wisdom of humans and machines) which has been shown to be superior to a machine-only solution [7, 8]. The customer remains in control over how much helpers and AI know about them. In principle, the app can be further integrated with smart customer devices, such as smart refrigerators, for automatic determination of needs and quantities on hand.

Another use of the app is in the analysis of historical patterns of customer purchases. As the project captures a wealth of customer experience with groceries, aggregate analysis of this data stands to generate unique and highly localized (e.g., district level, store specific) insights. These data can then be used by the partnering stores (which are already integrated into the app) for the improvement of the product offerings, and to anticipate and better react to future customer demand. This feature would also provide additional justification for the grocery stores to partner with GroceryBer.

The prototype for this project consisted of semi-functional webpages (with realistic graphics, navigation, interactive elements), but without database-connectivity - or a *horizontal prototype* (focusing on user interaction rather than low-level system functionality) [9]. The prototype created a realistic feel, showed proof of concept by construction [10] and allowed assessing a general user experience. The prototype was evaluated by an unbiased external expert judge – an academic with seven years of experience in managing and running real crowdsourcing projects. The project was also presented to a group of graduate students at a large public US university.

3   Implications and Significance

This project makes three contributions to the theory and practice of IS development. First, the project builds the case for broader consideration of indirect information capture in IS theory. Traditionally, information systems explicitly modeled (e.g., by designing appropriate database columns) the information to be captured and used in analysis and reporting. We believe with the rapid advances in computing technologies, proliferation of data mining and analytics, IS theory needs to expand and consider how to design systems that deliver data indirectly. The GroceryBer is a conceptual proof of the information as a by-product concept. Using the grocery context, we demonstrate that despite plethora of data sources, to generate more valuable customer insights and react to them in real time, one strategy is to design a real-time crowdsourcing system. The system (that could be profitable itself) then generates unique data that would be otherwise impossible or extremely costly to acquire. We hope that this project motivates future IS design research aimed at better understanding of the nature of indirect information capture, suggesting how to leverage this principle to develop IS more effectively and evaluate the merits of this principle against traditional direct information collection approaches.

Second, the project suggests three key design characteristics of data as a by-product in the crowdsourcing context: real-time integration with existing data sources (e.g., grocery store inventories, customer smart devices), extensive application of machine learning (e.g., to make real-time recommendations) and, since crowd-sourcing projects tend to have inherent human component, we suggest to integrate the human decision making as well resulting in a hybrid intelligence approach to IS design. These principles can be used in practice for developing similar applications. We also hope to examine these design principles in greater depth in the future.

Finally, this project offers a novel application of crowdsourcing. Much of existing crowdsourcing research tends to focus on the use of crowds for small, well defined tasks [11, 12]. In addition, a major application of crowdsourcing is in problem solving and surveillance activities done on behalf of an organization (e.g., reporting bird sightings, folding proteins) [13]. With this project we suggest that crowds can play a double role of physical delivery agents as well as intelligent advisors tightly integrated into the broader process. This expands the traditional crowdsourcing landscape, informs a boarder theoretical understanding of the crowdsourcing phenomena, as well as can be used by practitioners in implementing real-world crowdsourcing solutions.

References

1. Packer, G.: Cheap words (2014). http://www.newyorker.com/magazine/2014/02/17/cheap-words
2. Olivé, A.: Conceptual modeling of information systems. Springer, Heildelberg (2007)
3. Wand, Y., Weber, R.: On the deep structure of information systems. Inf. Syst. J. **5**, 203–223 (2008)
4. Krogstie, J.: Integrating the understanding of quality in requirements specification and conceptual modeling. ACM SIGSOFT Softw. Eng. Notes **23**, 86–91 (1998)
5. Provost, F., Fawcett, T.: Data Science for Business: What You Need to Know About Data Mining and Data-Analytic Thinking. O'Reilly Media Inc, Newton (2013)
6. Jones, C.: Uber, Lyft and Airbnb soar in popularity with business travelers. USA Today, 24 January 2016
7. Davis, E., Marcus, G.: Commonsense reasoning and commonsense knowledge in artificial intelligence. Commun. ACM **58**, 92–103 (2015)
8. Lukyanenko, R., Wiersma, Y., Parsons, J.: Is crowdsourced attribute data useful in citizen science? A study of experts and machines. In: Collective Intelligence 2016, New York (2016)
9. Bodker, S., Madsen, K.H.: Methods & tools: context: an active choice in usability work. Interactions **5**, 17–25 (1998)
10. Nunamaker, J.F., Chen, M., Purdin, T.D.: Systems development in information systems research. J. Manag. Inf. Syst. **7**, 89–106 (1991)
11. Nguyen, N.: Microworkers crowdsourcing approach, challenges and solutions. In: Proceedings of the 2014 International ACM Workshop on Crowdsourcing for Multimedia (2014)
12. Ipeirotis, P.G., Provost, F., Wang, J.: Quality management on amazon mechanical turk. In: Proceedings of the ACM SIGKDD Workshop on Human Computation, pp. 64–67. ACM (2010)
13. Lukyanenko, R., Parsons, J., Wiersma, Y.: The IQ of the crowd: understanding and improving information quality in structured user-generated content. Inf. Syst. Res. **25**, 669–689 (2014)

emotionVis: Designing an Emotion Text Inference Tool for Visual Analytics

Chris Zimmerman[✉], Mari-Klara Stein, Daniel Hardt, Christian Danielsen, and Ravi Vatrapu

Department of IT Management, Copenhagen Business School, Frederiksberg, Denmark
{cz.itm,mst.itm,dh.itm,cdfd.itm,rv.itm}@cbs.dk

Abstract. With increasingly high volumes of conversations across social media, the rapid detection of emotions is of significant strategic value to industry practitioners. Summarizing large volumes of text with computational linguistics and visual analytics allows for several new possibilities from general trend detection to specific applications in marketing practice, such as monitoring product launches, campaigns and public relations milestones. After collecting 1.6 million user-tagged feelings from 12 million online posts that mention emotions, we utilized machine learning techniques towards building an automatic 'feelings meter'; a tool for both researchers and practitioners to automatically detect emotional dimensions from text. Following several iterations, the test version has now taken shape as emotionVis, a dashboard prototype for inferring emotions from text while presenting the results for visual analysis.

1 Introduction

Emotion has become a popular topic in information systems research [1–6] as affective relationships are increasingly recognized as central to technology mediated interactions in general [7] and social networks in particular [8]. Emotions as "projections/displays of feeling" [9, 10] are the most visible layer of affect – explicitly shared in facial expressions, verbal and written communication. People go to social media in search of intensity, sensations and impressions that create affective jolts [8]. The resulting strong feelings are then often publicly shared (e.g., people voluntarily telling others 'how they are feeling' on Facebook). Due to this search for intensity, social media often invite intentionally provocative content and trolling behavior, rather than rational argumentation in a Habermasian public sphere [11].

While the uses and gratifications of social media include affective experiences, organizations seek to understand how their customers feel and which emotions they express online in relation to their brand. Such insights are used for improvements in marketing strategy, customer service, and the discovery of new business opportunities [12–15]. Opinions from the crowd are increasingly discovered with the help of automatic sentiment analysis. Yet state-of-the-art tools offer sentiment detection in the form of a polarity score, lacking context to what form of positivity or negativity was expressed. These results can potentially be misleading for practitioners [16]. Many research prototypes have overlooked fundamentals of information visualization by their own admission [17]; others have only attempted to pursue one angle of analysis [18]. Few research prototypes have

© Springer International Publishing Switzerland 2016
J. Parsons et al. (Eds.): DESRIST 2016, LNCS 9661, pp. 238–244, 2016.
DOI: 10.1007/978-3-319-39294-3_22

attempted multi-category emotion detection [19, 20]. If attempted, studies typically re-apply existing emotion classes from offline research (Ekman-6, Plutchik-8 or Scherer's emotion wheel) while leveraging generalized emotion lexicons (ANEW, OlympLex) that are not necessarily adept to online spaces. The dashboard prototype demonstrated herein differs in three fundamental ways from other existing tools. First, our training data set benefits from *specificity;* providing granularity of up to 143 discrete emotion types. Second, the tool offers *multi-dimensionality* by including both the valence and the arousal dimensions. Third, we offer a re-alignment in classification towards how people exhibit *emotions online*. Our tool reflects current emotion discourse online (particularly Facebook) which appears to be skewed towards high arousal and positive emotions (e.g., excitement) [15].

The artifact instantiates Action Design Research design principles from an ongoing engaged scholarship within a social media marketing agency [21]. Development cycles have been informed by research prototypes [22–24] and considers existing commercial tools such as Talkwalker, Topsy and Radian6 [25–27]. The emotionVis tool is accessible at cssl.cbs.dk/software/emotionVis (includes demo video).

2   Methodology: Artifact Design

Development began with data collection of 12 million public posts from Facebook that mentioned feelings. Of these, we used 1,618,499 posts, where the user tagged their text with one of 143 Facebook 'feelings tags' (feature since 2013) (Fig. 1). This provided us with a unique training set for our tool to detect emotion attributes from text. Standard approaches to text classification [28] involve the following steps: (1) Preprocessing: text is tokenized (so that words can be separately identified); (2) Feature Extraction: identifying word (unigrams, bigrams and trigrams) sequences; (3) Classification: a supervised machine learning algorithm is selected, which determines which combinations of features best predict the classification of interest. We followed the above steps to train four separate classifiers on our set of emotion-categorized posts.

Kimberly-Jade Maud 😊 feeling heartbroken with **Michael Maud.**
January 18 · 🌐

I normally hate status' like this, however, wanted to thank everyone for your messages of love and support during this difficult time.
It's never easy to loose a loved one, life can be so cruel at times and it has come as such a shock to all the family.

Fig. 1. Example of Facebook feeling tag used in training.

The first classifier detects individual emotions from the inputted text, leveraging 28 'Facebook feelings' with the most volume within our training set. The second classifier groups these feelings into 6 core emotions. It is common in emotions research to group discrete emotions into a smaller number of 'core' categories, such as joy, anger, sadness, fear and excitement [9, 29]. Our tool includes Joy, Sadness, Anger, Fear, Excitement and Empowerment, reflecting a wider range of high arousal, positive emotions – in line with the kinds of intense affective experiences

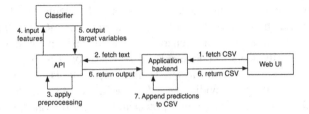

Fig. 2. Schematic diagram of the prototype.

people seek from and express on social media [8]. The third and fourth classifiers detect levels of valence (pos-neg sentiment) and levels of arousal from the inputted text. The resulting prototype consists of a backend and frontend (Fig. 2). The backend includes two Python Flask applications: an API interacting with the classifier and a web app interacting with the API. This app receives a CSV file from the user, extracts necessary data, sends it to the emotionVis API, adds classification scores to the CSV file, and returns the data to the user, along with computing the chart data for the dashboards. The front-end (UI) is made in HTML5, CSS and JavaScript. Bootstrap is used for the layout, while the D3.js and NVD3 visualization libraries are leveraged for the charts.

Action Design Research (ADR): The primary design consideration was to build a tool with value to Marketing and Social Media practitioners. ADR was used as a practical way of eliciting needs from the industry to inform the design [21]. Current development is taking place within a research environment while simultaneously testing the tool within a social media marketing agency. A survey was conducted among 30 practitioners at the agency to gauge which of the 143 feeling types were more relevant when making decisions. Early test versions of the tool were utilized by practitioners on a brand campaign by the electronics manufacturer Bang and Olufsen in 2015. In line with Sein et al.'s dual mission of making theoretical contributions while solving practitioner problems [4], we also see our tool as being useful for researchers who use similar datasets (post-level csv) from social channels (Facebook, Twitter, etc.). Design of the interface, thus, had these various users in mind.

Dashboard Affordances: The tool is intended to augment social media data that researchers or practitioners have at hand (e.g., post-level data exported from commercial tools as .csv files). Such data often provide details about the "who" and "when", which can be enhanced with "what feelings were felt" and topical clues as to why. The dashboard seeks to facilitate several affordances:

Emotional Alignment – A social media manager can compare the emotionality of postings made by the organization (e.g., happy or excited) with the emotionality of the comment chain generated in reaction to the published post.

Emotional Reverberation, Resilience, and Shifting – As emotions circulate on social media, they reverberate and intensify (e.g., a firestorm) or diffuse and wane. In downturns, brands may seek to rebound from negative emotional discourse. Sometimes the same objects can also elicit different emotions in different situations [30]. Our tool enables the tracing of 'emotional trajectories' within zoom-able time series/area charts [20]. In addition, as affect circulates, it creates an archive of expressed emotions [31]. Our tool affords tracing the *accumulation of emotions* over time.

Emotional Stickiness – As affect circulates, particular feelings can get 'stuck' to certain bodies, spaces, situations, etc. [8]. E.g., in a case of Marius the Giraffe, negative feelings got "stuck" to the scientific director of Copenhagen Zoo, who was the public face of the giraffe's controversial execution [32]. Term frequencies within emotion categories can unveil changing attachments between emotions and topics within text.

Design of the Prototype: The user begins by importing their own data (Fig. 3). Users are free to choose and indicate header names and the form of text file they are uploading (1). The layout design facilitates thematic progression in data exploration. Users first glance at the overall distributions of core emotions, followed by the breakdown of these groups into discrete emotions, and ultimately exploring individual posts and actors. Chart sophistication progresses at the same time (from bar charts to dual-axis to sunburst). As with other emotion-based tools [20], the color scheme has been carefully considered, while respecting existing connotations that humans identify with color. Two forms of bar chart show the **distribution of emotions** (2–3). A horizontal stacked bar chart shows a part-to-whole composition of core emotions. The ordering of emotions in this band (from most positive to negative) corresponds to the order of 28 sub-level emotions in the bar chart immediately below. The next layers illustrate **volumes over time** (4–5). Conversation volume is represented by gray bars in the background. This is overlaid with two lines that represent arousal and valence levels. A time slider encourages users to drill-down to specific windows in time.

A view displaying the **breakdown of a conversation (by core emotions) over time** follows. Individual emotions can be removed to isolate a stream of interest over time. A **post-level visualization** maps all posts within a conversation onto a two-dimensional (arousal and valence) scatterplot (6). This allows the user to see the emotional 'footprint' of the entire conversation. The practitioner can also see where their own published posts lie within the footprint – in comparison to the crowd – as visual feedback on emotional alignment. The sunburst diagram facilitates a **breakdown of core emotions** (7). One can see, for example, that a large portion of anger detected may have originated from annoyance, rather than disgust. This granularity elaborates on the unique footprint a conversation may hold. The last series of charts **rank people** in the conversation who express the highest average levels of each core emotion (8). These serve as actionable opportunities for social media managers to engage with people flagged as having particular emotions towards the brand.

3   Limitations and Future Perspectives

With the latest iteration of this prototype, opportunities for action research are expected to widen as practitioners begin to use the tool. EmotionVis has been tasked for reporting within a social media audit of a global hotel chain, as well as conversation monitoring

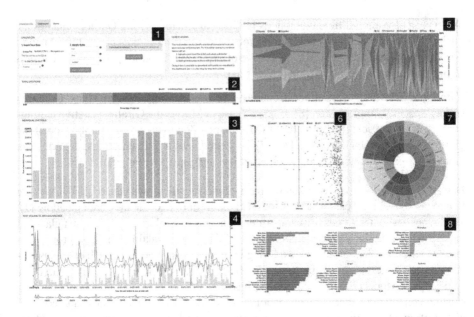

Fig. 3. The User Interface (UI) presents data for different affordances via specific visualizations (Color figure online).

during the European football championships (Euro 2016) by the tournament's main sponsor. Such applications will provide valuable future direction in the development of the prototype. Once the tool is directly connected to APIs from social media channels, it will also provide a real-time interface benefiting from consistent display in the dashboard. Currently the visualizations are also serving designers as self-assessment instruments to fine-tune the classifier. In future work, we will systematically assess the accuracy of detecting different emotions in test data.

References

1. Beaudry, A., Pinsonneault, A.: The other side of acceptance: studying the direct and indirect effects of emotions on information technology use. MIS Q. **34**, 689–710 (2010)
2. McGrath, K.: Affection not affliction: the role of emotions in information systems and organizational change. Inf. Organ. **16**, 277–303 (2006)
3. De Guinea, A., Markus, M.: Why break the habit of a lifetime? Rethinking the roles of intention, habit, and emotion in continuing information technology use. Mis Q. **33**, 433–444 (2009)
4. Stein, M., Newell, S., Wagner, E., Galliers, R.: Felt quality of sociomaterial relations: introducing emotions into sociomaterial theorizing. Inf. Organ. **24**, 156–175 (2014)
5. Stein, M., Newell, S., Wagner, E., Galliers, R.: Coping with information technology: mixed emotions, vacillation, and nonconforming use patterns. Mis Q. **39**, 367–392 (2015)
6. Zhang, L., Jiang, M., Farid, D., Hossain, M.: Intelligent facial emotion recognition and semantic-based topic detection for a humanoid robot. Expert Syst. Appl. **40**, 5160–5168 (2013)

7. Vatrapu, R.K., Suthers, D.D.: Technological intersubjectivity in computer supported intercultural collaboration. In: Proceedings of the 2009 International Workshop on Intercultural Collaboration - IWIC 2009, pp. 155–164 (2009)
8. Hillis, K., Paasonen, S., Petit, M.: Networked Affect. MIT Press, Cambridge (2015)
9. Ekman, P., Friesen, W.: Universals and cultural differences in the judgments of facial expressions of emotion. J. Pers. Soc. Psychol. **53**, 712 (1987)
10. Shouse, E.: Feeling, emotion, affect. M/C Journal **8**(8), 26 (2005)
11. Robertson, S.P., Vatrapu, R.K., Medina, R.: Off the wall political discourse: facebook use in the 2008 U.S. presidential election. Inf. Polity **15**(1–2), 11–31 (2010)
12. Goh, K., Heng, C., Lin, Z.: Social media brand community and consumer behavior: quantifying the relative impact of user-and marketer-generated content. Inf. Syst. Res. **24**, 88–107 (2013)
13. Holsapple, C., Hsiao, S., Pakath, R.: Business social media analytics: definition, benefits, and challenges. Bus. Soc. Media Anal. **2010**, 1–12 (2014)
14. Kurniawati, K., Shanks, G., Bekmamedova, N.: The business impact of social media analytics. ECIS **13**, 13 (2013)
15. Zimmerman, C., Stein, M., Hardt, D., Vatrapu, R.: Emergence of things felt: harnessing the semantic space of facebook feeling tags (2015)
16. Marcus, A., Bernstein, M., Badar, O.: Twitinfo: aggregating and visualizing microblogs for event exploration. In: Proceedings of the SIGCHI Conference on Human Factors in Computing Systems, pp. 227–236. ACM (2011)
17. Guzman, E., Bruegge, B.: Towards emotional awareness in software development teams. In: Proceedings of the 2013 9th Joint Meeting on Foundations of Software Engineering, pp. 671–674. ACM (2013)
18. Wensel, A., Sood, S.: Vibes: visualizing changing emotional states in personal stories. In: Proceedings of the 2nd ACM International Workshop on Story Representation, Mechanism and Context, pp. 49–56. ACM (2008)
19. Pu, P.: EmotionWatch: visualizing fine-grained emotions in event-related tweets. In: Proceedings of the in the 8th International AAAI Conference on Weblogs and Social Media (2014)
20. Zhao, J., Gou, L., Wang, F., Zhou, M.: PEARL: an interactive visual analytic tool for understanding personal emotion style derived from social media. In: 2014 IEEE Conference on Visual Analytics Science and Technology, pp. 203–212. IEEE (2014)
21. Sein, M., Henfridsson, O., Purao, S., Rossi, M., Lindgren, R.: Action design research. MIS Q. **35**, 37–56 (2011)
22. Hussain, A., Vatrapu, R.: Design, development, and evaluation of the social data analytics tool. In: Tremblay, M.C., VanderMeer, D., Rothenberger, M., Gupta, A., Yoon, V. (eds.) DESRIST 2014. LNCS, vol. 8463, pp. 368–372. Springer, Heidelberg (2014)
23. Zimmerman, C., Vatrapu, R.: Designing the social newsroom: visual analytics for social business intelligence. In: Donnellan, B., Helfert, M., Kenneally, J., VanderMeer, D., Rothenberger, M., Winter, R. (eds.). LNCS, vol. 9073, pp. 386–390Springer, Heidelberg (2015)
24. Flesch, B., Vatrapu, R.: Social set visualizer: a set theoretical approach to big social data analytics of real-world events. In: 2015 IEEE International Conference on Big Data (Big Data), pp. 2418–2427. IEEE (2015)
25. Trendiction, Talkwalker. www.talkwalker.com. Accessed 13 April 2015
26. Apple (purchased and closed in 2014), Topsy. www.topsy.com/analytics
27. Salesforce, Radian6. www.radian6.com. Accessed 13 April 2015

28. Pang, B., Lee, L., Vaithyanathan, S.: Thumbs up? Sentiment classification using machine learning techniques. In: Proceedings Conference on Empirical Methods in Natural Language Processing 6–7 July 2002, Philadephia, Pennsylvania, USA, pp. 79–86 (2002)

29. Parrott, W.: Emotions in Social Psychology: Essential Readings. Psychology Press, Abingdon (2001)

30. Kuntsman, A.: Introduction: affective fabrics of digital cultures. In: Karatzogianni, A., Kuntsman, A. (eds.) Digital Cultures and the Politics of Emotion, pp. 1–17. Palgrave Macmillan, Basingstoke (2012)

31. Cvetkovich, A.: An Archive of Feelings: Trauma, Sexuality, and Lesbian Public Cultures. Duke University Press, Durham (2003)

32. Zimmerman, C., Chen, Y., Hardt, D., Vatrapu, R.: Marius, the giraffe: a comparative informatics case study of linguistic features of the social media discourse. In: Proceedings of the 5th ACM International Conference on Collaboration Across Boundaries: Culture, Distance and Technology, pp. 131–140. ACM (2014)

Author Index

Printed in the United States
By Bookmasters